Change and Language

Papers from the
Annual Meeting of the British Association for Applied Linguistics
held at the University of Leeds, September 1994

Edited by

Hywel Coleman and Lynne Cameron

BRITISH ASSOCIATION FOR APPLIED LINGUISTICS

in association with

MULTILINGUAL MATTERS LTD

Clevedon • Philadelphia • Adelaide

British Library Cataloguing in Publication Data

A CIP catalogue record for this book is available from the British Library.

ISBN 1-85359-359-1 (pbk)

Published by the British Association for Applied Linguistics in association with
Multilingual Matters Ltd.

Multilingual Matters Ltd

UK: Frankfurt Lodge, Clevedon Hall, Victoria Road, Clevedon, Avon BS21 7SJ.
USA: 1900 Frost Road, Suite 101, Bristol, PA 19007, USA.
Australia: P.O. Box 6025, 83 Gilles Street, Adelaide, SA 5000, Australia.

Typeset by Wayside Books, Clevedon.
Printed and bound in Great Britain by the Longdunn Press, Bristol.

Contents

Change and Language: Editors' preface

HYWEL COLEMAN and LYNNE CAMERON
University of Leeds

Taking its cue from the theme of the 1993 BAAL Annual Meeting – 'Language in a Changing Europe' – the 1994 Meeting widened the scope to encourage investigation of the relationship between Change and Language in the broadest sense.

The Meeting was organised around the following three sub-themes:

(1) *Change, Language and Society at the End of the Twentieth Century*
(2) *Change, Language and the Individual*
(3) *Change, Language Education and the Developing World*

and this volume maintains that internal organisation.

Change, Language and Society at the End of the Twentieth Century

Papers in this sub-theme examined the ways in which social change brings about changes in language and language use. The focus, then, was not necessarily on planned change (as in the third sub-theme, below), nor was it primarily concerned with education, nor was it restricted to a particular geographical area.

Six papers dealing with this sub-theme have been selected for this volume. Fairclough's plenary identifies eight aspects of social change in the late twentieth century and then investigates the ways in which social change is constituted by changing discourse practices. Foster adopts an even broader historical perspective, exploring the concept that language is an evolutionary product; he concludes that 'languages are subject to the inconveniences of constant variability, and hence change; and . . . we retain a flexibility in our language use that confers on us the capacity for conscious linguistic innovation'.

Kennedy's chapter is a study of a particular case of planned language change in the UK which is intended to contribute to social change. Meinhof's chapter, on the other hand, traces the subtle ways in which language use in the films of Edgar Reitz mirrors social change in Germany during the twentieth century. We return to the UK in Rogers' chapter, where she identifies glaring examples of change failing to take place in educational practice, despite superficial changes in terminology. The final chapter in this section is Turner's study of the interface between British Sign Language and English among British Deaf people.

Change, Language and the Individual

The second sub-theme considered the twin issues of language and change in the context of the individual. This permitted examination of first, second and foreign language development in the individual learner. It was concerned with investigation of language change within the individual in the broadest sense: for example, to what extent and in what ways do native speakers change in their use of their mother tongue as they grow older and encounter change in life circumstances? Five papers representing this sub-theme have been selected for inclusion in this volume.

Catherine Snow's plenary paper opens this section with a meticulous study of the ways in which approaches to development in child language have themselves developed over recent years. Ben Rampton's chapter examines the phenomenon of 'language crossing' – the use of Creole, Panjabi or stylised Indian English – by members of other ethnic groups and, in doing so, begins to challenge some basic concepts employed in Second Language Acquisition research. The chapter by Raschka and Milroy takes as its research base members of another ethnic minority in the UK, the Chinese community in Tyneside, and demonstrates that language development is intimately connected with the social networks in which individuals involve themselves.

Whilst Raschka and Milroy's subjects have been in the UK for between 5 and 36 years, Tonkyn's chapter examines the English language development of a small group of international students at a British university. These are people who are exposed to English in Britain for a matter of weeks only. Tonkyn uses this opportunity to explore the suitability of a number of instruments in order to detect whether change takes place even in such a short period.

The chapter by Turner and Hiraga concludes this section with a comparative study of the assumptions regarding appropriate behaviour in lecturer–

student interaction in Japanese and British universities. Not surprisingly, perhaps, they discover that these assumptions reflect differing sociopragmatic principles. This finding is then related to the theme of the volume by raising the question as to how individuals who have to move from one academic context to another can be enabled to become aware of the differing socio-pragmatic assumptions and so ensure that their behaviour continues to be contextually appropriate.

Change, Language Education and the Developing World

This sub-theme explored the complex relationships between language education and social change in developing countries. Issues raised included the choice of national languages, the role of English as the medium of contact in development activities, and the role of agencies such as the British Council in language education in the developing world. The focus of attention in this sub-theme, therefore, was on the way in which language education and lan-guage policy influence, support or hinder the planned or deliberate social change which constitutes the essence of development activity. Three chapters in this collection represent this sub-theme.

D. P. Pattanayak's chapter, based on his plenary presentation, argues forcefully that the richness which linguistic and cultural pluralism represents must be defended against tendencies to homogenisation. Pattanayak's argu-ment thus resonates with Fairclough's discussion which opens this collection. Clinton Robinson's study picks up on some of the same issues and examines them in the specific context of Cameroon; he too argues that the variety of languages in Africa is a resource which we are foolish to neglect. Finally, the chapter by Cortazzi and Jin looks at a very particular aspect of the teaching of English in China; although at first sight they may appear to be upholding the hegemony of English which both Pattanayak and Robinson dread, in fact they too are arguing for pluralism, this time in recognising and making use of culturally appropriate pedagogic practices.

Alternative Perspectives

We have so far emphasised the division of this collection into three sub-themes. However, we must not neglect the fact that a number of other themes appear at different points. At one level, for example, it is striking how many of the contributors make use of educational contexts as the sites for their investiga-tions (see Fairclough, Rogers, Rampton, Tonkyn, Turner & Hiraga, and

Cortazzi & Jin, for example). This is understandable, for educational institutions are dedicated, *par excellence*, to the production of human change.

Another feature which recurs throughout the three sub-themes of the collection is the question of measuring change. This is tackled, in one way or another, by Kennedy, Snow, Rampton, Raschka & Milroy, Tonkyn, and Cortazzi & Jin. Another recurring concern is the issue of language change – change both in status and in corpus – being a mirror of social forces which are beyond the control of individuals and of relatively powerless social groups (see, for example, the contributions by Fairclough, Meinhof, Turner, Rampton, Pattanayak and Robinson).

Finally, all the work reported here is fired by the desire to explore the immensely complicated and symbiotic relationships between change in the individual, change in society, and change in language.

Acknowledgements

We are grateful to Ken Tait of the Computer Based Learning Unit in the School of Education, University of Leeds, for help with converting files into formats which we could use. We are also grateful to Jill Carroll and Christine Backhouse for clerical support.

Section 1:
Change, Language and Society at the End of the Twentieth Century

Introduction

The papers in this section address different aspects of the theme from very different angles, and at different levels of analysis; together they demonstrate the breadth of potential contributions that applied linguistics can make to understanding language use and language change in its social context.

Fairclough's plenary paper, 'Border Crossings: Discourse and social change in contemporary societies', presents an applied linguist's response to processes of social and cultural change in the late twentieth century post-modern, post-industrialised world. From the intersection of applied linguistics with social science, he identifies the interaction of discourse (and discourses) with change of various types – technological change, economic and social change, conversationalisation, marketisation and increasing reflexivity – in order to ask what theories of language and discourse, and what modes of language education are relevant in this scenario. Emerging changes in the grammar of English are traced to change in orders of discourse occurring in response to, and as constitutive of, socio-cultural change, providing support for his call for a critical discourse analysis that will complement and frame linguistic analysis.

Meinhof's chapter, 'Dialect as Metaphor', is a detailed investigation into the use of dialect change as a symbol of personal and social change over the period 1918 to 1982, as portrayed in the *Heimat* films. Such investigation of speech behaviour, at one remove from everyday life in its media representation, reveals something of the attitudes of individuals and groups to choice and use of language.

In Foster's paper, 'Language Change and Darwinian Principles', the analogy between language change and the processes of biological evolution

1

is explored, highlighting particularly the common features of redundancy and multiple functioning. Turner's paper on the risk of attrition for British Sign Language – 'Language Change at the British Sign Language/English Interface' – also uses analogy, this time with language attrition in small, localised minority language communities. He draws conclusions about the need for first language users of BSL to feel positively motivated to use and develop their language, in both signed and written modes, and across a range of genres, in order to prevent damage to the long-term viability of heritage BSL.

The papers by Kennedy ('"*La Crème de la Crème*": Coercion and corpus change') and Rogers ('Modern Foreign Languages and Curriculum Policy at 16+') both deal with aspects of language open to planned intervention, in social and educational contexts respectively. However, they report very different outcomes. Kennedy uses a corpus of newspaper advertisements to analyse changes in gender-specific language use brought about by the Sexual Discrimination Act of 1975. His data show how enforced changes in language use reflect and partly constitute legislated social change, and give rise to interesting questions about the long-term impact which such enforced change actually has on attitudes and behaviour.

Rogers' data, meanwhile, identifies a failure to change at more than a superficial level among a group of people who are potentially gatekeepers for change in language education: A-level examiners in Foreign Languages. By analysing documents issued by examining boards, she demonstrates how superficial changes in terminology are apparently not supported by underlying changes in understanding of language learning processes, and the confusion that results from this conflict.

1 Border Crossings: Discourse and social change in contemporary societies[1]

NORMAN FAIRCLOUGH
Lancaster University

Language in Sociocultural Change: A field of applied linguistics

John Trim in his address to the twentieth anniversary meeting of BAAL in 1987 (Trim, 1988) emphasised the broad view of applied linguistics accepted as the remit for BAAL by its founders. Indeed he referred to one important aspect of the 'field of application' which I am concerned with in this chapter in noting that it was 'a cause for great regret and deep concern if professional academic linguists are so absorbed by problems of government and binding in syntax that . . . all those concerned with the consequences of the increasing internationalisation of life, from the management of multinational corporations, the conduct of international and supranational organisations and authorities to the impact on individual lives of personal mobility and the need for access to information, must . . . fend for themselves and develop, ad hoc, their particular linguistic expertise'.

Contemporary processes of social and cultural change, including the internationalisation – or as it is now more commonly called 'globalisation' – of life, are a focus of increasing attention and concern amongst academic social scientists, in the media, and in everyday life. Responses to change are often coloured by nostalgia, anxiety, and even a bleak hopelessness. What is striking in the accounts of these changes by sociologists and others is the extent to which they involve and are constituted in language change, and in changing discursive practices. (These are not one and the same, as I argue later.) There is an opportunity and a responsibility here for applied linguistics. An opportunity, in that so far linguists have not made their mark to any degree in these academic and extra-academic debates and analyses, despite the fact that there are many issues where their insights would be valuable additions.

There is specifically here an opportunity for interdisciplinary work: if applied linguists are able to contribute relevant theories of language and frameworks for analysis, they may be able to rebuild bridges with social scientific colleagues which past disappointments and the excesses of formalism have burnt. There is a responsibility, in that (as Trim's remarks imply) ongoing change has all sorts of problematic language-related consequences for people's lives. Applied linguistics research might be able to help people towards a clearer view of the processes they are caught up in, and of alternative ways of acting, as well as contributing to the development of a language education agenda which is better suited to the times.

This field of application is a relatively new one for BAAL agendas, but it may perhaps prove to become an increasingly prominent one. It has already received some attention – for instance from Gunther Kress in his arguments for a social and historical linguistics (and his suggestion that BAAL is uniquely well placed in the UK to contribute to such a development, and is in fact doing so), in the first Pit Corder memorial lecture at the 1991 Annual Meeting (Kress, 1993a). And the Applied Linguistics Association of Australia published in 1993 a collection of three papers by Michael Halliday under the title *Language in a Changing World*, including his keynote addresses to the Ninth World Congress of Applied Linguistics in Thessaloniki in 1990, and the 1992 Annual Congress of the ALAA (Halliday, 1993). There is much in Halliday's papers that I agree with, and indeed I shall draw on them in this paper. But I do have one reservation. It strikes me that he is trying to make grammar stretch too far. The issues we are dealing with require in my view a systematic framework for discourse analysis, for the analysis of what I shall call 'orders of discourse', and of the potentially complex articulations of orders of discourse and their constituent discourses and genres in the production and consumption of texts. A framework for discourse analysis in terms of which sociocultural change can be explored in its discoursal aspects as the negotiation and restructuring of boundaries within and between orders of discourse: 'border-crossing'. A framework for discourse analysis complementing, and framing, a framework for linguistic analysis. I shall shortly spell this out further.

Social Change

I should begin with some necessarily limited and selective comments on social change in the late twentieth century, drawing particularly on some of the work on cultural change which is a major interest amongst social science colleagues at Lancaster University (Keat & Abercrombie, 1991; Keat, Whiteley & Abercrombie, 1994; Lash & Urry, 1994). Changes are often conceptualised in terms of a transition from modern to 'late modern' or 'post-modern' society. I prefer the former term, because I accept the argument that what is at issue is extreme developments of tendencies within modernity. My thesis here is that social change in contemporary society has a substantively – though not of course exclusively – cultural character, and that more specifically contemporary social change is substantively constituted by changing discursive practices. I assume here a constitutive theory of discourse – or more precisely a dialectical theory of discourse as both shaped by and shaping other facets of society and culture – social structures, social relations, systems of knowledge and belief, ideologies, identities, values.

(1) It makes sense to begin by referring to technological changes which constitute the basis for the massive economic, social, political and cultural upheavals we are living through, though they will not be a real concern here. Suffice to say, as many others have done, that the new technologies are leading directly to important border-crossings in their own right. Computer-mediated interactions for instance are leading to the emergence of new genres which combine characteristics of speech and writing, conversational discourse and public discourse. More generally, traditional and familiar distinctions (such as speech versus writing) and categories (such as authorship) may be radically affected by the new technologies. In the context of 'virtual reality', so may representation.

(2) Economic change is often discussed in terms of a late modern process of globalisation, the emergence of a global field of economic exchanges and flows at the expense of the national economies of modernity. (International exchanges and flows are of course not new; the concept of globalisation points to their distinctive contemporary forms.) Globalisation may be economically rooted, but it has also received increasing attention as a political and especially a cultural process (Robertson, 1992; Lash & Urry, 1994). But it is a mistake to conceive of globalisation as the economic, political or cultural unification of the world. Certainly inequalities in all these spheres are if anything widening rather than being ironed out – witness the condition of much of Africa. The point is rather that the fields for these processes are increasingly becoming global; thus it is becoming less easy to insulate national economies, states or cultures from the effects of – and from having effects on – those of other nations. Lash & Urry (1994) argue that there is a dialectic of globalisation and localisation, and that what we need to attend to is the emergence of new forms of relationship between the global and the local. There is some evidence that both the global and the local are gaining at the expense of the national, in the sense of the nation state, but certainly not in the sense of the nationality!

I want to suggest that a part of cultural globalisation is the globalisation of discursive practices. What I mean by that is that one can begin to discern a tendency for flows and movements in discursive practices to assume a global scale. There are maybe the beginnings if you like of a global order of discourse. This has economic roots, notably in the emergence of large international multi-media conglomerates. In the spirit of a dialectic between the global and the local, I am not suggesting a simple hunt for, let us say, influences from the discursive practices of American TV news broadcasting (though such influences are part of the picture, and the asymmetry suggested by this example is too – globalisation in some domains (profits are an exception) involves more intensive flows out of the major international economies than into them, and there is the added factor of the partial global hegemony of English). More to the point is the question of what internal processes and reactions are set off within various national orders of discourse by inward flows – it would be interesting to look in these terms for instance at conversationalisation, simulation of conversational interaction in public discourse, for instance in political discourse in the mass media. What impact have American or west European styles of conversationalised political discourse in the media had in for instance Japan or Brazil, and what reactances have they sparked off in their respective orders of political and media discourse? I recently had the opportunity for some informal and rough observation of mediatised political discourse in Brazil, for instance, and my preliminary impression is that significant elements of political 'publicity' comparable to practices in the USA or Britain have become articulated into a distinctive mix with elements of traditional 'charismatic' political rhetoric which are hard to find on British TV, and indeed make people feel distinctly uncomfortable here. (On globalisation, see also Slembrouck forthcoming).

(3) A well-charted economic shift is the relative expansion of service industries as compared with manufacturing. In service industries, the goods themselves may have a more or less symbolic or linguistic character – notably in the culture industries, where the goods are things like television programmes. More generally, the way the goods are 'delivered', and therefore attributes of those who deliver them, determine the quality of the service. The quality of air travel for instance is partly a question of the behaviour – and language – of cabin crews. This means that language is an important part of the goods, and is therefore subject to economic calculations, controls and intervention.

(4) We may think of such interventions in terms of the cultural keyword 'design'. My colleague Nigel Whiteley notes that 'the 1980s has witnessed

a boom in the growth and newsworthiness of design: the High Street has been visually transformed; design consultancies have mushroomed . . .; the Press has revelled in the epithet "designer"', and he quotes the DTI minister responsible for design speaking in 1985, 'the British Government regards design as a dominant factor that lies at the heart of product success'. A common view of design marries functionalism (does it work?) and 'aesthetico-moral principles (e.g. truth to materials, integrity of surface)' (Whiteley, 1991). Factors in the design of linguistic goods in service industry contexts are I suggest similarly both functional and aesthetic. Thus interview has long been a target for research, design and training in the light of functional considerations such as effectiveness in meeting institutional objectives – for instance in 'social skills training' associated with social psychology (Argyle, 1978). Aesthetic design of language would seem to be an issue in for example recruitment policies and training for waiters in restaurants, where the atmosphere, the social relations, and the staff themselves are now often almost as much part of the goods as the food. A recent research project on a 'fun', 'southern style' restaurant in Cambridge suggests that staff are appointed because they possess the right 'cultural capital' – 'they have to be informal, young, friendly, with the appropriate skills of emotional control, and with the right sort of body and skills in presenting it in their performances'. Preparation for work is talked of in terms of 'getting in the mood' (Lash & Urry, 1994: 202, reporting Crang, 1993). Aesthetic design here clearly involves cultivation and simulation of particular communicative styles (and the specific selections are adjusted to the overall ethos of the particular restaurant) for the values, forms of self and social relations which they are metaphors for. Language here clusters with curtains, wallpaper and table decorations. The aesthetic design of language is I suggest an increasingly prominent feature of contemporary orders of discourse, in line with what Featherstone (1991) calls the 'aestheticization of everyday life', corresponding to the acquisition by commodities in late capitalism of increasingly dominant 'sign value', in Baudrillard's terminology (Baudrillard, 1988). This is perhaps how we should frame 'the noticeable shift from verbal to visual forms of representation and communication' discussed by Kress (1993a, b).

(5) One widespread outcome of interventions to design service encounters is the conversationalisation of these public discourses. The engineering of informality, friendship and even intimacy entails a crossing of borders between the public and the private, the commercial and the domestic, which is partly constituted by a simulation of the discursive practices of everyday life, conversational discourse. This may be a matter of aesthetic

design, but with functional pay-offs in terms of effectiveness as variously measured. Conversationalisation can be linked to what Hochschild has identified as the 'emotional' nature of much labour in contemporary service industries (Hochschild, 1983): language and other semiotic resources in the management of affect, self-management on the part of service workers, as well as routinely manipulating the feelings of clients, all part of the service. Waiters in restaurants are a case in point. Emotional labour is an institutional appropriation of practices of everyday life, and it needs the language of everyday life. It has often been remarked that the burden of emotional labour in everyday life, especially in the family, has an unequal gender distribution, and is disproportionately carried by women. Service industries can be read in terms of a feminisation of labour, suggesting a certain gender bias to phenomena of conversationalisation. Finally, returning to the dialectic between globalisation and localisation, conversationalisation can partly be interpreted as a localising tendency – a revalorisation of vernacular language as part of a revalorisation of vernacular cultures, part of a reassertion of region and locality at the expense of the centralised nation-state. Conversationalisation entails diversification of practices, a plurality of conversational styles depending on social class and cultural membership as well as region. However, conversationalisation of public discourse is a selective construction and simulation of actual conversation which draws upon certain conversational practices but excludes others (including the conversational practices of minority languages and of particular classes and strata), and recontextualises and transforms the practices it draws upon. Moreover, the globalisation-localisation relation *is* a dialectic: conversationalisation also becomes an affectation of western culture projected as a model on a global stage. These comments also perhaps suggest the deeply ambivalent nature of conversationalisation with respect to social relations of power: it is a democratising, opening, movement which is however widely calculated and engineered top-down. There is a suspicion that informalised and conversationalised relations in public may be spaces of more penetrative forms of power (Foucault, 1979).

(6) The emergence of services as the dominant economic sector in the most advanced economies has been accompanied by a process of marketisation which has assimilated not only new service industries but also traditional ones, including public services and the professions, to a market mode of operation. Commodification, the generalisation of the capitalist commodity form to society as a whole, is an entrenched process in capitalism which was already described by Karl Marx. The experience of the past two decades, especially Thatcherism for us in Britain, is a further turn of

the screw. Contemporary forms of commodification reflect the relatively enhanced role in the economy of consumption, and its cultural consequences have been designated as 'consumer culture' or 'promotional culture' (Featherstone, 1991; Wernick, 1992). I want to suggest that the cultural change involved is partly a change in discursive practices: in particular, new service and older professional domains have been extensively colonised by the genres and discourses of the market, leading to profound transformations of their orders of discourse. The contemporary development of advertising as a genre makes the point: commodity advertising is now at the centre of a vast proliferation of semi-advertising forms in education, health care, the arts, and so forth, where the generic conventions of advertising are variously hybridised with the conventions of more traditional genres in these domains. An example of a semi-advertising genre is the contemporary university prospectus. In broader terms, there has been a colonisation of orders of discourse by the promotional functions of language, perhaps with major ethical consequences and pathological effects. For instance, the category of 'informative' discourse is widely problematised where 'telling' acquires an increasingly insistent undercurrent of 'selling'. Commodification of discourse certainly entails design, both functional and aesthetic. It is also closely tied up with conversationalisation: it is well known that a distinctive feature of modern commodity advertising itself is what Leech (1966) called its 'public-colloquial' character, a public language with features of private, colloquial, conversational language.

(7) Giddens has suggested that reflexivity is a fundamental defining feature of late modernity. The reflexive monitoring of action is often seen as intrinsic to ALL human activity. Late modernity is characterised by reflexivity in a special sense, which Giddens glosses as 'susceptibility of most aspects of social activity, and material relations with nature, to chronic revision in the light of new information or knowledge' (Giddens, 1991). Reflexivity is often discussed as things that scientists or social scientists do, but Giddens is pointing to reflexivity as a pervasive feature of the ordinary lives of ordinary people. Language too in late modernity is susceptible to chronic revision in the light of new information or knowledge, though we might wonder about the meaning of 'chronic' in the light of Halliday's comments about the 'inherent antipathy between grammar' – particularly its 'inner layer' – 'and design' (1993: 31). What I have said about design perhaps belongs under the general heading of modern reflexivity, and indeed I have referred elsewhere (Fairclough, 1992a) to the 'technologisation of discourse' as a distinctive feature of contemporary orders of discourse – a systematic, institutionalised, top-

down linking of research into, design and redesign of, and training in discursive practices. However, the emphasis in Giddens is on reflexivity in ordinary life, if you like as a 'bottom up' phenomenon. Seen in this way, reflexivity is a counter-weight to the bleak accounts of contemporary social change we are all familiar with. It emphasises the increasing cultural capital of ordinary people, and their agentive capacity, their capacity not only to understand but also to act upon, and act against, the structures which shape their lives. These social theoretical debates on reflexivity ought I think to inform our thinking about language awareness. Ordinary people – or perhaps rather particular classes or groups – are I suspect becoming more linguistically aware as part of modern reflexivity. This is evident in the increasing salience of language in the ways that social issues are interpreted and contested. One example is the focus on language within the feminist movement, another is the orientation to 'verbal hygiene' in 'self-help' materials described by Debbie Cameron in her address to the 1993 Annual Meeting (Cameron, 1994). I return to language awareness as an issue in language education below.

(8) Globalisation involves flows of people, ranging from large-scale migrations to a jet-setting cosmopolitan elite. Cultural diversity is an increasingly salient and unavoidable part of experience. It's increasingly salient from where I imagine most of us are standing because even countries with a determined monocultural tradition like Britain or Germany can no longer dodge it. If we view culture as a process as Brian Street recommended at the 1991 Annual Meeting (Street, 1993), diversity entails not static reproduction of difference, but cultural hybridity or syncretism (Robertson, 1992), which includes discursive and linguistic hybridity. Ben Rampton (1990) for instance describes incipient forms of language crossing in the emergence of a culturally complex British youth culture. Recent work in cultural studies has suggested a generalisation and centralisation of what have hitherto been seen as the marginal experiences of diaspora and cosmopolitanism as a way of refiguring the social subject in culturally diverse societies (see papers by Hall and Homi Bhabha in Rutherford 1990).

Language

I now want to ask two questions which bring the focus back to language. First, what sort of theory of language do we need to investigate these linguistic and discursive aspects of sociocultural change? Second, what particular contribution can an analysis of language texts make to research on sociocultural change?

With respect to the first question, I have already suggested that we need to distinguish linguistic analysis and discourse analysis (Fairclough, 1992a). We might say that there are two sorts of system which shape and are reshaped by practice: language systems, and orders of discourse. Both are constitutive in, and transformed within, social and cultural change. The concept of 'order of discourse' comes from Michel Foucault. I see an order of discourse as the configuration of discursive practices associated with a particular social institution or domain, specified by listing the set of practices, and the nature of the relationships and boundaries between them, including how closed or open the borders are. The main categories of discursive practices are for me genres and discourses. An order of discourse is a social order which is linguistically realised – we might see relationships between language on the one side and society and culture on the other as mediated by orders of discourse, rather than direct. At the most general level we can talk of a societal order of discourse, the overall configuration of a society's orders of discourse. One set of questions about social and cultural change has to do with changing relationships between orders of discourse, and between discursive practices within orders of discourse. For instance, the globalisation/localisation dialectic transforms relationships between societal orders of discourse, and, in so doing, relationships within each of them. Conversationalisation involves a restructuring of relationships between orders of discourse of everyday life and public life.

What then of the relationship between orders of discourse and language systems? Halliday suggests that a grammar is 'a theory of experience', 'a guide to action', 'a metalanguage by which we live'. His example of the 'growthism' that is inherent in the English classification of nouns into countable and uncountable, construing essential resources such as air or water as unbounded, seems to support this. But as his own analysis makes clear – for instance his endorsement of Bernstein's claims on class and code – a grammar is compatible with diverse theories of experience. I would still want to agree with Halliday's insistence on the ideological power of grammar, especially the inner layer of grammar. But should we not rather say that it is the syndromes of grammatical features which realise particular codes, discourses and genres that constitute so many theories of experience, rather than the grammar *per se*?

Analysis of orders of discourse can reveal the diverse theories of experience within a society, and, crucially, the shifting relationships between them. It strikes me that it is fruitful to reformulate Halliday's valuable analysis of the history of scientific discourse in these terms, i.e. in terms of a relationship between sociocultural change and language/grammar that is mediated by orders of discourse, rather than in terms of a direct relationship between society and grammar. Some of the more recent developments that Halliday refers to clearly involve border crossings between orders of discourse – the colonising spread of scientific discourse into the orders of discourse of administration, bureaucracy and management, and the recent widespread alienation of people from scientific discourse which seems to me to have to do with an opening of borders between scientific discourse and the discourse of everyday life, which the mass media are deeply implicated in. (Though this alienation is not just a discoursal development, it is a wider feature of late modern culture.) Also, there is a genealogical question to ask about how emergent scientific discourse drew upon and creatively rearticulated earlier orders of discourse – about the configuration of discourses and genres it was created out of.

The emergence and colonising spread of scientific discourse does not entail new grammar, as Halliday points out, but a reweighting of existing grammatical features, and a recasting of them into a new syndrome, a new pattern of co-occurrence which realises a new semantic style, a new discourse. The grammatical changes here seem to be consequential upon changes in the societal order of discourse – not simply the existence of a new discourse of science, but its hegemony over other discourses in fields such as chemistry or medicine, its marginalisation rather than destruction of these other discourses, and its colonising spread to orders of discourse in other social domains outside straight science. It is these changes in the societal order of discourse that brought a particular syndrome of grammatical features into prominence. You could then say the language and the grammar have changed after all: not only did the syndrome generate new constructions, such as the 'happening a caused happening x' clause type Halliday mentions, where 'two nominalized processes are linked by a verb expressing the logical relationship between them' (an example from Newton, for instance: . . . *all Bodies by percussion excite vibrations in the air*); there is also no clear way of dividing a shift in preferential patterns of use in the grammar from a change in the grammar.

There remains one key reason for claiming that the order of discourse has primacy over the grammar as the construct in terms of which we can chart discursive aspects of sociocultural change. Contemporary societies are, as I have suggested, overwhelmingly culturally and linguistically diverse. An order of discourse – for instance the order of discourse of a particular workplace, or more abstractly of 'the workplace' in contemporary society – will involve hybrid configurations of practices that have diverse cultural origins and which are realised in different languages and combinations of languages. The grammar of any particular language is a part, but only a part, of the picture.

My second question was about the contribution that analysis of language texts can make to research on sociocultural change. I have been discussing change in terms of border-crossing within and across orders of discourse. These border-crossings are of course effected in texts. The focus correspondingly is upon the hybridity of texts – how texts in contexts of change can mix together discourses and genres in creative and often complex ways, cutting across conventional boundaries within and between orders of discourse. Of course, not all texts are markedly hybrid, some are relatively normative. What I want to stress though is that textual hybridity is normal especially in a period of intensive and extensive sociocultural change. Degrees of hybridity show up in the intertextual analysis of a text – when one interprets how it draws upon the discursive resources of the culture – its orders of discourse. We might say that intertextual hybridity is realised in linguistic heterogeneity, which shows up in the linguistic analysis of a text. For example, one textual realisation of commodification, of the hybridisation of promotional and advertising discourse with professional and public service discourse, is hetero-geneity of interpersonal meanings and forms. For instance, in communica-tions between institutions and their publics or clients in a variety of domains, one finds heterogeneity in the textual construction of participant relations between the institutional addresser and addressees.

This can be illustrated by four texts, which I refer to here as A, B, C and D:[2] A is the written text from a page of a brochure about Barclaycard pro-duced in 1985, B is extracts from a brochure about the 'enterprise initiative' produced by the Department of Trade and Industry in 1988, C is an entry from the Lancaster University undergraduate prospectus for 1990, and D is an advertisement for academic posts by one of the new universities dating from 1992. Each of these manifests heterogeneity in the authority relations between addresser and addressee. In A, the institutional addresser (the bank) is both regulating – laying down rules for – the use of the Barclaycard financial service, and selling that service to potential consumers. The former entails the addresser as authoritor (the participant with authority) and the addressee as authoritee (the participant without it), but the latter entails the addressee as authoritor and the bank as authoritee. The heterogeneity shows up formally in realisations of obligation. The text alludes to many actions required of the client, yet only two are worded with obligational modalities – *you should keep*, and *it is important to ensure*. Elsewhere, requirements show up as imperatives or non-modalised declaratives mitigated with *just* – a favourite advertising device which conveys the core consumer value of effortlessness. Other requirements are located in non-finite clauses. There is thus textual heterogeneity in the realisation of obligations, but also textual compromise: the requirements are there, but they are not overtly worded as such.

In B, the addresser–addressee relationship is constructed both as an expert–client relationship and as an advertiser–consumer relationship (illustrated in the fact that the brochure is in part 'selling' the enterprise initiative). So we again have contradictory authoritor–authoritee relations, and textual heterogeneity. So too is C, where the institutional addresser (the university) is both regulating potential students – for instance in terms of what courses they can take – and selling itself to them. Here, the problematical requirements on potential students are handled by concentrating them in the diagrammatic part of the entry, which largely avoids explicit obligational modalities.

I see D as promoting the university while advertising the posts, so that authoritor–authoritee relations are again heterogeneous. One striking feature of D is its little speculative narratives with the potential applicant as hero, giving clauses modalised with *will* such *as you will be committed to teaching excellence*. These forms are alternatives to explicit obligational modalities. These are interesting because they mitigate an aggravated institutional intrusion into the person and personality of the applicant that I think is going on here. The institution is wanting to regulate the commitment of applicants, and other personal qualities – or qualities that used to be personal. Explicit obligational modalities would make this transparent. Recall also my observation earlier that conversationalisation might be associated with more penetrative forms of power.

Heterogeneity can be read as contradiction, and we might say that texts show up in the detail of their linguistic choices the contradictory, unresolved, unfinished nature of the social practices which they (help) constitute. These examples could I think be fruitfully analysed in these terms. What I would want to suggest about the special contribution that textual analysis can make to research on change is that textual evidence is particularly useful in revealing the messiness that is characteristic of real as opposed to ideal-typical processes of social and cultural change. Social theorists often provide us with the broad sweep, with what may sometimes amount to a persuasive definition and directionality in terms of which we can read – and perhaps ten years later totally reread – experience. Texts are a good corrective, helping us see the reality 'on the ground'. Processes of change are usually contradictory processes. They are also processes of struggle. The heterogeneity of texts may point us to this: to struggles over change between groups of people within or across institutions, to struggles within contradictorily constructed subjects (such as perhaps the collective subjects that produce texts like my examples) for whom change may mean insecurity and anxiety.[3]

I have found it useful to think of a critical discourse analysis of language texts as a mapping of three sorts of statement onto one another: statements about the language of the text, statements about the intertextuality of the text, and statements about the social and cultural practice within which the text is framed. Intertextuality mediates the link between language and society/culture. Statements about language connect the particular text to language systems, statements about intertextuality connect it to orders of discourse. Actually statements about intertextuality can be seen as just a part of a more broadly conceived mediating component which appertains generally to text-as-process – to processes of various sorts in the production, distribution, and consumption of texts.

Implications for Language Education

I here draw upon early discussions towards an 'International Multiliteracies Project' which will surface as a publicly available document in a few months time, as well as on published work in the field of 'critical language awareness' (Fairclough, 1992b). Kress (1993b) has recently suggested that we should be recasting the language curriculum in schools *now* in the light of our best guesses about what capacities people will need as citizens and workers in about 20 years time. Futurology is a risky business, but two predictions would perhaps attract fairly general agreement: that the next generation will need the capacity to live with, and inflect the direction of, rapid and constant change; and that they will need to be able to live with and articulate linguistic and cultural differences. With respect to language and literacy education, 'back to basics' is of course pretty irrelevant in such a scenario. But we should also be cautious about over-emphasising training in what are judged to be socially powerful genres. The issue of transfer becomes crucial, and more precisely the capacity of people to draw upon socially available conventions and orders of discourse, in all their cultural complexity, in creative ways. Of course, as Bakhtin pointed out with reference to genres, conventions 'must be fully mastered in order to be manipulated freely' (Bakhtin, 1986). So the issue is not alternatives to acquisition and training, but the articulation together of diverse activities within a pedagogy. Such a creative relationship to socially available orders of discourse needs to be based in self- and other-consciousness, and so a social framing including ideological critique of discursive practices and orders of discourse is another key activity in the pedagogy. Critical language awareness in language education is the necessary basis for the reflexivity and creativity we are already finding we need as workers, citizens, and in our ordinary lives; for self-defence, for responding to change, and for negotiating and contesting the directions of change. So far, these capacities are restricted to an educated elite. An argument, and a struggle, which now needs to be developed is that some sections within employers and the state, as well as learners themselves, may have an interest in generalising them.

Notes

1. I am grateful to Lilie Chouliaraki and Joan Pujolar for their valuable comments on an earlier version of this paper.
2. These examples have been more fully discussed elsewhere: example A in Fairclough, 1988, example B in Fairclough, 1991, and examples C and D in Fairclough, 1993.
3. Lilie Chouliaraki and Joan Pujolar point out that texts need their own corrective: we need to situate them as moments in contextualised interactions. One way of ensuring such contextualisation in analysis is to use a combination of critical discourse analysis and ethnography, as they do in their research.

References

Argyle, M. (1978) *The Psychology of Interpersonal Behaviour* 3rd ed. Harmondsworth: Penguin.

Bakhtin, M. (1986) *Speech Genres and Other Late Essays*. Austin: University of Texas.

Baudrillard, J. (1988) In M. Poster (ed.) *Selected Writings*. Cambridge: Polity Press.

Cameron, D. (1994) Putting our practice into theory. In D. Graddol and J. Swann (eds) *Evaluating Language: British Studies in Applied Linguistics* 8. Clevedon: Multilingual Matters.

Crang, P. (1993) A New Service Society: On the geographies of service employment. PhD Dissertation. Dept of Geography, University of Cambridge.

Fairclough, N. (1988) Register power and sociosemantic change. In D. Birch and M. O'Toole (eds) *Functions of Style*. Leicester: Pinter Publications.

— (1991) What might we mean by 'enterprise discourse'? In R. Keat and N. Abercrombie (eds) *Enterprise Culture*. London: Routledge.

— (1992a) *Discourse and Social Change*. Cambridge: Polity Press.

— (ed.) (1992b) *Critical Language Awareness*. London: Longman.

— (1993) Critical discourse analysis and the marketisation of public discourse. *Discourse & Society* 4.2: 133–68.

Featherstone, M. (1991) *Consumer Culture and Postmodernism*. London: Sage.

Foucault, M. (1979) *Discipline and Punish: The birth of the prison*. Harmondsworth: Penguin Books.

Giddens, A. (1991) *Modernity and Self-Identity*. Cambridge: Polity Press.

Hall, S. (1990) Cultural identity and diaspora. In J. Rutherford (ed.) *Identity: Community, culture, difference*. London: Lawrence & Wishart.

Halliday, M. (1993) *Language in a Changing World*. Occasional Paper no. 13. Sydney: Applied Linguistics Association of Australia.

Hochschild, A. R. (1983) *The Managed Heart*. Berkeley: University of California Press.

Homi Bhaba. J. Rutherford (ed.) (1990) Interview.

Keat, R. and Abercrombie, N. (1991) *Enterprise Culture*. London: Routledge.

Keat, R., Whiteley, N. and Abercrombie, N. (1994) *The Authority of the Consumer*. London: Routledge.

Kress, G. (1993a) Cultural considerations in linguistic description. In D. Graddol, L. Thompson and M. Byram (eds) *Language and Culture: British studies in applied linguistics* 7. Clevedon: Multilingual Matters.

— (1993b) Representational resources in the presentation of subjectivity: Questions for a multicultural society (MS).

Lash, S. and Urry, J. (1994) *Economies of Signs and Space.* London: Sage.

Leech, G. N. (1966) *English in Advertising.* London: Longman.

Rampton, B. (1990) The use of interracial Panjabi in a multilingual adolescent peer group. ESF Workshop on Code-Switching, Brussels.

Robertson, R. (1992) *Globalization: Social theory and global culture.* London: Sage.

Rutherford, J. (ed.) (1990) *Identity: Community, culture, difference.* London: Lawrence & Wishart.

Slembrouck, S. (forthcoming) Globalising flows: Promotional discourses of government in western European 'orders of discourse', to appear in *Social Semiotics.*

Street, B. (1993) Culture is a verb: anthropological aspects of language and cultural process. In D. Graddol, L. Thompson and M. Byram (eds) *Language and Culture: British studies in applied linguistics* 7. Clevedon: Multilingual Matters.

Trim, J. (1988) Applied linguistics in society. In P. Grunwell (ed.) *Applied Linguistics in Society.* London: CILT.

Wernick, A. (1992) *Promotional Culture.* London: Sage.

Whiteley, N. (1991) Design in enterprise culture: Design for whose profit? In R. Keat and N. Abercrombie (eds) *Enterprise Culture.* London: Routledge.

2 Language Change and Darwinian Principles

MICHAEL FOSTER
St Mary's University College

Introduction

The paleontologist Stephen Jay Gould, whose many books and essays are the original inspiration for this paper, wrote in *The Panda's Thumb* (1980: 57):

> If genius has any common denominator, I would propose breadth of interest and the ability to construct fruitful analogies between fields.

His own particular hero, Darwin, was a great metaphorical thinker and maker of analogies, and his theories partly owe their formulation to the fruitful analogies he was able to make with the *laissez faire* economic theories of Adam Smith, for instance, and also with the historical linguistics of his day. For example, in *The Descent of Man* (1871, quoted in Gould, 1980: 26) he writes:

> Rudimentary organs may be compared with the letters in a word, still retained in the spelling, but become useless in pronunciation, but which serve as a clue in seeking for its derivation.

This is a good illustration for both fields of the way that a complex history leaves behind its traceable remnants. It is not hard to see that there are other shared features in linguistic and evolutionary systems that have made such anologies popular, for linguists as well as biologists. Such features would include hereditary transmission, mutation, unpredictable variability in form, and change accelerated within isolated populations. A recent example, from the evolutionary side, is Steve Jones's 1993 book on genetics and evolution entitled *The Language of the Genes*, which makes use of the analogy throughout. In the introduction, for instance, he writes that 'Genetics itself is a language', with a vocabulary (genes) and a grammar (the rules for ordering them); he also speaks of evolution in both systems, and 'garbled transmission' of the reproductive message as a primary source of change.

The basis of the analogy that I would like to explore here is that languages and complex organisms share the principal pre-requisites for evolving systems of organisation: most importantly, redundancy of function and multiple use in individual structures. Creativity in evolutionary terms depends, says Stephen Jay Gould (1993: 97), on 'sloppiness, poor fit, quirky design, and above all else, redundancy'. These terms seem to me to be perfectly adequate for describing language structures. Gould illustrates his point by showing how the sound-transmitting jaw bones of early reptiles, by odd accidents of juxtaposition and redundancy, the leaving off of some functions and co-opting of others, migrated to become (eventually) the three bones of the mammalian inner ear. It is not difficult to see that there are parallels in the history of language change, as structures shift form, overlap, gain some functions and lose others. In both systems, change is unpredictable and contingent: existing structures are the serviceable results of local, *ad hoc* changes that have achieved a manageable coherence, and not – despite popular misperception – the optimal products of a relentless upward momentum, through lower forms to a triumphant perfection.

Further in this paper, I would like to look at ways in which language change and biological evolution share not only structural principles but also a common misfortune in the ways that they are misunderstood. There is a great potential for compounding error at the point where language and evolution are directly, rather than analogously, related; that is, where language is viewed as a product of biological evolution.

Fruitful Analogies: Redundancy, Contingency and Constraint

Gould himself, in an essay called 'The Senseless Signs of History' (1980), makes a sophisticated and instructive use of the language analogy when trying to explain why Darwin searched for 'oddities and imperfections' in the natural world – because 'Remnants of the past that don't make sense in present terms – the useless, the odd, the peculiar, the incongruous – are the signs of history' (p. 27). As Gould points out, 'words provide clues about their history when etymology does *not* match current meaning'. Historical systems, says Gould, are 'complex, contingent, interactive, [and] hierarchical' and nothing within such a system can escape the myriad oddities and compromises that are imposed by heritage. This trailing legacy of in-built constraints is one of the fascinating characteristics of both fields.

Gould's favourite example of ways in which 'past histories exert a quirky hold . . . upon an imperfect present' (Gould, 1987: 24) is the panda, and its strange array of adaptive and non-adaptive features (Gould, 1980). It has a carnivore's teeth, reflecting the carnivorous past that it shares with other bears. But it also has what is essentially a carnivore's gut – that is, its intestine is very short in relation to its body compared to other grass and leaf-eaters – and is therefore very ill-adapted to its new life as a herbivore, and especially a herbivore trying to get by on a nutrient poor diet of bamboo. The result is that it has to eat about fifteen hours a day, and prodigiously defecates all that semi-digested bamboo. Moreover, its chief source of food disappears at regular intervals during its flowering cycle. It is the panda's thumb that especially delights Gould. It is specially designed for the necessary but limited function of stripping off bamboo leaves, but it is not a true thumb; it had to be contrived out of a hypertrophied wrist bone since its original thumb had already been employed in the usual place in a carnivore's claw. An odd incidental byproduct of the new thumb is a slightly hypertrophied corresponding bone in the panda's foot that does not seem to confer any advantage, but whose embryological pathway is correlated with the development of the wrist bone.

Obviously, language change also works under historical constraints of various kinds. No language as we know it would be a communicative engineer's ideal, just as no engineer would make a thumb out of a wrist bone if he could go back and start the design from scratch. Both systems are 'making use of old junk', in Jean Aitchison's phrase (1991, p. 148). I am not going to be so bold as to set out the parameters of an ideal language, but presumably it would be that which best realises the advantages that language is recognised to confer. If that form includes regular patterning at phonological, morphological and syntactic levels, then already there is a problem. As Theo Venneman (1993, pp. 322–3) writes, 'the potentially antithetic nature of language changes on different parameters has been known to linguists for a long time'. That is, features that are valued at one level of the language hierarchy are warred against at another. Sound changes and morphological changes are often antithetical. The optimal syllable is a strong consonant followed by a sonorous vowel, but the optimal word contains a strong initial syllable with all others reduced. Syntactic patterns will inevitably throw together collocations that knock the phonological system (and the 'one-word, one meaning' ideal) awry. Our word production can be extraordinary, but the variety and combinations of sounds we make is limited; as listeners, our phonemic processing is also phenomenal, but limited. The speaker wants more speed (which means more rapid translation of thoughts to words, more rapid processing by the listener, and more abbreviation of syntactic and phonological rules); the listener wants more clarity (marked, easily perceived, redundant distinctions, without ambiguity). And against those competing demands, and within the restrictions imposed by mere linearity, an ideal pattern (whatever it might start out as) cannot hold. Furthermore, once changes in patterns have set in, they then belong, at a further hierarchical level, to a social semiotic, by which a whole new set of historical pressures is brought to bear. And hence the 'oddities, imperfections, and quirkiness' of our languages, in many ways a match for the panda. When Venneman (1993, p. 322) writes,

> In any system of sufficient complexity, any meliorative move may have bad consequences,

he could be speaking on behalf of biological systems as well as linguistic ones.

For Gould, one of the key consequences of historical complexity is that individual features may either become redundant or assume multiple functions. The principle is an easy one to grasp: sometimes a single function is performed by more than one feature (the nose and the tongue both judge taste; verbs and adverbs can both express time), and often a single feature performs multiple functions (the tongue is employed in tasting, chewing, and speaking; many words have multiple meanings, operate as verbs as well as nouns, etc.). This is what allows change without loss of function: the overlapping is inefficient and sloppy in economic terms, but it allows a single feature to be detached from an original purpose and re-employed elsewhere. Gould illustrates this (in the example I mentioned earlier) through the evolutionary process by which jaw bones became ear bones: the redundancy of gill arches in early fishes allowed those closest to the mouth to be re-employed as jaw bones; bone has the incidental property of being a good sound transmitter, allowing structural bones that happened to be in the right place to assume a secondary function in hearing.

Languages, of course, as John Ohala (1993: 263) says, 'teem with polysemy and homonymy'. Redundancy and multiple function might work to instigate change (in syntax, let's say) when it becomes possible to re-interpret a function in a new way (as a bracing bone was 're-interpreted' as a hearing bone). Jean Aitchison (1991: 93) quotes A. J. Naro (1981: 97):

> The change . . . sets in at the zero point of surface differentiation between the old and the new systems and so spreads to other points along the path of least surface differentiation.

Aitchison uses the example of 'can', which originally meant 'know' before a noun and 'know how to' before a verb. As the position of 'can' before a verb became re-analyzed as its chief function, 'can' became specialized as an auxiliary unable to stand alone.

An example of a contemporary change in progress is the reanalysis of the pronoun 'they' as a singular in contexts where the referent could be of either sex:

'When you see one of the cleaners, tell them what happened.'

The 'zero point of surface differentiation' is not hard to find in sentences like:

The bus driver told everyone they were making too much noise.

Mary saw everyone before John saw them.

using 'he' and 'him' in these cases is clearly impossible. 'They' is forced into service in spite of 'everyone's' grammatical singularity, and by analogy is made available in other contexts. The spread of the use of 'they' as a singular is no doubt accelerated by the social pressure to avoid 'he' and 'him' in ambiguous contexts as sexist.

Obviously, wherever there is the potential for variation there is a potential for change: where different sounds can be interpreted as the same phoneme, where differing groups of phonemes can be interpreted as the same word, and where different syntactic structures can serve the same function. On what all of this means to an investigator (and now on the linguistic side of analogy-making, looking in the other direction) Roger Lass (1993, p. 160) comments that:

> Linguistic reconstruction is a 'paleontological' operation . . . like either projecting an ancestor (what kind of fish do we need to give us an amphibian?) or filling in a missing but patently necessary stage (what comes between coelocanths and amphibians?).

So in pursuing subjects that exhibit in many ways similar structures, their investigators are pushed towards analogous methods: as John Ohala (1993, p. 266) says, language history, like paleontology, 'deals with a subject matter that is inherently inaccessible to direct study'. The linguist and the paleontologist make reconstructions from the available evidence (sometimes remnants, sometimes more or less whole skeletons) – and try to develop, by inferential methods, a coherent theory of change for systems that are inherently unstable (that is, they are undoubtedly subject to change) yet always in equilibrium.

To summarise, then, the main structural similarities between linguistic and biological systems are these:

(1) In both, redundancy and multiple function provide the potential field for evolutionary innovation.

(2) Both are complex historical systems within which change in one parameter can trigger cascading changes in other parameters with un-looked
for consequences.

Less Fruitful Analogy

There is an irritating consistency in the way that commentators see the final
products of these two historical systems as optimal outcomes. We clearly see
this in the ladder of evolution pictures in text books that show life emerging
from slime to gradually mount from single-celled organisms, to insects, fish,
amphibians, reptiles, mammals, and at last, *homo sapiens*. This is a sort of
species chauvinism that Gould is always warning against; life is no ladder, he
tells us, but a copiously branching tree with all contemporary forms as little
twigs at the ends of their own particular branches, and the primate branch is
an especially thin and precarious one. I always have the feeling, when I hear
the language experts on radio or television rhapsodizing about 'the mar-
vellously rich and expressive power of the English tongue' or lamenting the
exquisite precision under attack by (for example) American corruption of
the present perfect, that at the back of their minds is the evolutionary ladder
model of English (although in this case the ladder is endlessly being shaken
and the position on the top rung constantly under threat). The television
naturalist does not tell us about species whose ingenious specialization left
them vulnerable to extinction (natural selection, in their interpretation,
never gets it wrong), and the radio language expert does not tell us of the
traditional capacities for redundancy, vagueness and ambiguity in English,
or of its wonderful irregularities ('spots of corruption' Samuel Johnson said)
that are just as much a part of its historical legacy as the 'wonderfully rich
vocabulary' that is regularly being claimed for it.

This ignoring of historical contingency leads to what Gould (1987)
calls a Panglossian sentimentality – everything that is is for the best – in
popular views on natural history. The physicist Freeman Dyson (1981,
quoted in Gould, 1987: 205) gave a Panglossian explanation of linguistic
diversity that brings together the ideas of language change and biological
evolution:

> It is not just an inconvenient historical accident that we have a variety
> of languages. It was nature's way to make it possible for us to evolve
> rapidly . . . To keep a community genetically isolated and to enable it
> to evolve new social institutions, it was vitally important that the
> members of the community should be quickly separated from their
> neighbours by barriers of language.

But there is no such thing as long-range planning in natural evolution – Dyson
would have to take the bizarre position that some ancestral *individual* gained
a selective advantage by being unable to speak his community's language –
while inconvenient historical accidents are everywhere. It is easy selection
theories of this kind that Gould calls 'Just So Stories', and which he likens to
Dr Pangloss's noting how perfectly noses were created for glasses to sit on.
After convincingly demonstrating that languages do not improve by changing,
Theo Vennemann (1993: 324–5) cannot let the subject go on what might
seem a negative note, and he says that in fact he does believe languages get
better (though only in evolutionary time):

> I believe that languages get better over long periods of time as part of
> the evolution of the human race . . . and I believe that the individual
> changes which linguists study are the vehicles of the global type of change
> by which languages have slowly evolved and are still evolving, from the
> meagre communicative systems of early anthropoids . . . into ever more
> supple, ever more effective, ever more beautiful means of communica-
> tion of a future mankind.

Venneman seems to make the careless Lamarckian error of supposing that
acquired characters can be passed on genetically, although I suspect that there
has simply been a momentary lapse in attention. After a rigorous essay, he
seems to yield to the dangerous temptation of gazing into the mists of time,
past and future, where there is little to constrain glowing hopes in the one
direction or easy speculation about grunting anthropoid ancestors in the
other.

Derek Bickerton, in *Language and Species* (1990), tries more seriously
to trace the origins of language to a source in evolutionary history. However,
the course of his argument sometimes parallels the assumptions that grew
from the argument, made in the last century and continuing well into this
one, that 'ontogeny recapitulates phylogeny', i.e. that the development of
an individual member of a species recapitulated stages in the history of the
species (see Gould, 1977). The argument had some sound bases: the jaw
bones converting to ear bones is played out in every mammalian embryo.
However, it was eventually dropped as a doctrine in embryology, but not
before it had been taken up by analogy in other fields (e.g. by sociologists
who argued that childhood was a reliving of primitive stages of savagery; by
Freud, who thought that boys lived through a psychological recapitulation of
an ancient practice of sons ganging up to murder their father). Although
Bickerton (p. 115) recognises the dangers of accepting recapitulationism as
a principle of development, he assumes on the ground that it *may* be valid
here, that something like a primitive 'protolanguage' may be seen in the
asyntactic forms of chimpanzee signing, in child language in the two-word

stage, and in certain dysfunctional speakers such as Genie (the girl from Los Angeles who had been kept a virtual prisoner in her room until the age of thirteen, with almost no exposure to language). This reasoning risks repeating classic errors made during the time that the ontogeny/phylogeny argument enjoyed its widest acceptance: (1) that a dysfunctional modern adult could be taken to represent an earlier stage of human development; (2) that chimpanzees are a sort of ancestral pre-hominid, not contemporaries who have followed a different line of development; and (3) that the developmental process of a contemporary toddler might recapitulate the evolutionary course of the species.

M. A. K. Halliday also uses the recapitulation argument as a justification for studying the language development of children. In a paper given in 1970 (published in Kress, 1976), Halliday says that the social functions of children's language can be most clearly seen as a model for origins of grammatical structures because 'ontogeny does in some way provide a model for phylogeny' (1976: 17). In *Learning How to Mean*, Halliday (1975: 80) also refers to the child's 'glossogenic trail – which we may speculate on as the evolutionary path of human language'. This is putting himself on theoretical ground of very doubtful validity.

Gerald Edelman, in *Bright Air, Brilliant Fire* (1992), invokes Darwinian selection as a fundamental principle in neural development, but within this framework he has little to say on the subject of language. He confidently writes (1992: 127):

> We may reasonably assume [?!] that phonology arose in a speech community that used primitive sentences (perhaps resembling present-day pidgin languages) as major units of exchange. In such an early community, utterances correlated nouns with objects and led to the beginnings of semantics. Verbs followed.

This is entirely unsupported and not a great deal more convincing than Dyson on language divergence. (Pidgin first and *then* phonology?)

The Advantages of Retarded Development

However, I do think it is clear that language *is* an evolutionary product, and that its biological constraints are located within the ears and mouth and brain, and may somehow be revealed in attempts to describe a Universal Grammar (see Pinker, 1994; and Bickerton, 1990, for interesting arguments). An evolutionary account that may shed some light on properties of language emphasizes the primary role of neoteny in human development. Neoteny is the slowing down of embryological growth rates, resulting in the persistence of juvenile features into maturity. We are, by this account, apes that never grow up: the close resemblance of baby apes and humans is apparent to the most casual observer. Our thin skulls, our large craniums in proportion to our face and large brains in proportion to our bodies, our protracted dependency throughout an infancy that far exceeds that of other primates – all of these are 'co-ordinated by their common efficient cause of retarded development' (Gould 1977: 397). Gould (1977: 401) quotes M. Jacobson (1969) who points out that 'during ontogeny there is a progressive reduction of the capacity to form new neuronal connections and to modify existing ones'; this reduction occurs at different times in different classes of neurons, and those generated late in animals that mature slowly have the greatest modifiability. 'Modifiability of neuronal connections in the adult is . . . a continuation of developmental processes more pronounced in embryos'. We cannot draw any conclusions from this about the origins of language as such, but it is clear that the neotenous human infant with its still embryonic brain must generate a great part of the neuronal connections of its language late in its ontogeny and under environmental influence (which Edelman [1992] contends is the course for many aspects of brain development leading to consciousness). In regard to language, there seem to be two significant historical outcomes of our neotenous evolutionary inheritance and the consequent ability to create and to modifiy neuronal connections: first, languages are subject to the inconvenience of constant variability, and hence change; and second, we retain a flexibility in our language use that confers on us the capacity for conscious linguistic innovation.

References

Aitchison, J. (1991) *Language Change: Progress or decay* (2nd ed.). Cambridge: Cambridge University Press.

Bickerton, D. (1992) *Language and Species*. Chicago and London: University of Chicago Press.

Darwin, C. (1871) *The Descent of Man*. London: John Murray.

Dyson, F. (1981) *Disturbing the Universe*. New York: Harper & Row.

Edelman, G. (1992) *Bright Air, Brilliant Fire*. London: Penguin.

Gould, S. (1977) *Ontogeny and Phylogeny*. London: Belknap Press, Harvard University.

— (1980) *The Panda's Thumb*. London: Penguin.

— (1983) *Hen's Teeth and Horse's Toes*. London: Penguin.

— (1987) *An Urchin in the Storm*. London: Wm Collins.

— (1993) *Eight Little Piggies*. London: Jonathon Cape.

Halliday, M. (1975) *Learning How to Mean*. London: Edward Arnold.

Jacobson, M. (1969) Development of specific neuronal connections. *Science* 163, 543–47.

Jones, C. (ed.) (1993) *Historical Linguistics*. London: Longman.

Jones, S. (1993) *The Language of the Genes*. London: Harper Collins.

Kress, G. (ed.) (1976) *Halliday: System and function in language*. London: OUP.

Lass, R. (1993) How real(ist) are reconstructions? In C. Jones (ed.) *Historical Linguistics* (pp. 156–89). London: Longman.

Naro, A. (1981) The social and structural dimensions of asyntactic change. *Language* 57, 63–98.

Ohala, J. (1993) The phonetics of sound change. In C. Jones (ed.) *Historical Linguistics* (pp. 237–78). London: Longman.

Pinker, S. (1994) *The Language Instinct*. London: Allen Lane, Penguin.

Vennemann, T. (1993) Language change as language improvement. In C. Jones (ed.) *Historical Linguistics* (pp. 319–44). London: Longman.

3 *'La Crême de la Crême'*: Coercion and corpus change – an example from recruitment advertisements

CHRIS KENNEDY
University of Birmingham

Status and Corpus Planning

Language policy and planning is a deliberate process, often but not always carried out by governments, which forms part of a socio-economic and/or political agenda, and which has as its objective changes in the form and functions of a language or languages, and in the uses to which a language is put in the society in which the policy is being implemented. The term *'status planning'* is used where the intention is to change the status and functions of the language concerned. Decisions to use a particular language as the official language of a country for all administrative purposes, or as a medium of education and learning in schools, represent attempts to expand the uses of the language chosen and result in a loss of function for the language being replaced, and are examples of a status planning process. (See Baldauf & Luke, 1990; Kennedy, 1984; 1989 for examples.) In some cases, such changes in the status of languages place new linguistic demands on them. Thus, if a language is being used for the first time as a medium of formal education it is likely that the store of vocabulary items in the language will not be sufficient to respond to its new educational role, and vocabulary items used in the content areas of the curriculum such as history, geography and science will have to be created. Such change to the form of a language, whether at the lexico-grammatical or discoursal levels, is referred to as 'corpus planning'. Corpus planning may be carried out by Language Academies which provide dictionaries and word lists recommended for use in the new domains, with varying degrees of success (Cooper, 1989). The research I will report later touches on the degree to which such planned approaches to the corpus of a language succeed.

Corpus planning and corpus change

In the discussion so far, I have assumed that there is a cause–effect relationship between status and corpus planning in that a planned change in language status may result in a planned attempt at change in the form or corpus of the language. However, the two (status and corpus change) do not have to be so closely and sequentially related, nor is corpus change always a result of deliberate planning, since the corpus of a language is constantly evolving and changing in line with changes in a society's culture, without there being a major shift in a language's functions. There may of course be occasions when there is social or political pressure to intervene in this change process more directly in an attempt to force changes in the corpus and its use. Such forced change in linguistic behaviour is difficult to achieve if the change goes against the attitudes and beliefs of those being asked (or forced) to implement the change, or if the change is impractical. The failed attempt in 1994 by the then French Culture Minister, M. Toubon, to ban the use of English words in French newspapers and advertisements is a case in point. There may also be cases of less direct corpus change where the main objective is to change social behaviour, but given the close links between social and linguistic behaviour, a consequent 'indirect' effect on the corpus of the language occurs. The topic of this paper lies within this area.

Legislation is one way of changing both social (and linguistic) behaviour and may be enacted through national laws. Such laws, which are inherently coercive (Bennis *et al.*, 1976), can often affect particular groups or institutions, and may change in a small but significant way the language behaviour of those working in the institutions concerned. If the change is successful, we may expect to see a change in the language of the genres used professionally within the institutions concerned.

An Example of Coercive Language Change

It is corpus change achieved indirectly through coercive legislative means and the resultant changes in professional genres that I should like to describe in the rest of this article. The legislation concerned is the Sexual Discrimination Act 1975 and the particular genre I wish to investigate is that of recruitment advertisements. The two essential questions I shall deal with are: (1) Did the

Act trigger any linguistic changes in the genre under investigation, and (2) if so, what were they?

The Sexual Discrimination Act received Parliamentary Approval in October 1975 and the Royal Assent in November 1975. The Act forbade sexual discrimination in relation to employment, including discrimination in the recruitment process and the terms and conditions of the recruitment. Section 38 of the Act dealt specifically with discriminatory advertisements and made illegal: '. . . *an advertisement which indicates or might reasonably be understood as indicating an intention by a person to do any act which is or might be unlawful . . .*' (unlawful under the terms of the Act) (Sub-section 38.1). Sub-section (3) of section 38 goes on to specify some linguistic examples: '. . . *use of a recruitment description with a sexual connotation (such as "waiter", "salesgirl", "postman", or "stewardess") shall be taken to indicate an intention to discriminate . . .*'

The Corpus

I wished to investigate the genre of recruitment advertisements but restricted the investigation to a particular sub-genre where it was clear at the time of the Act that an employment culture existed in which one would expect to find sexual discrimination. The interest then would be to discover how the culture solved the (linguistic) problem of remaining within the law after the Act had been passed. I selected a profession which at the time of the Act recruited primarily from the female sex, and where both recruiters and the recruited expected and to some extent accepted this discrimination. (I am not necessarily expressing agreement with the norms of this culture, but stating a cultural reality – and one which the Act was attempting to change). The profession is that of Secretary/PA. My view was that in 1975, at the time of the Act, Secretaries/PAs would be primarily female and that recruitment advertising prior to the Act would clearly show this linguistically. I selected a specific and narrowly-focused sub-genre for reasons related to the quantity of data and the evidence I could draw from it, which I discuss in the next section. One particular newspaper was selected for the investigation, *The Times*. Each Wednesday, *The Times* has a special employment section devoted to the recruitment of Secretaries/PAs, entitled '*La Crême de la Crême*' and my data was drawn from display and semi-display, private sector, recruitment advertisements in this section of the newspaper. A sample advertisement, from October 1974, is presented below (names have been changed).

SECRETARY TO DIRECTOR

The Finance Director of Smiths Auto is looking for a Secretary to help him deal with his home and international business. Apart

from the usual secretarial duties, there is some schedule typing and
she will have scope to use her own initiative, will be responsible for
arranging meetings and dealing with his telephone enquiries. The
Offices are situated in Kerwick opposite Neaham BR. We require
a girl of 22 plus with good secretarial qualifications and we offer a
very competitive salary for the right candidate.

For further information please write or phone: Rachel Smith.

The Data

Table 3.1 shows the months from which I drew the data.

Table 3.1 Months in which data was published, with other significant events

OCT 74	OCT 75	NOV 75	DEC 75	JAN 76	OCT 76
	Act	Royal		Act	
	passed	assent		enforced	

Some 100 recruitment advertisements (approximately 8,000 words) were taken
from each of the months October 1974, October 1975, November 1975,
December 1975, January 1976 and October 1976 (i.e. six sub-corpora). This
produced a total of some 600 advertisements containing 48,000 words. We
can now see the reason for specifying as narrow a sub-genre as possible. The
quantity of the data collected is substantial (600 complete individual texts).
However, for the purposes of drawing evidence from a corpus, the main corpus
and the individual sub-corpora constitute a relatively small word count (each
individual text being on average 80 words long), and there is a risk that any
linguistic patterns discovered might be the result of chance. To minimise this
risk, which cannot be totally avoided without access to a larger corpus than
that presented, a narrow sub-genre was selected for investigation on the
basis that a specialised corpus was more likely to reveal reliable representative patterns.

The data from October 1974 was selected since it was published one
year before the Sexual Discrimination Act became law. This data therefore
provides a baseline of the linguistic situation from which comparisons with
data collected after the implementation of the Act can be drawn. October
1975 was the month the Act was passed and November 1975 the month of the
Royal Assent. The hypothesis was that there would be little difference in the
language used in the October 1974 advertisements and the advertisements

covering the period from October and November 1975. I believed that the data in December 1975 would begin to show some change, and that by January 1976 (when recruiters could be prosecuted for breaking the law), and certainly a year later in October 1976, significant changes would be in evidence. The data was typed into a computer data-base and concordanced using the Mini-Concordancer (1989) and Micro-Concord (1993) programs.

Culture and the Genre of the Recruitment Advertisement

Table 3.2 below summarises the parameters of the recruitment advertisement we are dealing with. Typically an agency or personnel officer has a vacancy and has to interest potential applicants at the same time as ensuring that there is a match between the position available and the applicants' qualities and qualifications, so that no time is wasted during subsequent interviews with unsuitable candidates. Formal qualifications and formal rewards are important (both aspects are found in the advertisements) but, since the applicant will have to work in a particular culture, we would expect, and indeed find, references to work environment; qualities other than those represented by formal qualifications; and a recruitment specification including some details of the person with whom the PA will be closely associated.

Table 3.2 Elements of a recruitment advertisement

Someone	Agency; Personnel officer; private sector business
looking for	matching exercise; degree of selling
someone	secretary/PA; qualities
to do something	high-level job spec
in a certain way	skills
somewhere	location and work environment
for someone	boss – status; qualities; activity
for something	salary/fringe benefits

Some of these elements form part of the genre of recruitment advertisements, whilst others are specific to the sub-genre represented by 'La Crème de la Crème'. While we might expect some elements not to be influenced by the Act's provisions, others, particularly those related to the applicant, and the applicant's qualities, might be expected to show changes. Space does not permit a full discussion of these parameters and the linguistic changes, if any, associated with them, and I shall concentrate on aspects related to the applicants and their qualities.

The Applicant

The recruiters themselves were aware of the implications of the Sexual Discrimination Act for their work. An extract from a December 1975 advertisement (a month before prosecution under the Act would come into force) reads as follows:

> *Good Bye Girls. My role as girl broker ends on 29th December with the Equal Opportunities Act and this is my last, last advertisement on behalf of other male chauvinist pigs, for 'attractive, elegant, charming, and intelligent career girls with good shorthand typing speeds . . .'.*

This extract not only shows an awareness of the legal implications of the Act but also of the sort of language which might cause problems under the Act. It is interesting that the linguistic stereotyping the recruiter employs is not consistent with the actual language used in the advertisements deriving from this period. Of the four epithets used as modifiers to the *career girls* headword (i.e. *attractive, elegant, charming,* and *intelligent, attractive* and *intelligent* are indeed used to describe the (female) applicants, though not as modifiers to the headword *career girls*. *Elegant,* in the data, collocates with *offices,* and *charming* is always associated with the (male) employer. Women, in the data, are not *charming*; men are. Women in the data possess *charm,* a male/female, active/passive distinction which unfortunately we do not have time to develop here.

Explicit reference

To see whether there was language shift and when it occurred in relation to the Act, those items referring specifically to females, whether nouns or pronouns, were identified. The following occurred in the data: *she, her, woman, girl, lady* (SET 1) (all referring to the applicant); and the alternative forms: *he/she; his/her; man/woman* (SET 2). Table 3.3 shows frequencies for each of the items above in each of the sub-corpora.

In the case of SET 1 we can see that there was little change in use in October 1974 (a year before the Act) and a year later (November 1975) as the Act was receiving the Royal Assent. However, December 1975 (the month after the Act received the Royal Assent) shows a sharp decrease in the use of each of the items except that of *woman*. By January 1976, when recruiters could be prosecuted under the Act, the frequency drops still further: *girl* (3 instances); *her* (1); and *she, woman,* and *lady* (zero use). The frequencies were substantially the same in October 1976. The figures from SET 1 clearly demonstrate that the Act had an impact on the language used in the recruitment advertisements examined, and did lead to a major shift in language use in this particular genre.

Table 3.3   Frequency of occurrence of specific nouns and pronouns

	OCT 74	OCT 75 Act passed	NOV 75 Royal assent	DEC 75	JAN 76 Act enforced	OCT 76
SET 1						
she	26	21	23	6	0	0
her	14	23	11	6	1	3
woman	3	5	3	3	0	1
girl	13	8	17	5	3	1
lady	6	3	4	2	0	0
Total	**62**	**60**	**58**	**22**	**4**	**5**
SET 2						
he/she	0	0	0	0	2	0
his/her	0	0	0	0	0	1
man/ woman	0	0	0	0	1	0
Total	**0**	**0**	**0**	**0**	**3**	**1**

The items in SET 2 in Table 3.3 are also interesting in this regard. The sub-corpora were examined to see whether recruiters had used the alternative forms which are available to indicate applicants of either sex. The forms *he/she*, *his/her*, and *man/woman* do occur in the form quoted here, but not prior to the Act. This is to be expected since SET 1 showed that the applicant, prior to the Act, was always assumed to be female, a fact made explicit in the advertisements, and at the time legal. SET 2 is, however, rarely used even after the Act. There are only two instances of *he/she* in the data from January 1976 and October 1976; and one each of *his/her* and *man/woman*. In other words, the strategy of using the *he/she* form and similar items in order to overcome the restriction on sexual preference imposed by the Act, was not employed. There may have been a number of reasons for this. It may have been regarded as stylistically awkward or wasteful of expensive space. Perhaps, however, a more likely reason was that the Act triggered a relatively simple linguistic change (deletion of explicit female reference) without changing the underlying attitudes of recruiters towards the sex of the applicant they still wished to attract. They still wished to attract female applicants and therefore did not wish to encourage male applicants, which use of the *he/she* alternative might have done.

Implicit reference

The data has shown that prior to the Act the applicant is always unambiguously marked as female, most obviously by the use of words such as *girl/woman* and the associated female pronouns. The Act also indirectly changed other less obvious references to the sex of the applicant. We shall look at three examples referring to the qualities expected of the applicant, the modifiers *attractive* and *young*, and the headword *initiative*. Data is taken from October 1974 and October 1976, representing the linguistic situation before and after the implementation of the Act.

Attractive

In the 1974 data *attractive* occurred nine times; in the 1976 data, six times. In the case of the 1974 data, four of the occurrences refer to a human quality and are associated with the female applicant. Thus we find the following examples:

October 1974 data
(1) '. . . *She will be intelligent,* **attractive***, and probably married* . . .'
(2) '. . . *tact essential, combined with* **attractive appearance** *and pleasant personality* . . .'
(3) '. . . *company president seeks* **attractive, efficient secretary** . . .'
(4) '. . . *advertising agency requires* **a really attractive well-groomed lady** . . .'

The remaining five occurrences of *attractive* in the 1974 data are used as modifiers to headwords relating to aspects of the job, specifically *fringe benefits* (1 occurrence); *offices* (2); *salary* (2).

In the 1976 data, after the Act's implementation, the use of *attractive* to describe a human quality is not found, each of the six occurrences referring solely to the job: *fringe benefits* (2 occurrences); *office* (1); *salary* (2); and *position* (1).

The recruiter could have used the epithet *attractive* without explicit linguistic reference to the sex of the applicant (see example *(3)* above: *attractive efficient secretary*. It would appear, however, that in the sub-genre concerned the word *attractive*, when describing a human quality, is associated, by recruiters, with female qualities, which limits its use in this particular context, a possible example of semantic prosody described by Louw (1991). Comparison with a much larger corpus of general English would reveal whether *attractive* is generally regarded as a female attribute or whether its use here is characteristic of the sub-genre concerned.

Young

In the 1974 data, there were 17 occurrences of *young,* seven of them referring to aspects of the employers or the firm (e.g. . . . *the President is* **young***,
personable and dynamic . . .*), 10 of them used as modifiers to the headwords
girl (1 occurrence); *lady* (2); *woman* (3), and *secretary* (4).

In the 1976 data, of the 12 occurrences of the item *young,* eight refer to
the employers or the firm, similar to the 1974 data. However, the use of *young*
in collocation with nouns explicitly referring to females is no longer found;
the remaining four occurrences are used as modifiers with *secretary* as headword. Clearly, the necessity to avoid explicit female reference through words
such as *girl/lady/woman* (see 7.1 above) has an effect on those modifiers
closely associated with them. In the case of *young woman* and *young lady,*
the modifier and headword constitute a linguistic unit in this context, and, in
these instances, it is the nominal group (modifier + headword) which no
longer occurs.

Re-phrasing

Our final example deals with a quality commonly mentioned in the advertisements, namely the item *initiative*, with 23 occurrences in the 1974 data
and 25 in the 1976 data. *Initiative* carries no semantic loading with reference
to the sex of the applicant and yet we find some interesting differences in the
use of the word in its context in the two different sub-corpora. In particular,
the phrase *ability/able to/can work on her own initiative* occurs six times in
the 1974 data. In line with data we have discussed above, we would expect
the possessive adjective *her* to be deleted in the post-1975 data and this is
indeed what occurs, with the possessive adjective being deleted (4); replaced
by *his/her* (1) and by *their* (1). At the same time, however, a new phrase – *a
rare chance/a great opportunity to use initiative* – occurs in the 1976 data and
not at all in the 1974 data. This could indicate that a linguistically minor lexico-
grammatical change may trigger a greater linguistic change in that a writer
may decide not to take the option of a single item deletion, but may seek an
alternative phrasing. Applied to the data presented here, the necessity to
delete '*her*' from the phrase *on (her) own initiative* may have caused the writer
of the advertisement to seek an alternative phrasing, *a great opportunity to
use initiative*, which has the effect of subtly changing the meaning. Thus in
the 1974 data *initiative* is viewed as a requirement for the job; in the 1976
data, *initiative* is assumed, and the job becomes a means to apply it. What we
may be seeing is a more radical change in the language where the recruiter
subconsciously reformulates whole phrases of the language as a consequence of
the necessity to drop one linguistic item from a phrase. Clearly more data is

required to prove this hypothesis, but such reformulations would confirm current thoughts on lexical 'chunking', the idea that we communicate in 'chunks' of language and that a change to one element of the chunk or phrase may trigger the production of a different phrase. Sinclair (1991), for example, believes in the 'idiom principle' and demonstrates how we cannot assign meanings to individual words without considering the co-text, the items that surround the individual word. We suggest here that a change in the co-text may have caused reformulation of a whole phrase.

Conclusion

Space restricts further discussion of the large amount of data gathered from the corpus which provides further evidence of change and of the linguistic strategies adopted by recruiters. However, even from the limited amount of data represented here, it is clear that an indirect effect of the legislation was to trigger changes in language use in the genre concerned. Three instances of change were presented, all related to characteristics of the applicant. In the first instance, explicit reference to the sex of the applicant was avoided; in the second, we saw that items not explicitly referring to the sex of the applicant but apparently carrying a particular semantic loading were avoided; and a third example raised the question whether whole chunks of the language were having to be re-cast.

There remains the question whether cultural change in the workplace also occurred as well as linguistic change. Some of the data indicated, perhaps not surprisingly, that the linguistic changes did not reflect major changes in attitudes. Additional data collected (but not discussed here) would also tend to support this interpretation. This raises the question of the influence and importance of the legislation and subsequent linguistic changes. Neither are sufficient to change attitudes, beliefs and behaviour but they are nonetheless a necessary and important part of the process of change as a means of awareness-raising and legitimisation of the issues.

Note

I am grateful to Debbie Langford for typing the data, to Catherine Kennedy for her legal assistance, and to John Sinclair for his helpful comments.

References

Baldauf, R. and Luke, A. (eds) (1990) *Language Planning and Education*. Clevedon: Multilingual Matters.

Bennis, W., Benne, K., Chin, R. and Corey, K. (eds) (1976) *The Planning of Change.*
New York: Holt, Rinehart and Winston.

Cooper, R. (1989) *Language Planning and Social Change.* Cambridge: Cambridge
University Press.

Kennedy, C. (ed.) (1984) *Language Planning and Language Education.* London:
Allen and Unwin.

— (1989) *Language Planning and Language Teaching.* Hemel Hempstead: Prentice
Hall.

Louw, B. (1991) Classroom concordancing of delexical forms. *Classroom Concordancing* ELR Journal 4, 151–78. ELR: University of Birmingham.

Miniconcordancer (1989). London: Longman.

Micro-Concord (1993). Oxford : Oxford University Press.

Sinclair, J. (1991) *Corpus, Concordance, Collocation.* Oxford: Oxford University
Press.

4 Dialect as Metaphor: The use of language in Edgar Reitz' *Heimat* films

ULRIKE HANNA MEINHOF
University of Manchester

Sociolinguistic and pragmatic research has long taken for granted that our linguistic behaviour not only reveals information about our social and regional background, but is equally responsible for a range of attitudes which we prompt in others. Accordingly, we judge our own ways of speaking and that of our respondees.

Attitudinal research as a sub-discipline in sociolinguistics and social psychology has for many years attempted to describe and predict the complex interrelations between linguistic and non-linguistic judgements and reactions. It has shown that positive or negative assessments of certain speech variables or varieties[1] can importantly influence either the retention of these speech forms or their abandonment.[2] The influences of attitudes on regional, supra-regional, national, cross-national speech variants and varieties have been extensively researched, with often highly ingenious indirect research methods aimed at highlighting differences in behaviour towards speakers of different speech forms – all else being equal.[3] Such ingenuity is necessary because our consciously held attitudes and evaluations do not (necessarily) equate with those we hold unconsciously, so that our linguistic attitudes are best inferred from our behaviour towards speakers of these varieties, rather than elicited by the more direct methods of questionnaires and interviews. Questionnaires and opinion polls about the (un-) desirability of certain dialects can only reveal simplistic stereotypes about these dialects, with a notorious discrepancy between folklinguistic notions about language and the assumptions and results of linguistic research.

The representation and evaluation of speech behaviour in fictional genres in literature, film, radio and television is therefore of considerable interest.

Coarse, over-generalized representations not only help to confirm stereo-typical attitudes towards these speech forms. The way fictional characters are made to speak and communicate can also show up what counts as situa-tionally (in-) appropriate for authors, producers or actors. How far do fictional accounts of dialectal or colloquial variation correspond to sociolinguistic reality? Do they appear simplified, idealized, comically exaggerated, or otherwise distorted, and why? How are the characters placed through their speech forms? With questions such as these, we can assess the role which lan-guage behaviour plays in the genres themselves, whether they be naturalistic, symbolic, allegoric or ironic. This essay will concentrate on the fictional repre-sentation of language varietes in two recent German films, which are, in my view, amongst the most sensitive and intelligent representations of language we have seen in the history of German film-making: Edgar Reitz' use of lan-guage in his two *Heimat* films.

Both – the 15½ hours long *Heimat* of 1984, and the 25¼ hours long *Zweite Heimat* of 1992 – have been reviewed in the international press and journals with enthusiasm, and in the case of *Heimat*, some antagonism as well. The extensive commentaries, especially in relation to *Heimat*, have emphasized other themes than the use of language, though there are excep-tions such as Peter Buchka's insightful comment about *Heimat* in the Süd-deutsche Zeitung, that the representation of Schabbach as 'a melting pot of dialects' made German history more noticeable than the use of the many historically accurate props.[4] And Pflaum, in his study of the New German Cinema, compares the use of more genuine dialect speech in the critical films of the 'Left' – such as Martin Sperr's *Jagdszenen aus Niederbayern* (*Hunting Scenes from Lower Bavaria*) from 1968 – with the 'synthetic standardized imita-tion of the original dialect'[5] in the hugely sentimental so-called 'Heimatfilme' of the 1950s.[6] But these are exceptions. This relative neglect of the language use in *Heimat* is perhaps not surprising, given the importance of other themes. Telling German history from 'below', in epic form from 1919 to 1982, as the story of a few ordinary people in one village, Schabbach, and naming such a film 'Heimat' – a deeply problematical title for Germans[7] – was an unusual, provocative endeavour, touching on central taboos. Unsurprisingly then, the critical academic response largely focussed on issues of historical repre-sentations and memory.[8]

However, studying the role of language in these films can give many insights into the strategies which Reitz uses in showing precisely that history. The changes that gradually infiltrate the insulated pre-modern, rural world of *H1* are not only represented by changes in the object world of the people of Schabbach, as in the gradual emergence of the signs of modernity: radio, telephone, motorway, television; they are on a more intimate level symbolized by changes in their language. Similarly, the world of the big cities of *The Second Heimat* – Munich, Amsterdam, Venice, Berlin – is not only shown to be cosmopolitan, broken-up, post-modern by the life-style of the protagonists, their avant-garde art, their disruptive disillusioning lives; it is again reflected in the language of the characters. Change in both films is thus always inextricably linked with changes in language and changes in the attitudes towards language.

Together, the speech varieties of the different characters comprise a wide range of ways of speaking: from different traditional dialects and colloquial speech varieties to standard speech – a range unprecedented in German film. This not only shows Reitz' ability to closely chart a sociolinguistic history of twentieth century Germany; it also makes language use one of the most potent symbols in the narrative structure. The way the characters speak, change, reject or retain their speech varieties throws into focus questions of belonging and not-belonging, of rootedness and alienation, of tradition and change.

The Schabbach at the beginning and at the end of *Heimat* is a very different place. In episode 1, the place to which Paul returns in 1919, at the end of the First World War, is a closed rural community where everyone speaks the same dialect, the 'Hunsrück Platt'. On the sociolinguistic map of Germany the speech variety of the fictional Schabbach is easily identifiable as belonging to the Hunsrück barrier, a dividing line on the Frankonian dialect continuum between the more northern Rhine and the more southern Mosel-Frankonian. It is set off against standard German by a range of phonological, morphological, syntactical, and lexical features. Key variables include, for example: /dat/ instead of /das/ (Engl.: this/that); /wat/ for /was/ (Engl.: what); /esch/ or /eisch/ for ich (Engl.: I); /sin/ for /bin/; /hääm/ for /heim/ (Engl.: home), as well as a whole range of distinct dialect words, such as the many non-standard expressions for adverbials of place, and for wild berries, which Hermann celebrates in a chorus piece performed at the end of *Heimat*.[9]

Modernisation and an increasing connection to the outside world come through the expanding network of modern means of communication. With it, too, come different ways of speaking. Different dialects, colloquial speech and standard German speech forms appear side by side, as more and more characters appear and settle in Schabbach from other parts of Germany; such as Martha from Hamburg with her low German variants, Otto who speaks standard German, his Upper-Saxon speaking assistant Pierritz, and most notably Lucie, with her Berlin Urban Vernacular speech, who deeply resents the insularity of the village, longing first for the great world of the Nazi officials, and later, for the great world of the American dream.

The Schabbach of modern times has ceased to be a homogeneous speech community. But this development does not take us on a nostalgic trip from an idyllic past to the lost idyll, as some critics suggested.[10] It is true, that with its old traditions superseded by pastiche and fairground drunkenness, the modern Schabbach seems a much more brash and vulgar place: Maria's younger son Ernst literally sells off the past by taking down the old beams and doors from century-old farm houses, replacing them by plastic versions and Hollywood swings, with particular pride in a spray that imitates the scent of old wood. But the old Schabbach in the first sequence is, nevertheless, both a place of reassurance and one of imprisonment. Security and warmth are the positive terms which comprise at the same time their negative counterparts in enclosure, xenophobia, and aggression against outsiders. This ambivalence between valuing old traditions whilst, at the same time, showing the inflexibility that comes with it, is powerfully expressed in the symbolic role which the Hunsrück dialect has in the film. Dramatically these ambivalences emerge most notably in the different ways in which the two 'Weggeher', ('the ones who go away') reject Schabbach. Paul, Maria's husband, who walks away from Schabbach at the end of episode one, not to return for another 20 years, and Hermann, Maria's son by Otto, both escape the narrowness of the village, both return briefly: one as a successful business man in America, the other as a successful musician. How they cope with their departure from – and their return to – Schabbach is symbolized by what happens to their language.

Episode no. 8, entitled 'The American', brings Paul's first return visit from the United States after a 20-year absence. His return is celebrated by many of the villagers, especially Lucie, as a triumphal event. But his behaviour is subtly marked by various linguistic and communicative incompetences. Silently observed through the eyes of Maria, he is placed as an arrogant, vulgar show-off who cannot find a language to express himself in. This shift in perspective contrasts sharply with his first homecoming from the war in the very first episode, when his ambiguous vision of Schabbach as a place of security and of entrapment was the one which the film privileged; then he understood better than the villagers the ambivalences entailed in the enclosure of Schabbach. This time, he understands less; incapable of assessing his own behaviour or that of the others, he tries to bridge the distance by vulgar superficialities, but fails in the essential relationships with his family. These failures as a father, son, and grandfather, as husband and friend are marked by various inadequacies in his way of speaking. Examples of these are manifold: he mixes German dialect forms with American idioms (see below); he uses inappropriate linguistic registers, as in his bragging speech to the Schabbach people; he misunderstands pragmatic cues, as when he tries to climb into Maria's bed when all she does is offer him a blanket. But all of these mis-firings are not only signs of linguistic inadequacy; they also signal a deeper emotional incompetence. He is easier with Lucie's admiring waffle and her son's memorized list of US States, the American officer's welcome, than he is with his own family. When his daughter-in-law Martha tells him about his granddaughter, he asks (in English) 'What happened?'; when he stands next to his own son Ernst in a night-club he fails to recognize him; and when Marie-Goot, his sister-in-law, is devastated about his wanting to leave prior to his mother's funeral, he explains that his residence permit has expired in the following confusing way:[11]

Paul: Mei Aufenthalterlaubnis is expired.
Marie-Goot: Was is expired?
Paul: Marie-Goot, mei residence permit is abgelaafe.

But it is his behaviour towards Maria which focuses his inadequacies most sharply. The following transcript comes from a scene where he and Maria visit his father's grave, and shows Maria trying to make Paul talk to her about his disappearance.[12]

Maria: Paul, jetzt han isch mir die ganz Zeit wo du da bist fescht vorgenomme, dich dat net zu frage, aber jetzt muß isch disch doch frage. Warum bist de damals von uns fortgange, Paul? Die Kinner ware doch so scheen? Und eisch, han isch der net gefall, Paul? Isch hans net verstande. Isch han simuliert un simuliert, un isch hans einfach net verstande. Manschmal han isch gemeent, der is krank im Kopp. Sag mers jetzt, Paul, eisch bin doch net dumm- eisch wills doch nur wisse. Oder hots was mit den Fraue zu tun. Eisch wills doch nur begreife.
Paul: Maria, wie soll ich der det nur erklären. Dat war damals hier-
Maria: Ach Paul, dau brauchst mer nix zu erklären. Laß et sin, Paul.
Paul: Isch weiß es net, Maria. Isch weiß es wirklich nit. Vielleischt nur, damit isch jetzt hier bin un euch alle helfe kann.
Maria: Mir brauche kei Hilf, Paul.
Paul: Isch versteh dat Deutschland hier net mehr.
Maria: Wenn isch dich da stehe seh, Paul. Die Leut in deiner Fabrik ham sicher an große Respekt vor dir.
Paul: Oh yes, and die brauche mich aach.

Paul is incapable of seeing the difference between Maria's wish to know, asking him to tell her ('sag mers'), to talk about himself, and his attempt to explain to her ('wie soll ich Dir dat nur erkläre . . .'). The latter she rightly rejects for its condescending tone, just as she rejects his arrogant rationalisation that what he really wanted underneath was to be able to help them. This sequence at the grave-yard, which ends again in his typical English and German mix – 'Oh yes, and die brauche mich aach' – epitomizes a shallowness which marks him out in all the remaining sequences of *Heimat*. With Paul, then, we encounter the negative side of the new, symbolized by the collapse of all communicative means. The mixture between the old and the new renders him incapable of expressing himself. In contrast to Maria, he has no language for his experiences and his emotions.

Against this negative evaluation of the 'Weggeher' Paul, we find the positive side of change represented in Hermann. Hermann, too, loses touch with Schabbach. After the expulsion of his lover, Klärchen from Schabbach, he too makes a deliberate break; but in contrast to Paul he finds a personal resolution between the old and the new. Again this is metaphorized by language, here by his achieving a synthesis between a new form, atonal music, and the rediscovery of his old Hunsrück dialect. In the final episode of *Heimat*, (no. 11), which contrasts well with the church-yard scene transcribed above, Hermann visits Maria's grave after her funeral and is addressed by an old man sitting on a bench.[13]

Old man: Hermännsche, suchst de jemannen? Kann isch der helfe?

Hermann: Wo liegt denn hier meine Verwandtschaft?

Old man: Ach, überall- druhe, unne, drohe, dronne, vore, hinne, lo, und do, und hie. Hermännsche, kennscht de kee Hunsrücker Platt me?

Hermann: Verstehe tu ichs schon noch, aber mit dem Schwätze da haperts scho.

Old man: Dat lernscht de a noch. Knebbersche, Krieschele, Wele un Schlehe, kennscht de dat noch?

Hermann: Knebbersche, das sind so kleine wilde Kirschen, die kenn ich noch von einem Gedicht von Hoffmann:
'Dat Hannekesche hot obe im Kirschbaum gsesse
un hat Knebbersche, so kleene Kirsche gesse.'

Old man: Und Krieschele?

Hermann: Das sind Stachelbeere.

Old man: Und Weele?

Hermann: Das sind Heidelbeere.
'Weele, Weele, Heidelbeere,
wer will sich die Schmiß beschmeere'
Das hammer immer als Kinner gesunge im Wald.

Old man: Un Schlehe, dat is der Hunsrücker Wein, der is so sauer, det zieht der die Tint im Arsch zsamme. Komm Hermännsche, da setz dich he, wir weile noch e bißche beisamme. Hermännsche, wo bischt de denn eigentlich dran?

Hermann: Ich bin jetzt in München. Ich bin immer unterwegs, überall.

Old man: Überall.
'Vatter, Mutter, Kind
Unkel, und Gesind,
warn frieher all beisamm im Haus
heit sins in de ganze Welt verstraut'
. . .

Old man: Hermännsche, hoscht de se all gfunde, wo de gsucht host, de Verwandten.

Hermann: So ungefähr. De Goot und de Pat-

Old man: Jo Hermännsche – im Himmel do schwätze se Hunsrücker Platt.

I quoted these two passages at some length because they sum up the difference between Paul's and Hermann's return. Hermann's return to Schabbach does not in any way symbolize a return to old values and traditions, but offers a synthesis in a new form. Those dialect words which the old man at the graveyard brings back to Hermann's memory, and his departing call 'Im Himmel do schwätze se Hunsrücker Platt' ('In heaven, they speak in the Hunsrück dialect') are used by Hermann as the centre of a modern choral piece. In the last moments of *Heimat* we hear this piece performed in an old cave in the Hunsrück, but it is broadcast by radio. With this composition and its performance, which combines dialect words with atonal music, and the acoustics of an old cave with the technology of broadcasting, Hermann has finally found a language for both old and new.

To summarize what has been said so far: the changes in the village of Schabbach during this century are powerfully presented through the way a homogeneous dialect community is seen to gradually break up. Making the rural dialect a symbol for coherence to the old values works so well, precisely because the symbolic is anchored in close observation of sociolinguistic reality in Germany. None of the characters use clichéd or idealized forms of speaking.

However, this perceptive use of language must not disguise the fact that in *Heimat* we are not dealing with a documentary piece about a German village, but with a complex symbolic journey through memory, loss and renewal. What is so impressive here is that Reitz shows in dramatized form how closely the language we speak is tied up with our subjectivity, our social and personal identity, and our integrity. The language the characters speak becomes a sensitive measure for us to judge them by. This is never spelled out directly by any of the characters, nor by the narrator Glasisch; they do not talk about identity or lost values; no metapositions about the significance of our language get articulated. Instead they are left implicit in the dramatisation.

In this respect the narrative strategies of *Heimat 1* contrast sharply with those of *Heimat 2*. Here the central characters explicitly take stances about all that is left implicit in *Heimat*.[14] They argue about history, politics and life-styles, they critically assess or dismiss their relationships with their parents and relatives, or explain their preoccupations with various forms of artistic expressions; they analyze, criticize, assess.

In their discussions and reflections, the central metaphors of both films are articulated and explained, including that of the role of language itself. And language is once more indicative of the ambivalences of change. The young artists in the centre of *Heimat 2*, brought to Munich from all over Germany and abroad, are self-conscious about their ways of speaking, whether they speak a particular rural dialect as in Hermann's case, or 11 languages (including music) as in Juan's. How the way we speak places us in the eyes of others, how our subjectivity is bound up with our language, how painful it is to break away from this and find a new way of speaking, all this becomes in *Heimat 2* part of the characters' conscious concern; inversely, the risk of not belonging is shown in Juan's (unsuccessful) attempt to blend into the foreign culture by losing his accent and learning all the languages he speaks to perfection. But he, more than anyone else, knows this and spells it out for us. In interpreting the role of language in *The Second Heimat*, we find the characters – most notably Hermann himself – taking up the place of the analyst, assessing the way it places them, and discussing their own solutions to these problems.

The Hermann of *Heimat 2* who arrives in Munich in the first episode hears with dismay his own speech. He hates the way it sounds and what he associates with it, rural backwardness, 'dungheap stink' (135), 'Scheißhausparolen' (224).[15] When students at the Academy of Music laugh at him as he answers in dialect the calling out of his number – 'Eisch! Dat sin eisch!' (121)[16] – he knows they are laughing because his rural speech sounds comical in the cosmopolitan university environment. Learning to speak standard German (in a wittily ironic sequence at a drama school, scene 136) is thus not only the obvious way to rid himself of the 'dungheap stink' of his language, but equally represents his break with the 'terrible Hunsrück' (102). Speaking standard German marks for him this new departure.[17]

> Ich wollte auch so sprechen wie diese Kinder aus den guten Familien, die aus den Städten kamen. Ohne diesen Misthaufengeruch meines Bauerndialekts. Ich wollte sprechen, wie es geschrieben stand. Die Sprache der Dischter- Scheiße, der Dichter und Denker. (135)

But this attempt to break with the past is not without its ambiguities; the celebration of the typical postmodern condition, to be without roots, 'to give birth to yourself a second time' (810) as Hermann puts it, is upsetting, lonely, even ridiculous, and never without pain.

Again the use of language, in particular Hermann's slipping between his newly acquired standard and the speech from home, becomes indicative of these ambivalences. When he falls ill, for example, his struggle to break free from the dialect is undermined as he misses the closeness and comfort of home. (He shouts out in dialect that he wants to go home: 'eisch will häam', 250.) At other times, too, he falls back into his native dialect, such as when he is invited to eat potato dumplings which remind him of home, though he quickly corrects himself again and switches back to standard German.[18] Most clearly his ambivalence is shown in his relationship with and ultimately disastrous marriage to Schnüßchen. Because although he resents the 'Hunsrück lavatory speech' of Clemens (226), and dismisses – albeit humorously – Schnüßchen's Hunsrück dialect,[19] he is nevertheless seduced by the simple security she seems to offer against the tortured unfulfillable relationship he has with Clarissa. But even this ambivalence is consciously expressed as when he says to Schnüßchen: 'Schnüßchen, irgendwie wirfst du mich um Jahre zurück.'[20]

As in the first *Heimat*, Hermann struggles to find some resolution by integrating music and language. In *Heimat 2* this is a conscious endeavour, as becomes obvious in the following explanation he gives to his 'landlord', the Kohlen-Josef, an old Bavarian coal-merchant, as he plays him his newest ultramodern composition on his guitar:[21]

Hermann: Das hier, das wird ein Stück für Cello und Sprechgesang . . . ich geh doch da in diese Schauspielschule und mach so Sprechkurse . . . Und da kriege ich so Übungstexte.
[Recites a set of absurd sentences all with alliterating [ʃt], which he accompanies with his guitar. The guitar strings have a picture of a famous Munich church and a coin stuck through them which changes the sound of the guitar . . .]
Wenn sie sich vorstellen, daß die ganze Stadt voll ist mit Menschen, die solche Texte sprechen und sich damit quälen. Die kommen vom Land in die Stadt, um das Mitreden zu lerne. Das ist ein Chor von Leidenden. Das möchte ich hörbar machen. (255)

This comment of Hermann's beautifully sums up what he feels about the pain induced by the changes he is going through. Such observations are typical for the conscious understanding the characters of *The Second Heimat* are allowed to articulate, as against the implicit significance which language has for the characters in the first *Heimat*. Taken as complementary, the portrayal of language in both films is an outstanding representation of the roles which language plays in the life of an individual and of a community. The symbolic significance which the retention, change, desired or undesired loss of one's way of speaking has is brought into sharp focus by detailed observations of sociolinguistic processes, in a comprehensive and subtle manner which is unparalleled in the history of German film.

Notes

1. Following standard sociolinguistic practice, a variety of a language is a particular geographically or socially determined regular way of speaking. Typical distinctions for German are traditional dialects ('Mundarten'), colloquial speech (relatively closer or nearer to standard), and standard speech (Hochdeutsch). For discussion of this terminology in contrast to the English sociolinguistic tradition, see Barbour and Stevenson, 1990 (chapter 5).
2. Cf. Labov's seminal work (for example in Labov, 1972); Schlobinski's work on Berlin (as in Schlobinski, 1987); Aitchison, 1992; and Barbour & Stevenson, 1990, for useful summaries.
3. For an excellent summary of such work see Fasold, 1984 (chapter 6).
4. P. Buchka, *Süddeutsche Zeitung* 214, 15 & 16 September 1984; my translation. Reitz' film has great visual persuasiveness, but its centre is language, the dialect. In the course of history, Reitz has turned his little Hunsrück village into a melting pot of dialects. With this, he has made history perhaps more visible, or rather more audible, than with the many historically appropriate props.
5. Pflaum, 1985 (English version 1990: 32). Films of Hauff, Herzog and Schlöndorff at least make the attempt to have their characters speak once again in a genuine dialect, and in so doing they provide a contrast to the standard German of the upper classes. A central concern of the new 'Heimat' film was, after all, to compose scenes and to depict events that had been ignored by the writers of 'official' history, who had never belonged to the lower classes. In this regard, the attempt to revitalize the genre was also the desire to present history from a different point of view, and this new perspective definitely incorporates the events and experiences of the year 1968.
6. See also Hugh Herbert in *The Guardian*, to my knowledge the only review of *The Second Heimat* which noted the symbolic significance of language: 'Reitz does introduce what looks like an important underlying theme: how language defines us . . . Hermann meets a young Chilean musician who speaks eleven languages – the 11th being music – and whose romantic imagination counterpoints Hermann's narrower, mechanistic attitude . . . The concern with both musical and spoken language is an extension of *Heimat 1*'s underlying theme about the century's obsession with faster communication. But language is more personal, more deeply etched in the programmed part of us. Hermann is acutely aware of his Hunsrück dialect, and takes elocution lessons to expunge it.' (*The Guardian*, 19 April 1993, II, 6–7).
7. The term *Heimat*, translatable as 'homeland', 'home country', 'fatherland', etc, arouses unfortunate associations since the Third Reich's appropriation of the term in connection with a 'Blut und Boden' (blood and earth) ideology, and a claim of this homeland for the Aryan race. Reitz' use of the term for his films is thus a deliberate linguistic reclaiming of a problematical German expression.
8. For key references, see Hansen, 1985; Elsaesser, 1989; Kaes, 1987, 1989; Santner, 1990; Wickham, 1991; the excellent bibliography in Töteberg, 1993; and my own article on the subject (Meinhof, 1994).

9. For discussions of the Hunsrück dialect see Diener, 1971; Wiesinger, 1983; and Newton, 1990.

10. For highly polemical accounts see some of the extracts printed in Hansen, 1985, and Saalmann, 1988.

11. Phrases occurring in English in the original are set in italics:
Paul: My residence permit is *expired*.
Marie-Goot: What is *expired*?
Paul: Marie-Goot, my *residence permit* has expired.

12. The following translation is taken from the BBC's English subtitles:
Maria: Paul, the whole time you've been here I was determined not to ask you, but now I must. Why did you leave us, Paul? The children were so lovely. And me? Didn't you like me, Paul? I didn't understand it. I tried to, but I simply didn't understand it. Sometimes I used to think: he's not right in his head. Tell me now, Paul. I'm not silly. I just want to know. Or did it have something to do with a woman. I just want to understand.
Paul: Maria, how am I to explain it to you. At that time, here . . .
Maria: You needn't explain anything to me, Paul. Forget it, Paul.
Paul: I don't know, Maria, I really don't know. Perhaps only that I'm here now and can help you all.
Maria: We don't need any help, Paul.
Paul: I don't understand this Germany any more.
Maria: When I see you standing there, Paul, I'm sure your workers respect you very much.
Paul: Oh yes, and they need me, too.

13. The following translation is from BBC subtitles:
Old man: Little Hermann, are you looking for someone? Can I help you?
Hermann: Where are my relatives buried?
Old man: All over. *[Points in different directions using Hunsrück dialect words for place adverbials.]* . . . Hermann, don't you know the Hunsrück dialect any more?
Hermann: I understand it, but speaking it is the trouble.
Old man: You'll learn it all again, 'Knebbersche', 'Krieschele', 'Weele' and 'Schlehe'. Do you still remember?
Hermann: 'Knebbersche' are little wild cherries, I know that from a poem by Hoffmann *[Recites two lines from poem about a little girl eating little wild cherries.]* . . .
Old man: And 'Krieschele'?
Hermann: They are wild gooseberries.
Old man: And 'Weele'?
Hermann: They are bilberries . . . *[Recites an old nursery rhyme about bilberries.]* We used to chant that as kids in the forest.
Old man: And sloes, that's the Hunsrück wine. So sour, they shrivel your arse and your shirt tail with it. Sit down, little Hermann, we keep each other company a bit . . . Hermann, what are you doing now?
Hermann: I'm in Munich now, but I'm always travelling all over the place.
Old man: All over. *[Recites in rhyme:]*
Father, mother, children, uncles, and the farm hands
They used to be in one house, now they're shattered across the world.
. . . Did you find all your relatives?
Hermann: Just about. 'Goot' and 'Pat'.
Old man: Yes, Hermann, in heaven they speak in Hunsrück dialect.

50 CHANGE AND LANGUAGE

14. For a further discussion of these strategies, see Meinhof, 1994.
15. The number references in brackets refer to the number of the scenes as indicated in the printed text of *Heimat 2* (Reitz, 1993).
16. Standard German would have been 'das bin ich' (It's me).
17. The following is my translation:
    I wanted to speak like those children from the good families, who came from the cities; not with the dungheap stink of my peasant dialect. I wanted to speak in the way it was written down, the language of the *poets [spoken in dialect]* – shit, the *poets [spoken in standard]* and thinkers.
18. Scene 553:
    [in dialect:] '. . . aber wir sagen Krumbeereklöß, wenn Ihnen dat wat sagt. Isch han schon lang net mer so ebbes geß.' *[continues in standard German:]* 'Ah, ja, also, wir essen sowas manchmal auch im Hunsrück.'
    English translation:
    [in dialect:] '. . . but we say potato dumplings, if that means anything to you. It's ages since I've eaten these.' *[in standard German:]* 'Ah, yes, we occasionally eat that kind of thing in the Hunsrück.'
19. Hermann to Schnüßchen, Scene 810:
    'Also, weißt do, Schnüßchen, du mit deinem Hunsrücker Platt. Wenn ich verliebt bin, da kann ich dat überhaupt net leiden. Dat kühlt misch dann rischtisch ab . . .'
    Translation:
    'You know, Schnüßchen, you and your Hunsrück dialect. When I'm in love, then I can't stand it at all. It really puts me off.'
20. 'Schnüßchen, somehow you throw me years back' (Scene 810, my translation). The BBC subtitles translate Hermann's phrase 'Schnüßchen, irgendwie wirfst du mich um Jahre zurück' as 'Schnüßchen, somehow you turn back the clock by years'. This translation misses the negative connotation of the German 'zurück-werfen'.
21. My translation:
    This piece here is going to be for cello and speech-song. . . . I go to a drama school to take speech lessons. . . . And I get these exercises to do. . . . Just imagine that the city is full of people who speak such texts and torture themselves with them. They come from the country to the city to learn to speak *['mitreden lernen' is ambiguous and also means 'to find a voice']*. It's a chorus of martyrs. I want it to be heard.

References

Aitchison, J. (1992) *Language Change: Progress or decay?* Cambridge: Cambridge University Press.
Barbour, S. and Stevenson, P. (1990) *Variation in German: A critical approach to German sociolinguistics*. Cambridge: Cambridge University Press.
Buchka, P. (1984) Weggehen, um anzukommen. *Süddeutsche Zeitung,* Nr 214. München.
Diener, G. W. (1971) *Hunsrücker Wörterbuch mit Mundartproben*. Niederwalluf.
Elsaesser, T. (1989) *New German Cinema: A history*. New Brunswick: Rutgers University Press.
Fasold, R. (1984) *The Sociolinguistics of Society*. Oxford: Blackwell.
Hansen, M. (1985) Dossier on Heimat. *New German Critique* 36, 3–24.
Herbert, H. (1993) The second Heimat. *The Guardian* II, 6–7. London.

Kaes, A. (1987) *Deutschlandbilder: Die Wiederkehr der Geschichte als Film.* München: Edition Text und Kritik.
— (1989) *From Hitler to Heimat: The return of history as film.* Cambridge, MA: Harvard University Press.
Labov, W. (1972) *Language in the Inner City.* Oxford: Blackwell.
Meinhof, U. H. (1994) Told and untold stories: A comparison of Edgar Reitz' two 'Heimat'-films. Paper delivered at the EFTSC Conference 'Turbulent Europe: Conflict, identity and culture'. British Film Institute, London, July 1994.
Newton, G. (1990) Central Frankonian. In C. V. J. Russ (ed.) *The Dialects of Modern German: A linguistic survey.* London: Routledge.
Pflaum, H. G. (1985) *Deutschland im Film: Themenschwerpunkte des Spielfilms in der Bundesrepublik Deutschland.* München: Max Hueber Verlag.
— (1990) *Germany on Film: Theme and content in the cinema of the Federal Republic of Germany.* Detroit: Wayne State University Press.
Reitz, E. (1993) *Die zweite Heimat: Chronik einer Jugend in 13 Büchern.* München: Goldmann Verlag.
Saalmann, D. (1988) Edgar Reitz' View of History: The new religion of regionalism and the concept of Heimat. *Germanic Notes* 19(1), 8–14.
Santner, E. L. (1990) *Stranded Objects: Mourning, memory, and film in postwar Germany.* Ithaka: Cornell University Press.
Schlobinski, P. (1987) *Stadtsprache Berlin: Eine soziolinguistische Untersuchung.* Berlin: de Gruyter.
Töteberg, M. (ed.) (1993) *Edgar Reitz: Drehort Heimat.* Frankfurt/M.: Verlag der Autoren.
Wickham, C. J. (1991) Representation and mediation in Edgar Reitz's Heimat. *The German Quarterly* 64(1), 35–45.
Wiesinger, P (1983). Die Einteilung der deutschen Dialekte. *Dialektologie* 1(2): 807–900.

5 Modern Foreign Languages and Curriculum Policy at 16+: Plus ça change

MARGARET ROGERS
University of Surrey

Introduction

In this paper I would like to discuss what I consider to be a number of inconsistent and initially puzzling features of modern foreign language (MFL) policy at 16+ in England, the jurisdiction of the School Curriculum and Assessment Authority. The main issue is the treatment of grammar in the context of a communicative approach to language teaching, an approach which is given full acknowledgement in official documents. I intend to suggest that the handling of grammar has hardly moved beyond the attitudes of traditional grammar, and a rather behaviouristic view of language learning. This will be illustrated by looking at the new subject core for MFLs, at some aspects of Advanced Level GCE marking criteria, and at a selection of Chief Examiners' subject reports. Attention will be focused in the main on production of the foreign language, since it is here that use of grammar is most easily observed. The language of illustration will be German.

The 1993 Subject Core for Modern Foreign Languages: Background

The first common core for Advanced Level GCEs in foreign languages – *Common Cores at Advanced Level* – dates back to 1983 (GCE Examining Boards, 1983). Its motivation was, according to the Introduction to the document by H. F. King, the desire of higher education authorities 'to establish what was common ground amongst their new entrants' (1983: 1). Around the common core, it was intended that a degree of inter-board variation be maintained. The core itself was said to represent those parts of the syllabuses which 'appeared to be indispensable' (1983: 7). The core was produced by analysing A-level syllabuses currently on offer; the Working Party consisted of the GCE boards, members of HMI, the Schools Council, the Standing Advisory Committee on University Entrance, the CNAA, and specialist subject teaching associations. The new syllabuses were implemented between 1984 and 1987.

The recent new subject core for MFLs (A/AS) appeared in December 1993 and is published by the SCAA (School Curriculum and Assessment Authority, 1993). The 1993 document is longer than its 1983 predecessor and consists of two parts: Introduction and The Core. In contrast to the 1983 version, where pressure from the higher education sector was acknowledged as a principal factor in driving the change, in this case the main influences seem to be from below, centring around the GCSE examination, which was sat for the first time in 1988. 'Earlier developments' on which the document is said to build include: the GCSE National Criteria for French (1985) and the National Curriculum Order for modern foreign languages (1991).

The SCAA document will form the basis of new A-level syllabuses from 1997. It is therefore of some concern that the new subject core contains a number of puzzling formulations. In my view, these suggest a fundamental confusion at 16+ about the relationship between grammar and 'communicative competence' and the nature of language learning. The document does indeed build on previous practice, as we can see from Mitchell's (1994) critical analysis of the treatment of grammar in GCSE syllabuses. She points out that the 'Structures and Grammar' (*sic*) section of the GCSE syllabus for German of the Southern Examining Group is almost exclusively based on the traditional scheme of parts of speech, namely: Articles, Nouns, Pronouns, Verbs, Adjectives, Adverbs, Prepositions, Conjunctions, with Word Order thrown in for good measure. By contrast, information on sentence grammar, such as negatives and interrogatives, is scattered throughout other sections of the syllabus and may be found in Language Functions and General Notions, leaving the impression that grammar has all to do with morphology and very little to do with sentences, let alone discourse or text. We shall see that similar conceptions of grammar are prevalent at A-level.

The 1993 Subject Core for Modern Foreign Languages: Content

The SCAA document (SCAA, 1993) explicitly places the A/AS subject core in the communicative tradition of language teaching, citing the 'teaching of communicative skills and the use of the target language' as evidence of good classroom practice on which the core builds (Section 1.3). Yet nowhere in the document does the term 'communicative competence' appear. Instead, there are several references to something called 'linguistic competence', e.g. 'The skills of listening, speaking, reading, and writing should not be regarded as discrete but as integrated elements in the development of linguistic competence' (Section 1.5). 'Linguistic competence' is said to be one of two 'complementary core elements', the other being 'knowledge of contemporary society'. The question then arises: how does SCAA's conception of linguistic competence, which is undefined, relate to the well-documented concept of 'communicative competence' (Hymes, 1972) which is the central notion normally associated with a communicative approach to language teaching, along with the various 'functions' originating from Speech Act Theory (see, for instance, Searle, 1972). Indeed, linguistic competence might reasonably be interpreted as grammatical competence or knowledge of the formal language system, i.e. as a component of overall communicative competence, since Hymes' communicative competence encompasses four types of knowledge, namely: the formal possibility of something (grammar); its feasibility (e.g. in terms of memory or processing capacity); its appropriacy in relation to a context; and what I understand to be its probability of use. Unfortunately, this is nowhere clarified in the SCAA document.

It is surprising that the sociolinguistic notion of communicative competence – a model of language *use* – appears to play such a shadowy role in the SCAA document. It is equally surprising that the view of language learning which appears to underlie the core is reminiscent of a behaviourist orientation, MFLs being described as 'linear subjects': 'Due recognition should be given to the progression and gradation which are a feature of linear subjects like modern foreign languages' (Section 1.5).

What is meant by 'linear subject'? I can only assume that this is a lingering reflection of a particular assumption about the nature of language learning which is seen as an additive process in which new bits of language are added to the current stock of the learner's knowledge without there being any qualitative change in the system or part of the system so far established. In my reading, it implies that 'bits' are learned in discrete succession. If a process is 'linear', then any backsliding (i.e. errors) needs to be explained by reference to factors outside the language system. This usually means that it is the learner's fault. As we shall see from the discussion of examiners' reports below, this view is pervasive when it comes to discussing 'linguistic competence'.

The Core of the document (Section 2) is divided into three sub-sections: knowledge and understanding (2.1), concepts and skills (2.2) and assessment objectives (2.3). The motivation for this division – particularly between 2.1 and 2.2 – is unclear. For instance, in Section 2.1 'knowledge of contemporary society' is mixed in with various aspects of language use, including not only comprehension but also production. The sub-section on concepts and skills (Section 2.2) appears equally muddled, linking together concepts of 'linguistic structure' and 'cultural understanding'.

The third sub-section on assessment objectives (Section 2.3) requires that candidates 'demonstrate their knowledge of contemporary society and their linguistic competence' in five ways. One of these objectives causes particular concern in the context of an apparently communicatively-based approach:

- manipulating the target language accurately in spoken and written forms and in ways which demonstrate a capacity to choose appropriate examples of lexis and structures and to transfer meaning from and into the target language;

Two words cause particular difficulties here: 'manipulate' and 'transfer'. The motivation for using the word 'manipulate' in the context of a communicative approach is unclear (why not 'use'?). It suggests a rather semantically-empty handling of form, but this seems not to be intended, since the 'transfer of meaning' is later mentioned. 'Manipulate' has strong associations with drill exercises and form, but not with meaning. For instance, writing about the teaching of modern languages, Hawkins uses a medium-message continuum to describe classroom activities; medium-focused activities are said to be those 'in which the pupil concentrates on *manipulating* the sounds and the grammar patterns, as in a paradigm drill' (1981: 246, emphasis added).

The second cause of concern is the phrase 'transfer of meaning' (why not 'express meaning'?). On the one hand, the phrase might be intended to refer to translation and interpretation exercises in the sense of 'decode' and 'encode', but this seems unlikely, since translation/interpretation does not feature large in the catalogue of communicative activities. On the other hand, the phrase might just refer to comprehension exercises using foreign-language texts ('transfer meaning from the target language') and the production of foreign-language speech or writing ('transfer meaning into the target language'). But there are two objections here. Firstly, comprehension skills are covered by two other assessment objectives, and so this would be a duplication (perhaps it is). Secondly, the so-called stimulus materials for production exercises or tests are often in the foreign language in any case; so in what sense is there any 'transfer', unless the student is expected to use English as a kind of translational interlanguage? Again, this seems unlikely in the context of a communicative approach. And, in any case, it is nonsense to talk of 'transferring meaning *from* the *target* language' (emphasis added).

One of the crucial problems underlying this apparent lack of coherence seems to be the fact that the interaction of grammar, or the formal language system, with the rules of language use (production and comprehension) is not well defined. The warning issued by Canale & Swain (1980: 6) some 15 years ago in their well-known paper on the theoretical bases of communicative language teaching and testing has not been heeded: '[. . .] if a communicative approach to second language teaching is adopted, then principles of syllabus design *must integrate* aspects of both grammatical competence and socio-linguistic competence' (authors' emphasis). This is clearly not the case in the new SCAA document which reads as if it had been repeatedly re-edited, leaving both inconsistencies and traces of earlier versions: the more it is amended, the less coherent it becomes. This state of confusion is a source of considerable concern in view of the document's central importance to the definition of future syllabuses, and hence to the teaching and testing of modern foreign languages at 16+.[1]

In fact, the confusion exhibited in the SCAA document turns out to be a continuation of current examining practice at GCE Advanced level. This continuity can be traced through marking criteria for examiners and Chief Examiners' subject reports.

Grammar and Communication in Marking Criteria

One of the main problems encountered when developing marking criteria – the general principles rather than specific marking schemes – is the need to judge how the whole language performance may be divided into discrete parts. Different examining boards find different solutions. For instance, it is not uncommon to find that similar criteria are given different labels (e.g. 'Range of expression' – 'Appropriateness of language' – 'Quality of language/ fluency', referring to the lexical and grammatical range of the candidate's performance). The grouping of criteria also varies. So where one board may emphasise the role of fluency in the assessment of language 'quality', another may stress grammar.

In the following, reference is made to the marking criteria published by three examining boards:

- the Advanced Level GCE Syllabus in Modern Languages for 1994 and 1995 issued by the University of Oxford Delegacy of Local Examinations (Oxford, 1991a)
- the Advanced Level GCE Syllabus in Modern Languages for 1995 published by London Examinations (London, n.d.)

- and the 1993 GCE Mark Scheme for German from the Northern Examinations and Assessment Board (NEAB, n.d. (1993)).[2]

As far as I can ascertain, these are the only boards which actually publish their marking criteria in any detail.

A recurring problem is how to deal with the relationship between grammar and communication. London, for instance, assesses its Paper 4 (Guided Writing and Essay) according to two sets of criteria: Content and Language (London Examinations, n.d.: 16–7). Language is somewhat confusingly exemplified as 'grammar, structures, lexis' where 'grammar' is presumably limited to morphology. Yet when the language criteria are examined more closely, each range of marks is in the first instance characterised by a statement about 'communication' (emphasis that of the original):

1–4   Candidates achieve a *limited degree of communication*; they show a limited knowledge of basic aspects of grammar and are occasionally accurate [. . .]

5–11 *Some communication* is achieved; candidates show some knowledge and accurate use of basic grammar, possibly with occasional indications of a wider range [. . .]

12–15 *A reasonable degree of communication* is achieved and often sustained; there is a fair knowledge and accurate use of grammar and structures [. . .]

And so on.

The wording of these criteria is suggestive of a more or less direct link between the degree of grammatical *accuracy* achieved and the efficacy of the *communication*. There is no mention, for instance, of the functions or notions which usually form the basis of communicative language teaching.

Marking criteria need to be expressed concisely, but concision is hard to reconcile with explicitness. Consequently, many assumptions are left implicit and the criteria must be interpreted by the examiner in the light of his or her own assumptions. Are all examiners agreed, for instance, about the definition of 'basic structures', 'complex structures', 'complex sentences', and 'elementary errors' as mentioned in the marking criteria for essays in German on prescribed texts (Paper 1, Section A, 'Command of language' and 'Accuracy of language'; NEAB, n.d. (1993): 3–4)? It seems unlikely. Little clarification is available elsewhere; regarding the NEAB Paper II (based on written material), we are told that a 'very good/good' German essay has the following characteristics: 'nouns with correct genders, used consistently; clear word order; agreement of verb and subject; correct use of the passive; [. . .]' (NEAB, n.d. (1993): 17).

Elsewhere, in connection with its Paper 4 for 1994 and 1995 (topic-based writing in German), Oxford attempts to define – within the criteria on 'Range of expression' – the concept of 'simple linguistic structures' and 'complex structures' (Oxford, 1991a: 27). These turn out, rather unenlighteningly, to be respectively: 'well-known constructions; no object pronouns' and 'object pronouns, less common constructions'.

The issue of communication arises not only in connection with grammar, but also in its relation to content. The NEAB criteria for marking the content of essays on prescribed texts can be illustrated by the following extracts from the bottom and top of the scale (NEAB, n.d. (1993): 4):

VERY POOR shows little knowledge of the work; largely or totally ignores
(0–7)   the specific question

EXCELLENT detailed and noteworthy display of relevant knowledge;
(30–35)   impressive organisation of material

If, however, we compare these criteria to those listed under the heading 'Communication' – specifically for the role-play – in the 1993 NEAB Oral Examination (NEAB, n.d. (1993): 28), we find that there is considerable similarity (6 is the maximum number of marks available):

0 totally unable to supply any useful information. Finds nothing of interest or substance to say

6 supplies all the information necessary for a full and accurate performance of the task. Uses all or virtually all the possibilities offered or available to develop the exchange

Reading further, we discover, however, that it is an accompanying set of criteria for the role-play, namely 'Responsiveness', which actually seems to be about communication. Indeed, the criterion for the award of the maximum mark is phrased precisely in terms of communicative functions (NEAB, n.d. (1993): 29):

0 totally unable to communicate other than with one word answers

6 native or near-native ability to communicate. Is able to interact on equal terms with the examiner, and to take the initiative by asking questions, disagreeing, countering views . . .

It seems then that considerable confusion reigns in the marking criteria examined in a number of respects, including, in particular, the relationship of communication to grammar and to content, and the nature of grammatical concepts such as 'simple' and 'complex'.

Grammar and Communication in Chief Examiners' Subject Reports

Subject cores, syllabuses and marking criteria are not the only places where confusion over the role of grammar in a communicative approach is to be found. Chief Examiners' post mortems, published annually by each board, are equally revealing. This is particularly well illustrated in the 1993 subject report for German from the London Examinations Board (London, 1993: 15) referring to the guided writing and essay paper, where 'grammar' initially appears to be interpreted as communicative functions:

> This paper tests accuracy as well as communication and therefore candidates need to become as proficient as possible in German grammar. The Examiners noted weakness in expressing agreement/disagreement, general uncertainty about all types of pronouns, confusion about when to use *müssen* and *dürfen*, and a lack of awareness of the difference between *wurde* and *würde*.

In fact, the wording of many comments to be found in contemporary examiners' reports as well as syllabuses in general indicates an unconventional understanding of grammar. For instance, the 1994 NEAB syllabus (NEAB, n.d. (1994): 346) talks of testing candidates' ability 'to handle competently the necessary grammar and syntax implicit in the above list of skills' (see also NEAB, n.d. (1995): 7). Meanwhile, the 1992 Associated Examining Board Examiners' Report (AEB, 1992: 21–2) classifies candidates' errors as being due to 'grammatical and syntactical inaccuracy on the one hand and sheer inaccurate learning or carelessness on the other'. 'Grammar', therefore, seems to exclude syntax, which is itself ill-defined.[3] Indeed, comments on 'main weaknesses' in German in a range of examiners' reports stress inflectional morphology as a particular source of error. Typically, these reports point to aspects of nominal and verbal morphology, with the occasional mention of word order, mirroring closely the 'Structures and Grammar' (*sic*) section of the Southern Examining Group German GCSE syllabus critically reviewed by Mitchell (1994). The following are typical examples: 'case usage, adjective endings, plural of nouns, formation of tenses, knowledge of parts of strong verbs, word order (especially position of the verb), when to use "zu" with infinitives and when not; correct use of das/daß + relative pronouns; appropriate possessives' (AEB, 1991: 18); 'adjectival endings and the cases following prepositions [. . .], the use of capital letters [. . .], the genders and plurals of common nouns' (Oxford, 1991b: 26). Reports from other boards contain a similar emphasis (e.g. London, 1992: 12; NEAB, 1993: 15).

While errors of inflectional morphology are defined in some detail in the examiners' reports, even down to the level of particular tokens, the precise nature of what examiners consider to be the more 'advanced' structures of the language generally remain a mystery, as was the case for the marking criteria discussed earlier. The 1991 and 1992 Oxford subject reports, for instance, talk of 'typically German "ambitious structures"' (Oxford, 1991b: 25) and 'complex linguistic structures' (Oxford, 1992: 26), but offer no examples or definitions of what these might be.

In reading these reports, one is left with the feeling that ideas are being expressed in a kind of pseudo-terminology which is intended to create an aura of expertise – 'lexis', 'idiom', 'complex linguistic structure', 'competence' – but which actually masks a lack of it, anticipating the lack of clarity observed in the more recent new subject core.

Explanations and Remedies in Chief Examiners' Subject Reports

As interesting as the descriptions of 'gross errors' in these reports are the explanations and remedies suggested for them. These may be viewed as a kind of window on assumptions about language learning, reflecting again what the School Curriculum and Assessment Authority document (SCAA, 1993) refers to as the 'linear' nature of foreign language learning. Through their comments, the examiners show that they regard inflectional morphology as 'basic' or 'elementary', and yet research in language learning shows that aspects of inflectional morphology in German are among the most persistent sources of error for teenage second language learners (Wichter, 1982). The view of this error type as 'basic' or 'elementary' also considerably underestimates the linguistic difficulties of endings which enter into complex syntagmatic as well as paradigmatic relations (Rogers, 1987).

The catalogue of attempted explanations for such errors is, for what it is worth, at least consistent with the assumption that inflectional morphology is basic and therefore, we are supposed to infer, 'easy'. The blame for the errors is consequently put firmly at the learner's door. Some typical attempts at explanations by Chief Examiners are shown below. They are sometimes mixed with proposed remedies, presumably as advice for teachers to pass on to their students in future years. The remedies again make it largely the learner's responsibility to fix things:

There was inaccuracy too – showing evidence of either ignorance or extreme carelessness [. . .] (Oxford, 1992: 26)

In many cases it was clear that the grammar had not been thoroughly learnt or understood, which is regrettable. In others, however, there

> seemed to be a total disregard for grammatical structure. This lack of discipline was often, but by no means always, compounded by careless presentation of work [. . .] (Cambridge, 1993: 18)

> To improve marks, candidates are advised to ensure full learning of lexical items and idioms, i.e. genders, plurals, cases required, specific word order patterns, etc. and quite simply pay far more attention to writing accurate and correct language. (AEB, 1992: 23)

The 'linear' understanding of language learning referred to is exemplified by phrases such as those used in the 1991 AEB report (AEB, 1991: 17) including a 'lack of accurate learning', 'half learned items', 'poorly applied grammar', betraying a clear unfamiliarity with any notions of learning development.

In this context, I would like to consider one particular phenomenon which is mentioned in several reports in connection with noun genders and plural formation. It concerns, as far as I can tell, exclusively masculine and neuter nouns. The nub of the problem seems to be that candidates place an -e on the end of these nouns, a typical plural ending, and then treat each noun as if it were feminine singular:

> It does now appear that there is a growing tendency amongst the weaker English learners of German to come across plural forms of masculine and neuter nouns ending in '-e', to half learn these items and to end up believing that these words are feminine singulars. [. . .]: *eine Spiele, eine Grunde, eine Vorteile, eine Nachteile, eine Probleme, eine Dinge.*
> (AEB, 1993: 28; see also Oxford, 1991b: 25; AEB, 1992: 23; NEAB, 1993: 15)

Now, it seems that there is some kind of regular pattern here. I would hazard an interpretation of this as follows: if you are not sure of the gender, use a kind of generic form ending in -e. Why this particular form is chosen is not clear from the Examiners' descriptions, but it might be worth noting that children learning German as their first language choose [∂] as their preferred adjectival ending when these begin to emerge at around the age of 2;0 (MacWhinney, 1978: 62). Perhaps the [∂] suffix is in some way particularly salient in German, and the A-level foreign language learners generalise it across the whole NP, using the letter -e in their written German. Whatever the eventual explanation, there appears to be a regularity here in the learners' treatment of a certain class (as they perceive it) of nouns. If there is a regularity, then it seems to have something to do with learning rather than 'lack of discipline', or 'half learning'.

Conclusion

All in all, the view which I have presented here is not very encouraging for the immediate future of modern foreign language testing by the English examination boards. I can only speculate that the kind of views about grammar which have been described here will persist if the examiners, syllabus designers and policy makers remain poorly informed about language learning processes and about language itself, both system and use. Until this changes, what remains is a communicative 'approach' which is in reality bolted on to an underlying view of language and language learning which has scarcely changed for many decades.

Notes

1. Similar criticisms can be levelled at the GCSE criteria for Modern Foreign Languages Draft Proposal (SCAA, 1994).
2. The year of publication of Northern Examinations and Assessment Board documents is often not given; references are therefore given to the year to which the document relates. Thus 'NEAB, n.d. (1993)' refers to the 1993 GCE Mark Scheme for German which in fact was published prior to 1993.
3. The following comments can be noted by way of example: 'knowledge of the structures and syntax of the German language' and 'German is a more structured language than English' (Joint Matriculation Board, 1992: 46); 'mastery of German grammar and constructions' (NEAB, 1993: 15); and 'knowledge of German grammar, structures and syntax' (NEAB, 1992: 67).

References

Canale, M. and Swain, M. (1980) Theoretical bases of communicative approaches to second language teaching and testing. *Applied Linguistics* 1/1, 1–47.

GCE Examining Boards of England, Wales and Northern Ireland (1983) *Common Cores at Advanced Level* (with an Introduction by H. F. King).

Hawkins, E. (1981) *Modern Languages in the Curriculum*. Cambridge: Cambridge University Press.

Hymes, D. (1972, originally 1971) On communicative competence. In J. Gumperz and D. Hymes (eds) (1972) *Directions in Sociolinguistics* (pp. 269–93). New York: Holt, Rinehart & Winston.

MacWhinney, B. (1978) The acquisition of morphophonology. *Monographs of the Society for Research in Child Development* 43, 1/2, Serial No. 174.

Mitchell, R. (1994) Grammar, syllabuses and teachers. In M. Bygate, A. Tonkyn and E. Williams (eds) *Grammar and the Language Teacher* (pp. 90–104). New York: Prentice Hall.

Rogers, M. A. (1987) Learners' difficulties with grammatical gender in German as a foreign language. *Applied Linguistics* 8/1, 48–74.

School Curriculum and Assessment Authority (1993) *Subject Core for Modern Foreign Languages. GCE Advanced and Advanced Supplementary Examinations*.

— (1994) *GCSE Criteria for Modern Foreign Languages Draft Proposals*.

Searle, J. (1972, originally 1965) What is a speech act? In P. P. Giglioli (ed.) *Language and Social Context* (pp. 136–54). Harmondsworth: Penguin.

Wichter, S. (1982) Zur Morphologie türkischer Lerner der zweiten Generation. In K. Detering, J. Schmidt-Radefeldt and W. Sucharowski (eds) *Sprache beschreiben und erklären* (pp. 439–49). Akten des 16. Linguistischen Kolloquiums Kiel, 1981. Band 1. Tübingen: Max Niemeyer Verlag.

Examination Board Publications

Associated Examining Board (1991) *Reports of Examiners. June Examination 1991. Section 2 Languages. Advanced Level/Advanced Supplementary.*

Associated Examining Board (1992) *Reports of Examiners. June Examination 1992. French, German and Spanish. Advanced Level/Advanced Supplementary.*

Associated Examining Board (1993) *Reports of Examiners. June Examination 1993. French, German and Spanish. Advanced Level/Advanced Supplementary.*

Joint Matriculation Board (1992) *GCE Examiners' Reports 1991. Modern Foreign Languages.*

London Examinations (1992) *Subject Report German (Advanced Supplementary and Advanced Level).*

London Examinations (1993) *Subject Report German (Advanced Supplementary and Advanced Level).*

London Examinations (n.d.) *GCE Modern Languages Advanced Supplementary and Advanced Level. Syllabuses May/June 1995.*

Northern Examinations and Assessment Board (1992) *Reports on the 1992 GCE Examinations (Languages). Advanced; Advanced Supplementary; Special.*

Northern Examinations and Assessment Board (1993) *GCE 1993. Report on the Examination. German (Advanced; Advanced Supplementary; Special).*

Northern Examinations and Assessment Board (n.d., 1993) *Mark Scheme GCE 1993 German (Advanced).*

Northern Examinations and Assessment Board (n.d., 1994) *General Certificate of Education Syllabus Offprints (1994) Modern Foreign Languages.*

Northern Examinations and Assessment Board (n.d., 1995) *General Certificate of Education Syllabuses for 1995: German (Advanced; Advanced Supplementary; Special).*

University of Cambridge Local Examinations Syndicate (1993) *German. Report on the June 1993 Examination.*

University of Oxford Delegacy of Local Examinations (1991a) *General Certificate of Education Advanced Level. Modern Languages Summer Examinations 1994 & 1995.*

University of Oxford Delegacy of Local Examinations (1991b) *Chief Examiners' Reports. Advanced Level. Modern Languages. Summer 1991.*

University of Oxford Delegacy of Local Examinations (1992) *Chief Examiners' Reports. Advanced Level. Modern Languages. Summer 1992.*

6 Language Change at the British Sign Language/ English Interface

GRAHAM H. TURNER
University of Durham

Introduction

'As long as there are Deaf people on earth, there will be signs . . .' This canonical statement, from American Deaf[1] man George Veditz (1913), has long stood as a marker of the faith Deaf people have in the durability – against often overwhelming odds (Taylor & Bishop, 1991; Lane, 1992; Lee, 1992) – of the signed languages they use.

Deaf people are people who undertake their interaction with the world principally on the basis of vision. They are people who simply cannot – 'no matter how much distorted, filtered, amplified sound can be generated by an electro-acoustical transducer stuck into their ears' (Stokoe, 1978: 4) – hear and use speech. They will, however, always need to communicate. Signing comes naturally and is efficient. A powerful combination of factors thus assures believers of the longevity of signed languages.

But what exactly is it that will survive? This paper suggests that the sociolinguistic circumstances of the Deaf community in 1990s Britain raise a degree of concern as to the long-term viability of heritage British Sign Language (BSL). It will be seen that linguistic and socio-cultural vitality for BSL-users are tightly co-inherent.

The Language Interface

There is a growing literature concerned with the matter of language shift or attrition (Dorian, 1981; Schmidt, 1985; Seliger & Vago, 1991). The primary concern of such analyses is the shifting of the structure of one language in contact situations with a second language.

Factors in language shift

What sociolinguistic factors have been identified as characteristic of language shift situations? Julianne Maher has focused discussion of contact-leading-to-shift situations on so-called *enclave* communities, i.e. 'communities where speakers of one language, A, are surrounded and/or dominated by speakers of a different language, B, in a defined political or geographic area' (1991: 67).

The essential characteristics of such a community are said to be:

- that it is *multilingual* (in the broadest sense);
- that language A is natively used by a significant *number* of people;
- that users of A constitute a *minority* of the polity (where this minority may be either numerical or socio-political or both);
- that the A-using community has been relatively *isolated* from other A users for 100–400 years (approximately).

Anne Schmidt's description (Schmidt, 1991) of language shift in Boumaa Fijian and Dyirbal identifies a number of sociolinguistic factors linked to linguistic consequences as outlined above. These include:

- *intermarriage:* women bring with them into marriage the speech habits of their birth village and transmit either these or Standard Fijian to their children, ie they do not transmit Boumaa Fijian;
- *compulsory education:* the Fijian education system promotes and uses Standard Fijian: the all-English curriculum provides a negative force for Dyirbal, replacing Dyirbal with English and creating and reinforcing the impression that Dyirbal is unimportant;
- *the Church:* promotes Standard Fijian forms in the Bible, prayer books and services;
- *the media:* radio programmes are in Standard Fijian/English; videos are in English; newspapers are in Standard Fijian/English: watching television presented in an L2 becomes a frequent pastime;
- *literature:* in the Dyirbal case, Schmidt notes (1991: 118) that 'All-English literature not only confirms English as a prestigious language, but also glossy magazines and books create desires, images and expectations': these are widely associated with the language in the context of which they are presented.

The lack of use of written texts in the L1 – and, at the extreme, the absence of a writing system with which to express the L1 as text – may also be highly significant. In a sociolinguistic decay/maintenance index, the presence of a writing system, and the choice of a system 'belonging to' the L1 as opposed to one imported from an L2, are – other things being equal – indicators of relative health.

Pathways

Maher's crosslinguistic account of contact and shift offers several insights into the pathways of the process. One of these is couched in functional terms: 'As language A dies out, speakers use it in fewer and fewer sociolinguistic contexts; it is suggested, therefore, that the need for stylistic variants in language A is reduced. Moreover, among intimates, context predetermines much of the message. The need for more formal, elaborated or context-independent speech varieties is, therefore, limited' (Maher, 1991: 80). Alternatively, one could look for explanations arising from acquisition of the L1 in the multilingual setting: 'Intergenerational language change in bilingual communities is seen in these terms as the result of inadequate exposure to language A for latter-generation children' (Maher, 1991: 81).

As a symptom of the process of decay, Dressler (1991: 103) highlights, amongst others, the lack of puristic reaction against encroachment from L2 formulations: '(Pre)terminal speakers fail to notice such "corruptions", and healthy speakers seem to have given up correcting them.' Nevertheless, there is a genuine paradox in the feelings minority-language users have about candidates for possible puristic reaction: there is liable to be a desire to adopt loanwords and structures from the majority language as prestige markers even as the very same elements are condemned as foreign elements destroying the purity of the minority language (Romaine, 1989).

As the process of shift runs its course, Schmidt observes (1991: 120–22) that one of the results is an 'economy of distinctions'. The changing language variety may have a diminishing role as a vehicle for communicative interaction, but it continues to play an important part in maintaining group identity. The principle of economy of distinctions holds that speakers economise on the number of distinguishing features, finding a lowest common denominator of items which mark their speech as distinct.

The reality of this pattern in the perception of language users is evident from the fact that speakers frequently perceive their language as 'healthy' as long as certain formal markers of the language continue to be used. Even a non-fluent semi-speaker, who has lost many distinguishing features of traditional language variety X and who has minimal proficiency in the code, will be regarded as a 'speaker of X' if he or she employs a few salient symbols of the language.

Parallels?

Firstly, does the British Deaf community constitute an 'enclave language community'? Look again at the criteria:

- *multilingual* – Clearly the British Deaf community is multilingual, although the balance between its two primary languages – BSL and English – is extremely uneven. (Reuben Conrad's finding, for example, that the average reading age of the deaf school-leaver is approximately eight-and-three-quarters (Conrad, 1979), suggests that skills in English cannot typically be described as altogether fluent.);
- *numerous* – Whilst it is difficult to know what counts as a 'significant' number of users, the widely cited and accepted figure of approximately 50,000 people whose first or preferred language is BSL seems to satisfy the criterion;
- *minority* – Given these numbers, plus factors like the complete absence of Deaf people in institutions such as the Houses of Parliament, and the small numbers of Deaf people who reach prominent positions in other social institutions, it seems clear that the British Deaf community satisfies this criterion on both numerical and socio-political grounds;
- *isolated* – A little trickier, this one, but the apparent family resemblances between New Zealand Sign Language, Auslan and BSL seem to indicate that these do share common origins. If this is accepted, then certainly the communities involved have been severely isolated for a long time.

Sociolinguistic parallels

And so to the potential sociolinguistic parallels. To what extent do these appear to match the characteristics of language shift circumstances elsewhere? Consider:

- *intermarriage* – Although statistics are not available to confirm this, a large proportion of Deaf people do indeed take spouses who bring to the family an additional, dominant language to which children are exposed;
- *education* – Whereas in times gone by (see Brennan, 1992: 4–5), the residential school for deaf children was the place where (in informal communication in the peer group as opposed to classroom interaction) signing skills were most often developed and refined, current practice rarely allows for extensive use of BSL in the schools. Many deaf children are placed in small groups in partially hearing units (PHUs) attached to mainstream schools; there and in wider school environments they are much more frequently taught using some combination of oral methods and manual English (English presented using the visual-gestural modality) than using anything approaching fluent BSL. In any case, no matter what the communication practices are,

it is incumbent upon the school, under the terms of current national educational policy (which certainly reflects public opinion as far as signed language is concerned), to promote the English language above all;

- *the Church* – Not such a significant factor with regard to the British Deaf community, it is still nevertheless true that 'church signing' is widely considered to show an enduringly close correspondence with the English texts which its relatively frozen forms often follow;
- *the media* – Such signing as does appear on television (radio and newspapers can carry none) often shows evidence of L2 (English) influence: whether this is attributable to the use of autocue facilities based on English texts, to an attitude that considers television to be an occasion for formal signing and English-influenced formulations to be most appropriate in formal contexts, or some other factor or factors, is unclear. Meanwhile, the remainder of television, film and video viewing is dependent upon subtitling, i.e. English. The presence of Deaf people embodying Deaf values and norms is extremely rare, reinforcing the desirability for contact with the wider world of English skills;
- *literature* – There is only the tiniest amount of BSL literature (i.e. signed literature on video) available: the texts that surround Deaf people in everyday life are overwhelmingly presented in English. In respect of theatre and poetry, the situation is a little more promising: still, in terms of broadcast or published work, the list is very short;
- *writing system* – There is no writing system (i.e. conventional script for everyday communication) for BSL: if a British Deaf person wishes to write, it will probably be in English.

One additional influential factor may be noted. Interaction between L1 users and L2 users is regularly mediated by the services of interpreters providing simultaneous interpretation translation between BSL and English. Most use English as their preferred language, and primarily have English-speaking communities as their 'home' communities. As brokers between language groups, who tend to be seen by members of the minority group as knowledgeable individuals, it is possible that they play a significant role as weak ties between signing and speaking social networks (cf. Milroy, 1987).

Further parallels

With reference to functional limitations, the perceptions of native signers suggest that there are many environments in which heritage BSL gives way to a more English-influenced type of signing. There comes to mind here an oft-cited example of the then administrative head of the British Deaf Association being 'caught' (in a televised debate on the issue of the acceptability of English-influenced signing) using just such a contact variety herself while in the midst of a passionate defence of heritage BSL. Such examples are not hard to find.

The role of inadequate intergenerational exposure is particularly significant, for here we see a uniquely constant factor, insofar as, some 90% of the time, the deaf child in Britain is born to hearing parents whose first language is English. The result is that there is minimal exposure to BSL in the family. The incidence of the deaf child being born to two Deaf parents, and therefore being as certain as can be of early exposure to fluent BSL in the home, is about one in 20.

Although a strain of puristic reaction can be seen in the British Deaf community, its manifestation tends towards either of two extremes. On the one hand, there is a sweeping general condemnation of the signing of some individuals as being typical of the signing seen as imported into the Deaf community by hearing professionals (commonly referred to as 'missioner signing' or 'social worker signing'). On the other hand, we see the dislike of particular signs seen as distinctly 'non-Deaf' or 'unnatural'.

The principle of economy of distinctions is again, in this context, a double-edged sword. On the one hand, the 'non-Deaf' signs mentioned immediately above; on the other, shibboleths used consciously or subconsciously to identify signers as 'one of us'. In both cases, a small number of features and elements repeatedly stand duty as indicating clear distinctions between those who really know the language and those who do not.

Turning finally to self-perceptions, given that the everyday signing of many qualified teachers of BSL (who are, in the community context, relative experts on the structure of the language, and who continue to act as professional 'teachers of BSL') is similarly influenced, it must be acknowledged that contact signing is, in the British context, not incompatible with 'authenticity' as a BSL user.

Education and language shift

It is worth a slight rallentando here to underline the role of educational practices in this sociolinguistic picture. Problems of this order can only arise in bilingual contexts, and the primary locus of bilingual development for the majority of Deaf people is the school. When deaf children who have a reasonable, age-appropriate grasp of BSL are schooled under a bilingual approach that advocates the use, in careful distribution, of both BSL and English, and the result over time is a generation of bilingual young people whose signed language usage unmistakeably shows the effects of shift under the sheer, blunt, irresistible weight of the English language juggernaut, the question must arise: *is this what was intended?*

Life Goes On

The primary countervailing pressure at present is the determination in some quarters of education for deaf children to develop an unwaveringly additive form of bilingualism. The adoption of additive bilingual practices in schools could bring immense benefits, forming (as 'institutional support') the first of three factors identified by Giles *et al.* (1977) as being of importance in language maintenance. Here Cummins & Swain's (1986: 101–10) three principles for 'bilingualism without tears' should also be noted:

- the principle of first things first; ensure that the child's L1 is adequately developed before worrying about progress in L2;
- the principle of bilingualism through monolingualism; the development of bilingual skills will be enhanced by the separated use of the two languages by teachers;
- the principle of bilingualism as a bonus; let students know how and why bilingualism will work for them: believe it, and it will become a self-fulfilling prophecy.

The second factor, demographic concentration, is rather difficult to fulfill, as the Deaf population in Britain is spread evenly from region to region. Keeping open the residential schools for deaf children would perhaps be the most realistic option, thus giving the children early opportunities to acquire the linguistic habits, including a solid grounding in BSL as an L1, which would stand them in good stead for future educational and bilingual success.

The tallest order

The third factor, status, is the tallest order, since there is no way of manufacturing it. The status of this minority language in the eyes of the majority language users is likely to remain as it currently is – small, curious and vaguely fascinating – for the time being. Of greater importance is the issue of status in the eyes of the minority language's own constituency: in this case, the status of BSL in the eyes of the Deaf community. Jim Cummins (1986: 22) points to the fact that 'widespread school failure does not occur in minority groups that are positively oriented towards both their own and the dominant culture, that do not perceive themselves as inferior to the dominant group, and that are not alienated from their own cultural values'. The current climate within the Deaf community is one in which the choice of young Deaf people increasingly to spurn the embrace of their local Deaf clubs clearly shows dissatisfaction with the practices seen as constitutive of adult Deaf cultural behaviour. Deaf children must be given some motivation, some reason to continue to know about the culture and use the language, some reason to *need* to do so. The alternative, in a bilingual environment, is that the L2 will indeed overwhelm the L1: what else will stop English (be it orally, manually or graphically coded) from being the only language the child needs to know in order to be in the world?

Motivation

Where could such motivation be generated? Look back to the sociolinguistic circumstances that accompany language shift and reverse the patterns:

- let BSL be used by parents of deaf children; if they are hearing, let them be taught BSL as a second language by fluent BSL-using Deaf teachers;
- let deaf children be educated using BSL as the language of instruction;
- let BSL be used in institutional contexts such as the Church;
- let the media produce television programmes aimed at the Deaf community in richly woven BSL, and let programmes not made with a Deaf audience in mind be translated thoroughly and presented by fluently signing interpreters or additional on-screen presenters;
- let the literature of BSL – narrative, poetry, theatre, comedy – be collected, recorded and published for the benefit of all who care to watch and share;
- and let experimentation with BSL writing be encouraged wherever there is curiosity as to the potential benefits and applications of the medium.

Steps such as these would seem at least to be worthy of consideration. BSL is between a horrifying rock and a terrible hard place. On the one hand, those who would be native users of the language – children whose deafness means that signed communication is more accessible and thus more natural to them than spoken communication – frequently do not, under present acquisitional circumstances, learn or use the language fluently. On the other, the status quo both in the Deaf community and in the wider polity is indelibly marked by the fact that English is the major world language, with all the breadth of scope which that implies, while BSL is used by a tiny minority of the population and is sorely lacking in status even among its natural constituency. The first step towards stemming what may be a significant shift is a relatively simple matter of *awareness*.

Note

1. Following a convention proposed by James Woodward (1972), the uppercase *Deaf* is used to refer to a particular group of people who share (signed) linguistic

and cultural patterns. The lowercase *deaf* is used to refer to the audiological condition of not hearing and to people who share this condition. Deaf children who, as described in this paper, are likely to have hearing parents, frequently do not embrace the linguistic and cultural patterns of the Deaf community until adulthood. I therefore use the lowercase *deaf* to refer to children.

References

Brennan, M. (1992) The visual world of BSL: An introduction. In D. Brien (ed.) *Dictionary of British Sign Language/English* (pp. 1–33). London: Faber and Faber.

Conrad, R. (1979) *The Deaf School Child: Language and cognitive function*. London: Harper and Row.

Cummins, J. (1986) Empowering minority students: A framework for intervention. *Harvard Educational Review* 56:1, 18–36.

Cummins, J. and Swain, M. (1986) *Bilingualism in Education: Aspects of theory, research and practice*. London, Longman.

Dorian, N. (1981) *Language Death: The life cycle of a Scottish Gaelic dialect*. Philadelphia, PA: University of Pennsylvania Press.

Dressler, W. (1991) The sociolinguistic and patholinguistic attrition of Breton phonology, morphology, and morphonology. In H. Seliger and R. Vago (eds) *First Language Attrition* (pp. 99–112). Cambridge: Cambridge University Press.

Giles, H., Bourhis, R. and Taylor, D. (1977) Towards a theory of language in ethnic group relations. In H. Giles (ed.) *Language, Ethnicity and Intergroup Relations* (pp. 307–48). London: Academic Press.

Lane, H. (1992) *The Mask of Benevolence*. New York: Alfred A. Knopf.

Lee, R. (ed.) (1992) *Deaf Liberation*. Middlesex: National Union of the Deaf.

Maher, J. (1991) A crosslinguistic study of language contact and language attrition. In H. Seliger and R. Vago (eds) *First Language Attrition* (pp. 67–84). Cambridge: Cambridge University Press.

Milroy, L. (1987) *Language and Social Networks*. Oxford: Basil Blackwell.

Romaine, S. (1989) Pidgins, creoles, immigrant, and dying languages. In N. Dorian (ed.) *Investigating Obsolescence: Studies in language contraction and death* (pp. 369–84). Cambridge: Cambridge University Press.

Schmidt, A. (1985) *Young People's Dyirbal: An example of language death from Australia*. Cambridge: Cambridge University Press.

— (1991) Language attrition in Boumaa Fijian and Dyirbal. In H. Seliger and R. Vago (eds) *First Language Attrition* (pp. 113–24). Cambridge: Cambridge University Press.

Seliger, H. and Vago, R. (1991) The study of first language attrition: An overview. In H. Seliger and R. Vago (eds) *First Language Attrition* (pp. 3–16). Cambridge: Cambridge University Press.

Stokoe, W. (1978) Sign Language Research: What it knows and whither it leads. Supplement to *British Deaf News* 9:8.

Taylor, G. and Bishop, J. (eds) (1991) *Being Deaf*. Milton Keynes: Pinter Publishers in association with the Open University.

Veditz, G. (1913) *The Preservation of Sign Language* (film). Silver Spring, MD, National Association of the Deaf.

Woodward, J. (1972) Implications for sociolinguistic research among the deaf. *Sign Language Studies* 1, 1–7.

Section 2:
Change, Language and the Individual

Introduction

The papers in this section range across first and second language development, across young children to adolescents to university students and adults. Linking them together is their concern to improve the descriptive and explanatory powers of methodology for measuring language development in the individual, to 'sharpen the axes', in Catherine Snow's analogy. Snow's opening plenary paper – 'Change in Child Language and Child Linguists' – sets the tone by reviewing changes in methodology within the field of child language studies over the last 30 years, and highlighting in particular the shift from the description of successive states through the single measure of MLU (mean length of utterance), to the assessment of change through an array of measures. In addition to the systems traditionally measured – phonology, lexis, morphology, syntax – she reports research with mothers and children that demonstrates further domains that seem to develop independently: conversation, extended discourse and pragmatic skills. Such results are worthy of attention from researchers into second language development, where complex interacting systems of language use and development are also at work and in need of description and measurement.

The papers by Tonkyn ('The Oral Language Development of Instructed Second Language Learners') and by Raschka and Milroy ('Developing Grammars in Their Social Context') both provide a glimpse of this complexity in their measures of second language growth in very different social contexts. Raschka and Milroy report on a project with women from the Tyneside Chinese community, involving analysis of grammatical patterns within conversational data. Interestingly, the field of first language development provides them with a tool, which they modify to measure syntactic development within social contexts, finding that syntax interacts in development with conversation skills, and that social contact with L1 English speakers is an important indicator of language proficiency.

While Raschka and Milroy's subjects had received no formal language instruction, Tonkyn's students were engaged in a ten week intensive English course. Again employing a measure of grammatical complexity, Tonkyn found that development was not unitary but that apparent trade-offs were manifested between improvements in complexity, accuracy and fluency. Once again, improving our capacity to measure growth in different domains of language would be valuable, in this case to allay uncertainty about potential language skills development through formal instruction.

The language skills of university students, this time from a sociopragmatic angle, are investigated in 'Elaborating Elaboration in Academic Tutorials' by Turner and Hiraga, who analyse the elaboration strategies which students use and report using in tutorials. The sociopragmatic assumptions that students bring to tutorials appear to affect the interaction pattern between tutor and student, and presumably may also influence the probability of effective learning outcomes, at least in the short term as students adjust to new expectations.

Social issues are central too in Rampton's chapter, 'Crossing: Language across ethnic boundaries', which presents an analysis of the interaction of multiracial adolescents engaged in peer talk across and between languages and social boundaries, demonstrating the language phenomenon which he labels 'crossing'. At the level of discipline perspectives and methodology, Rampton suggests the time is ripe for crossings between SLA and code-switching research.

From the theme of individuality and language change emerges a developmental picture of multiple complexity, with integration and interaction between sub-fields of language study offering opportunities to construct improved measures of language change.

7 Change in Child Language and Child Linguists

CATHERINE E. SNOW
Harvard Graduate School of Education

Introduction

Thirty years after the rebirth of child language as a field of study, it makes sense to take stock of where the field is. What have we learned in the last 30 years about how to study language development? In a volume devoted to the topic of change in language, it is eminently appropriate to include some consideration of how the child's language system changes during the first years of life – a developmental period during which change is rapid, exciting, and informative. In addition to discussing the kinds of changes that occur in children, I will take the opportunity in this chapter to discuss more generally how change can best be studied in the field of child language, and how the procedures used in the field have themselves changed over the last 30 years. In other words, I will combine a focus on how child linguists have changed their methods and approaches with information about how children change.

Traditional methods in the field of child language are by now familiar to any undergraduate psychology or linguistics major – a prototypical method consists of collecting a corpus of utterances from a child, taking a set of those utterances from a single developmental period, and then writing a grammar that characterizes them. When this method was used for child language by Roger Brown in the early 1970s (see also, for example, Braine, 1976; Ervin-Tripp, 1973), it proved illuminating in several ways: it demonstrated that traditional methods of linguistic description could be applied to child language and that a child's language even at early stages of development was systematic, organized and rule-governed. It provided ways of comparing children with one another and of comparing children's linguistic systems with adult natural languages.

There are also limitations inherent in this sort of method, though. First, the method forces one to describe a status, not a process of change – successive grammars characterize successive steady states, and leave quite open the question of how one system is reorganized into its successor. In this regard these methods reflect the limitations of traditional linguistic approaches, within which stability rather than variation or change is presupposed as the normal state for languages. Furthermore, this method concerns itself almost entirely with a description of grammar – syntax and morphology. Changes that occur in other areas of language – the propositional meanings uttered, the words used, the communicative intents expressed, and so on – are not described at all.

A somewhat hidden assumption underlying the analytic methods used most widely in child language research in the 1970s was that language was a single phenomenon – that it was an integrated, organized, monolithic system showing more-or-less straight-line development. This presumption led to the field's widespread reliance on a single developmental index – mean length of utterance (MLU) – for characterizing child language level. MLU has become the gold standard of child language measures – used to characterize children's language level in essentially all standard descriptive research, and to match children for language level in comparing children with handicaps to normally developing children (see, for example, Miller & Chapman, 1981). MLU works well as a general developmental indicator, but I would argue it obscures developmental processes by averaging over several disparate underlying changes (see Rollins, Snow & Willett, 1995, for an elaboration of this argument). Thus, while MLU is a good practical tool for generally characterizing a child's language level, it is not helpful in illuminating what aspects of the child's language change or how those changes occur as children grow. To illustrate this point, Snow & Pan (1993) plotted the MLU of a small group of 20-month old children against a pure measure of morphological sophistication – a score indicating what proportion of the child's noun phrases had all the required morphological markers. Children with identical MLUs were found to differ enormously in their morphological sophistication. This is not entirely surprising, of course : a child can lengthen her MLU by adding words rather than bound morphemes to utterances. But for those of us interested in processes of development, it suggests that independent measures of lexical length and morphological sophistication may reveal differences among children and influences on change that are obscured if we assume MLU is indexing what is important about development in language (Rollins, Snow & Willett, 1995).

Changes in the study of child language during the last 30 years rest on a number of methodological advances. First, moving beyond the single subject case study method required some mechanism for sharing transcript data and thus aggregating larger numbers of subjects than single researchers or laboratories could process. By virtue of the development of the Child Language Data Exchange System (CHILDES; MacWhinney, 1994; MacWhinney & Snow, 1985, 1990) this is now possible; furthermore the availability through CHILDES of transcript analysis programs that fully or partially automate many standard analyses makes the use of larger data sets feasible.

Second, we have started to develop a wide array of core measures of language development, measures which represent purer measures of different components of language ability than does MLU. The core measures (Pan, Snow & Willett, 1994) are designed to be relatively simple to compute, and yet to generate a profile of functioning across a number of different areas of development. More on this later.

Third, research in recent years has expanded beyond the grammatical boundaries that characterized early child language research to focus attention on areas not previously studied: in particular, within the domain of pragmatics, to develop ways of assessing children's control over a variety of communicative intents, over the rules of effective and polite conversation, and over the rules for producing extended discourse. Our goal is to create and test developmental indices for each of these various understudied areas, so that they are as likely to be attended to in studies of language development as are the more traditionally studied areas of syntax, morphology, and lexicon.

Finally, methods for assessing change rather than simply for describing status are just starting to be used in the field of child language. The introduction of statistical methods appropriate for the study of change (for example, growth modelling using regression or hierarchical linear modelling; see Rogosa & Willett, 1985; Willett, 1988, 1989, 1994) enables us now to describe change with great precision, to utilize fully the longitudinal data sets that have always been the bedrock of child language research, and to utilize as outcome measures highly reliable estimates of rate of growth over a period of time rather than much less reliable estimates of status at a particular age.

In this paper, I will summarize some findings from research which demonstrate these various methodological advances. We have analyzed language data from a group of children in an attempt to develop measures that are relatively pure estimates of different linguistic subsystems (lexical, morphological, syntactic, conversational, and communicative), in order to see whether it makes sense to treat language development as a single system or whether, conversely, we need to think about analyzing the developing language system as a composite of somewhat independently growing rule systems.

A Longitudinal Study of Language Development

A group of 52 mothers and children were observed in a laboratory setting engaged in dyadic play when the children were 14 months old. As many as possible of the dyads were brought back to the lab when the children were 20 and 32 months old as well; ultimately, we have complete data for 36 dyads. These are all English-speaking children with no evidence of medical risk or developmental delay, from lower- to upper-middle class families (see Pan, Snow & Willett, 1994, for more details of procedure and of the data summarized here).

Transcripts of the children's and their mothers' language were made from videotapes of the play sessions. We then attempted to develop or find relatively easily computable developmental indices for each of the following language domains: lexicon, syntax, morphology, and conversational skill. I will present each of these in turn. It should be noted that programs available through CHILDES were crucial in enabling us to calculate the measures presented here; see Pan (1994) for an introduction to the CLAN procedures.

Phonology

Phonology is a notably difficult domain in which to carry out careful assessment; the transcripts we were working from were for the most part orthographically, not phonetically, transcribed, and thus incapable of supporting a detailed phonological analysis. However, a relatively simple measure of phonological precision on the part of the child speakers is provided by simply counting what percent of utterances produced are intelligible. It can be seen from Table 7.1 that at 14 months a very high proportion of child utterances were unintelligible, while at 32 months the proportion had declined dramatically. Intelligibility is useful in revealing considerable individual differences among children at the younger ages, but declines in utility as all children approach high levels of intelligibility at 32 months.

Lexicon

Lexical development has traditionally been assessed in children using tests – tests of comprehension like the Peabody Picture Vocabulary Test (the child points to one of four pictures on hearing the word) or of confrontation naming, like the Expressive One-word Naming Test. More recently, parental report instruments (Dale, Bates, Reznick & Morisset, 1989) have been used to assess the vocabulary of young children, whose lexicons are still sufficiently restricted that their mothers have some chance of knowing what words the child has used. Our approach to assessing vocabulary growth from spontaneous speech involved counting how many words (tokens) and how many different words (types) children used in a standard length of time. These indices showed statistically significant change with age (see Table 7.1 for mean scores

Table 7.1   Means and standard deviations for core measures at three ages

| | Age | | |
Measure	14 months	20 months	32 months
Intelligibility	0.35 (0.33)	0.74 (0.20)	0.88 (0.11)
Word tokens per 10 minutes	7.53 (6.82)	69.52 (55.29)	215.16 (76.10)
Word types per 10 minutes	3.66 (2.68)	30.10 (20.83)	84.29 (26.79)
NP saturation	0.02 (0.14)	0.16 (0.17)	0.69 (0.22)
Mean length of utterance	1.13 (0.37)	1.33 (0.31)	2.26 (0.65)
IPSyn	— —	22.44 (8.26)	49.68 (14.10)
Mean length of turn	1.22 (0.43)	1.45 (0.37)	2.83 (0.95)
Mean length of turn ratio	0.05 (0.06)	0.12 (0.07)	0.42 (0.05)

at ages 14, 20 and 32 months), and reliable, linear growth for individual children (see Table 7.2 for estimated monthly growth rates). It would obviously be desirable, particularly at older ages when tests become usable, to relate these measures derived from spontaneous speech to other, more structured assessments of lexicon. There has been little work done in the field of child language to relate structured assessments to assessments based on spontaneous speech; this is clearly an area for further research and instrument development.

Morphology
As indicated above, we use a procedure for assessing morphological development that resolves many of the practical problems associated with trying to do morpheme-by-morpheme analysis (Brown's 1973 method) on relatively short speech samples. We simply identify NPs, PPs and VPs in the speech sample, then calculate a proportion of those that are missing some morphological marker over the total (see Pan & Elkins, 1989 for detailed coding

Table 7.2 Monthly growth rates for core measures at three ages

| | Estimated monthly rate of observed growth | | Estimated reliability |
Measure	Mean (st. dev.)	Range	
Intelligibility	0.030 (0.016)	−0.013 to 0.051	—
Word types per 10 minutes	4.634 (1.426)	1.679 to 6.881	0.721
Word tokens per 10 minutes	12.003 (4.132)	3.476 to 20.655	0.765
Mean length of utterance	0.089 (0.049)	0.027 to 0.274	0.706
Mean length of turn	0.099 (0.056)	−0.011 to 0.292	0.507
Mean length of turn ratio	0.016 (0.010)	0.001 to 0.047	0.735

procedures). A fully marked constituent is referred to as 'saturated'; Table 7.1 presents mean scores on noun-phrase saturation (VPs have not yet started to show significant developmental change during the period under study) at the three ages; since NP saturation could not be estimated at 14 months for most children because most children produced too few NPs, there are insufficient data points to estimate monthly growth rates. It can be seen from Table 7.1 though that NP saturation increases from 20 to 32 months.

Syntax
While we also use the standard measure of syntactic growth, MLU, for purposes of comparison with other studies, we include data on a purer, type-based measure of syntax developed by Scarborough (1990), called the Index of Productive Syntax (IPSyn). The IPSyn score is calculated by giving the children credit for certain structures if they occur in at least two different utterances; the structures are scaled, so that occurrence of more complex ones implies control over the simpler ones. Scores on both the IPSyn and MLU can be seen to change significantly with age (Table 7.1); growth rates for IPSyn could not be estimated because the children produced too few utterances to calculate IPSyn at 14 months, but MLU is estimated to grow at 0.9 morphemes per month (see Table 7.2).

Conversation
While a full representation of children's conversational skills requires coding for categories like initiations and provision of expected responses, a quick and dirty index of conversational participation is provided by assessing the child's Mean Length of Turn (MLT) as well as by determining a ratio of child's to mother's MLT (see Snow, 1977 for justification for this approach). Presumably as children become conversationally more competent, the ratio of child to mother MLT approaches 1.0. It can be seen from Table 7.1 that child MLT approaches the mother's over the time period in question while remaining less than half as long, and from Table 7.2 that growth in MLT-ratio occurs at a rate of about 0.016 units per month.

Relation among these measures
A key question motivating our attempt to measure development in the various language domains independently was to be able to see whether, in a group of normally developing children, the various domains grew in synchrony or not, and whether early status within particular domains predicted later status within those same or other domains. The first question, that of developmental independence, is addressed by estimating correlations among growth rates, on the presumption that if these are closely linked systems they would grow at similar rates (and of course status measures do show generally high correlations at each of the ages, in particular at 20 months, when most of the inter-correlations among these measures are high and significant; see Pan, Snow & Willett, 1994). Table 7.3 presents correlations among the growth rates;

Table 7.3 Correlations among monthly growth rates for core measures at three ages

Monthly rate of growth	*Word types*	*Word tokens*	*MLU*	*MLU5*	*MLT*	*MLT ratio*
		— Monthly rate of growth —				
Word types		0.85***	0.25	0.41**	0.25	0.50**
Word tokens			0.17	0.32	0.47**	0.66***
MLU				0.81***	0.39	0.04
MLU5					0.37	0.09
MLT						0.72***

* $p < 0.05$, ** $p < 0.01$, *** $p < 0.001$

it can be seen that correlations are high only between very closely related measures – word types to word tokens, IPSyn to MLU, but that correlations across the domains are only modest. Thus we have to conclude that there is considerable practical as well as theoretical value in being able to assess these domains independently.

As to the question of prediction, we present correlations from 14 month measures to later status in Table 7.4. It can be seen, first of all, that we have here a pattern of homotypic discontinuity: in other words, measures in one domain predict outcomes in a different domain rather than themselves (see Bates, Bretherton & Snyder, 1988 for similar findings). Second, it can be seen that the 14 month measures having to do with lexical skill are the best at predicting later outcomes; this finding, if replicated with larger samples, should have some relevance to the early identification of children who might benefit from language intervention.

Once again, though, it should be remembered that I have presented here measures based exclusively on spontaneous speech; a full description of language development and certainly a full-scale assessment of an individual

Table 7.4 Correlations between core measures at 14 and at 32 months

Measure at age 1;2	Intell.	Word types	Word tokens	MLU	IPSyn	NPSAT	MLT	MLT ratio
				Measure at age 2;8				
Intell.	0.04	0.04	0.14	0.04	0.04	0.15	0.20	0.00
Word types /10 mins	0.13	0.31	0.32	0.51**	0.53***	0.45**	0.45**	0.09
Word tokens /10 mins	0.14	0.35*	0.35*	0.35*	0.41*	0.41*	0.35*	0.19
MLU	0.16	0.26	0.38*	0.25	0.20	0.24	0.31	0.27
MLT	−0.17	−0.07	0.08	0.01	−0.11	0.03	0.09	0.05
MLT ratio	−0.16	−0.02	0.10	0.08	−0.05	0.04	0.05	0.10

* p < 0.05, ** p < 0.01, *** p < 0.001

child should incorporate measures from elicited speech situations and comprehension as well, so as to vary systematically the degree to which the child is receiving contextual support for the production of various forms.

The Neglected Domain of Pragmatics

I have presented eight measures of child language development that are all relatively easy to compute (once the gargantuan task of preparing transcripts is finished) and all of which show change over time as well as individual differences at given ages. Thus, these measures are useful developmental indices and potentially useful clinical indicators as well.

In addition to generating 'core' measures such as those presented above, though, we have been trying to design ways of reflecting development in domains that have been relatively understudied in child language. In particular, the domain of pragmatics, though much discussed, remains outside the mainstream, in part because of persistent theoretical divisions within the field (see Ninio & Snow, in press a, in press b) and in part because of the practical difficulties associated with assessing pragmatic skill.

Ninio & Wheeler (1984b; see also Ninio & Wheeler, 1984a) presented an unusually comprehensive and elaborate theoretical framework and associated method for coding communicative intent, which has been a basis for work in our lab on the development of communicative abilities. A major insight incorporated into the Ninio & Wheeler system was that communicative intent needed to be coded at different levels: they distinguish two major levels, the *interchange* and the *speech act*. The interchange codes the socially agreed upon communicative activity, i.e. what kind of communication we agree we are engaged in here. Examples of interchange type include NIA (negotiate immediate activity), DJF (discuss joint focus of attention) and DNP (discuss the nonpresent). The speech act level, on the other hand, reflects the individual speaker's illocutionary force, e.g. YQ (ask a yes–no question) or ST (make a statement).

We have used a somewhat abridged, but still extensive, version of the Ninio & Wheeler coding for pragmatic intent (Ninio, Snow, Pan & Rollins, 1994) to code the utterances of children and mothers in our longitudinal sample. A full report focusing on the repertoires of speech acts used by children at different ages is available (Snow, Pan, Imbens-Bailey & Herman, 1995), and one on the mothers' repertoires is in press (Pan, Snow, Imbens-Bailey & Winner, in press). Here I will confine my discussion to the quantitative measures that emerged from the analysis – measures which we argue reflect children's pragmatic development. The five measures we derived from speech act coding were the following: number of communicative attempts per minute, percent interpretable, number of interchange types produced at least twice, number of speech acts produced at least twice, and number of interchange-speech act combinations produced at least twice, which we refer to as pragmatic flexibility.

Table 7.5 presents the mean scores on each of these five measures for the children at 14, 20 and 32 months (from Snow *et al.*, 1995), together with the mothers' mean scores addressing 32-month-olds (from Pan *et al.*, in press; the mothers' scores showed no difference as a function of child age). It can be seen that all the child measures show considerable developmental change. That communicative attempts increase so strikingly is particularly interesting, considering that in coding communicative attempts we were extremely generous, giving credit for gestures, for uninterpretable vocalizations, and so on. Thus, the 14 month olds could have used their limited linguistic capacities to express communicative attempts quite easily, and it is striking that they chose to communicate as little as they did.

These varying measures of pragmatic skill show reasonable intercorrelations, though the correlations among the three type measures are much higher than those with communicative attempts and interpretability (Table 7.6). Including MLU in the correlation matrix shows clearly that there is considerable independence between the syntactic/morphological skills most often considered in studies of child language and the pragmatic skills we assess here.

Table 7.5 Means and standard deviations for summary pragmatic measures at three ages

Pragmatic measures	*Children at age*			*Mothers*
	14 months	*20 months*	*32 months*	
Communicative attempts per minute	4.37 (2.6)	7.91 (2.8)	11.2 (2.8)	19.3 (4.3)
Proportion of attempts interpretable	0.47 (0.23)	0.79 (0.16)	0.94 (0.03)	—
Number of interchange types	4.0 (1.8)	6.92 (1.9)	8.5 (2.0)	11.4 (1.4)
Number of speech act types	3.79 (2.5)	10.5 (3.5)	14.4 (2.7)	19.2 (2.7)
Pragmatic flexibility	5.13 (3.5)	14.2 (5.5)	22.7 (5.6)	34.2 (5.5)

Table 7.6 Associations among pragmatic measures and MLU at three ages

14 months	Interpretable	Interchange types	Speech act types	Pragmatic flexibility	MLU
Communicative attempts/min.	−0.16	0.45**	0.44**	0.41**	−0.19
Proportion interpretable		0.23	0.18	0.16	0.35*
Interchange types			0.79***	0.75***	−0.07
Speech act types				0.86***	−0.06
Pragmatic flexibility					−0.10

20 months	Interpretable	Interchange types	Speech act types	Pragmatic flexibility	MLU
Communicative attempts/min.	0.22	0.63***	0.52***	0.65***	0.07
Proportion interpretable		0.47***	0.60***	0.51***	0.27
Interchange types			0.78***	0.85***	0.32*
Speech act types				0.91***	0.44**
Pragmatic flexibility					0.37**

32 months	Interpretable	Interchange types	Speech act types	Pragmatic flexibility	MLU
Communicative attempts/min.	0.02	0.38*	0.59***	0.64***	−0.26
Proportion interpretable		0.37*	0.04	0.25	0.13
Interchange types			0.60***	0.76***	−0.06
Speech act types				0.80***	−0.18
Pragmatic flexibility					−0.14

* $p < 0.05$, ** < 0.01, *** $p < 0.001$

Later pragmatic development
Of course, pragmatic development does not end with the establishment of an adult-sized repertoire of communicative intents. Children also need to learn how to express those communicative intents conventionally and politely, a vast and vastly understudied area of development. Furthermore, children need to learn the pragmatic rules underlying effective connected discourse: how to express relations among utterances so that the listener understands about sequences of events, interprets referents correctly, and can assess the speaker's point of view. Furthermore, children need to learn about genre differences, to identify when they are supposed to provide descriptions versus narrations versus explanations, and how these various language forms are structured (see, for example, Snow, 1987).

All of these developments start in the 3rd or 4th year of life, and continue for years, in some cases through adulthood; the minimal attention given to them here should not be taken to indicate a belief that they are trivial or irrelevant to a comprehensive view of how language develops (see Ninio & Snow, in press b).

Conclusion

The goal of this paper has been to provide an overview of how children's language changes, and how those changes have been and can be measured. There are many reasons why we need to do a better job of measuring change in children's language: because describing normal development is prerequisite to understanding or explaining it, because we need norms if we are to identify children with language delay or disability, because we need to know how to match normally developing to language-handicapped children in order to pursue research on the characteristics of language disabilities, but most importantly because the way we assess language change reflects our underlying theories about the nature of the language system. Using a single measure to indicate a child's language level suggests we believe language is a monolithic system. I have proposed here that we need instead to think of a child's language status as a profile reflecting performance on a set of skills that are theoretically and empirically distinct.

Of course, the methodological underpinnings of a field are not typically a very glamorous place to be working. I am reminded of the story about a farmer hard at work chopping wood; a passerby mentioned to him that his axe was rather dull and should be sharpened. The farmer responded that he had far too much wood to chop to have time to stop and sharpen his axe. Child language researchers have been busy over the last 30 years filling up journals, generating hypotheses, informing our understanding of how children learn to talk – but doing it with tools that, we now realize, have needed sharpening. I argue here that it is time we stopped and sharpened our axes before returning to our primary mission, that of describing and explaining child language development.

Note

The ideas and data presented in this paper are the collaborative product of work I have been privileged to participate in with Barbara Alexander Pan and other members of the research team working on Foundations for Language Assessment in Spontaneous Speech, including Pamela Rollins, Jane Herman, Alison Imbens-Bailey, Lowry Hemphill, Brian MacWhinney, Heidi Feldman, and Jean Berko Gleason. Special mention should be made of our intellectual indebtedness to John Willett, for his patient tutoring in theory and methods for measuring growth. The research efforts summarized here were supported by NIH through HD23388, and are reported in more detail in manuscripts submitted to *First Language* and *Social Development*.

References

Bates, E., Bretherton, I. and Snyder, L. (1988) *Individual Differences and Dissociable Mechanisms*. New York: Cambridge University Press.

Braine, M. (1976) Children's first word combinations. *Monograph of the Society for Research on Child Development* 41, Serial Number 164.

Brown, R. (1973) *A First Language: The early stages*. Cambridge, MA: Harvard University Press.

Dale, P., Bates, E., Reznick, S. and Morisset, C. (1989) The validity of a parent report instrument. *Journal of Child Language* 16, 239–49.

Ervin-Tripp, S. (1973) Some strategies for the first years. In T. E. Moore (ed.) *Cognition and the Acquisition of Language*. New York: Academic Press.

MacWhinney, B. (1994) *The CHILDES Project: Computational tools for analyzing talk* 2nd edition. Hillsdale, NJ: Lawrence Erlbaum Associates.

MacWhinney, B. and Snow, C. E. (1985) The child language data exchange system. *Journal of Child Language* 12, 271–95.

— (1990) The child language data exchange system: An update. *Journal of Child Language* 17, 457–72.

Miller, J. F. and Chapman, R. S. (1981) The relation between age and mean length of utterance in morphemes. *Journal of Speech and Hearing Research* 24, 154–61.

Ninio, A. and Snow, C. E. (in press a) The development of pragmatics: Learning to use language appropriately. In T. Bhatia and W. Ritchie (eds) *Handbook of Language Acquisition*. New York: Academic Press.

— (in press b) *Pragmatic Development*. New York: Westview Press.

Ninio, A., Snow, C. E., Pan, B. A. and Rollins, P. (1994) Classifying communicative acts in children's interactions. *Journal of Communications Disorders* 27, 157–88.

Ninio, A. and Wheeler, P. (1984a) Functions of speech in mother–infant interaction. In L. Feagans, G. J. Garvey, and R. Golinkoff (eds) *The Origins and Growth of Communication*. Norwood, NJ: Ablex.

— (1984b) A manual for classifying verbal communicative acts in mother–infant interaction. *Working Papers in Developmental Psychology, No. 1*. Jerusalem: The Martin and Vivian Levin Center, Hebrew University. Reprinted as *Transcript Analysis* (1986) 3, 1–82.

Pan, B. A. (1994) Basic measures of child language. In J. L. Sokolov and C. E. Snow (eds) *Handbook of Research in Language Development Using CHILDES*. Hillsdale, NJ: Lawrence Erlbaum Associates.

Pan, B. A. and Elkins, K. (1989) An alternative measure of morphological development in young children's spontaneous speech. Paper presented to the New England Child Language Association, Boston, MA.

Pan, B. A., Snow, C. E., Imbens-Bailey, A. and Winner, K. (in press) Communicative intents expressed by mothers in interaction with young children. *Merrill-Palmer Quarterly*.

Pan, B. A., Snow, C. E. and Willett, J. B. (1994) Modeling language growth: Measures of lexical, morphosyntactical, and conversational skill for early child language. Submitted to *Journal of Child Language*.

Rogosa, D. R. and Willett, J. B. (1985) Understanding correlates of change by modeling individual differences in growth. *Psychometrika* 50, 203–28.

Rollins, P. R., Snow, C. E. and Willett, J. B. (1995) Morphological and syntactic skills co-determine MLU. *First Language*.

Scarborough, H. (1990) Index of productive syntax. *Applied Psycholinguistics* 11, 1–22.

Snow, C. E. (1977) The development of conversation between mothers and babies. *Journal of Child Language* 4, 1–22.

— (1987) Beyond conversation: Second language learners' acquisition of description and explanation. In J. Lantolf and A. LaBarca (eds) *Research in Second Language Acquisition: Focus on the classroom*. Norwood, NJ: Ablex.

Snow, C. E. and Pan, B. A. (1993) Ways of analyzing the spontaneous speech of children with mental retardation: The value of cross-domain analysis. In N. Bray (ed.) *International Review of Research in Mental Retardation* 19, 163–92. New York: Academic Press.

Snow, C. E., Pan, B. A., Imbens-Bailey, A. and Herman, J. (1995) Learning how to say what one means: A longitudinal study of children's speech act use. *Social Development*.

Willett, J. B. (1988) Questions and answers in the measurement of change. *Review of Research in Education* 15, 345–422.

— (1989) Some results on reliability for the longitudinal measurement of change: Implications for the design of studies of individual growth. *Educational and Psychological Measurement* 49, 587–602.

— (1994) Measurement of change. In T. Husen and T. N. Postlethwaite (eds) *The International Encyclopedia of Education* 2nd edition. Oxford: Elsevier Science Press.

8 Crossing: Language across ethnic boundaries

BEN RAMPTON
Thames Valley University

Introduction

This paper is in four parts. The first provides a brief sketch of the research that the paper draws on. The second illustrates a sociolinguistic practice that hasn't yet been adequately recognised, which I shall refer to as 'crossing'. The third section develops the account of crossing by comparing it with Bakhtin's notion of double-voicing, and, in the last part, I shall suggest two ways in which crossing might be a useful concept for applied linguistics.

The Research Base

This paper draws on research which examines the part that language plays in the emergence of multi-racial urban youth culture in Britain. More specifically, the research focuses on 'language crossing' – the use of Creole by adolescents of Asian and Anglo descent, the use of Panjabi by Anglos and Afro-Caribbeans, and the use of stylised Indian English by all three – and it uses the methodologies of ethnographic and interactional sociolinguistics to examine four closely inter-related dimensions of socio-cultural organisation:

- language, seen both as a central element in social action, and as a form of knowledge differentially distributed across individuals and groups;
- the interaction order mapped out by Erving Goffman;
- institutional organisation, encompassing domains, networks, activity types, social roles and normative expectations;
- social knowledge, specifically as this relates to race and ethnicity.

Two years of fieldwork focused on one neighbourhood of the South Midlands, with 23 eleven to thirteen year olds of Indian, Pakistani, Caribbean and Anglo descent in 1984, and approximately 64 fourteen to sixteen year olds in 1987. Methods of data-collection included radio-microphone recording, participant observation, interviewing and retrospective participant commentary on extracts of recorded interaction, and the analysis was based on about 68 incidents of Panjabi crossing, about 160 exchanges involving stylised Indian English, and more than 250 episodes where a Creole influence was clearly detectable. (For a full account, see Rampton, 1995a.)

Crossing: Some examples

Here are three examples of crossing. The first one involves Panjabi:

Extract 1

Participants: Raymond [An/AC M 13; wearing radio-mike], Ian [An M 12], Hanif [Bangladeshi M 12], others

Setting: 1984. Coming out of lessons into the playground at break. Ian and Ray are best friends. Stevie Wonder is a singer whose song 'I just called to say I love you' was very famous. Ray has a bad foot – cf. line 17. (Extr. III.13)

```
 1 Ray:   IA::N::
 2 Hanif: (              )
 3 Ian ((from afar)) RAY THE COO:L RAY THE COO:L
 4 Hanif: yeh Stevie Wonder YAAA ((laughs loudly))
 5 Ray:            ⌈ it's worser than that
 6 Ian ((singing)): ⌊ I just called to say
 7 Hanif: ha (let's) sing (him) a song
 8 Ian: I hate you
 9 Hanif: ((loud laughs))
10 Anon ((coming up)): (   ) are you running for the school (.)
11 Ray: huh
12 Anon: are ⌈ you running for the school=
13 Ray:      ⌊ no
14 Anon:= ⌈ I am
15 Ian:   ⌊ he couldnt run for th- he couldnt ⌈run for the school
16 Ray:                                       ⌊SHUT UP =
```

17 Ray: =I couldn-I don wan- ⌈ I can't run anyway
18 Hanif: ⌊ right we're wasting our ⌈ time=
19 Ian: ⌊ I did=
20 Hanif: = ⌈ come on (we're) wasting our time=
21 Ian: ⌊ you come last ( )
22 Hanif: = ⌈ [mʌmʌmʌ:]
23 Anon: ⌊ I came second
24 Ian ((singing)): I just called to say ⌈ I got ⌉ a big=
25 Ray: ⌊ I hate you ⌋
→ 26 Ian: =[lʊ ɬa:]
    ((Panjabi for 'willy'))
27 Hanif and others: ((loud laughter))
28 Ray ((continuing Ian's song)): so's Ian Hinks (1.5)
29 ((Ray laughs)) no you haven't you got a tiny one (.)
30 you've only got (a arse)

In this extract, Ian mixes Panjabi with Stevie Wonder in some jocular abuse directed at his good friend Ray. When he starts out in lines 6 and 8, he seems to be identifying himself with the first person expressed in the song, but when he repeats it in lines 24 and 26, it looks as though he's putting the words in Ray's mouth rather than claiming the 'I' for himself – certainly, Ray's retaliation in line 28 suggests that it's him that has been attributed the item in Panjabi, not Ian. Whatever – indeed maybe because of this perspectival switch – Ian comes off best in their brief exchange of ritual abuse: Ian's [lʊɬa:] upstages Ray's effort to preempt him in line 25; it is Ian who wins an enthusiastic response from third parties in line 27; and, in lines 29 and 30, Ray evidently judges his own immediate retort (line 28) as itself rather weak.

The second example involves a variety I have called 'stylised Asian English':

Extract 2

1987. Cyril [AC M 15 wearing radio-mike] is outside. Surjit [In F 15] approaches with a few friends [F]. In line 5 another boy (AnonM) arrives. Surjit is rumoured to have a boyfriend in his twenties. (Extr. III.4)

1 Surj ((from some distance)): hello Cyril:
2 Cyr: hello are you alright Surjit (.)
3 ?Surj: innit (1.5)
4 Cyr: remember the boyfriend (3.0)

      5 AnonM: Surjit (   )
      6 AnonF: ⌈ good mornin'
→   7 Cyril ((loud)): ˌtwenty ˌone ˌ**years** ˌoˊ:ld (1.0)
                         [twenti wʌn jiəz o::ld]
      8 AnonF: show him show him
      9 AnonM: alright Cyril right
     10 Cyril ((to AnonM)): dont mess ABOUT dont mess

This episode illustrates the banter that adolescent males and females frequently exchanged when they passed one another in school yards and corridors. In one variant of this, a lot of entertainment lay in the use of affiliative guises to publicly disclose embarrassing personal information about the addressee, and, after an initial greeting, Cyril begins this by introducing the topic of Surjit's boyfriend. Eliciting no audible response, he then elaborates in line 7 by specifying the boyfriend's exceptional characteristic – his age – and he encodes this in stylised Asian English. Rather than casting the boyfriend's maturity as a source of admiration and prestige, evidence from other interactions, interviews and other sources overwhelmingly suggests that the effect of this code-switch is to introduce a sense of comic anomaly. It is not exactly clear what happens next, but it looks as though this now sparks off some playful physical retaliation, with AnonM, I think, acting on Surjit's behalf.[1]

      Here is the third episode:

Extract 3

Participants: Asif [Pa M 15], Alan [An M 15], Ms Jameson [An F 25+], and, in the background, Mr Chambers [An M 25+]

Setting: 1987. Asif and Alan are in detention for Ms Jameson, who was herself a little late for it. She is explaining why she didn't arrive on time, and now she wants to go and fetch her lunch. (Extr. II.17)

     80 Ms J: I had to go and see the headmaster
     81 Asif: why
     82 Ms J: (   ) (.) none of your business
     83 Alan: a- about us (   )
     84 Ms J: no I'll be ⌈ back
                ((1.))
     85 Asif: ⌊ hey how can you see the=
                             ((f.))

86   =headmaster when he was in dinner (.)

87 Ms J: that's precisely why I didn't see him
                ((1.))

88 Asif: what (.)

89 Ms J: I'll be back in a second with my lunch ⌈ (   )
90 Asif: ⌊   NO [ʔ]=
                                                       ((ff.))

91   =dat's sad man (.) (I'll b   ) =
                ((f.))

92   =I ⌈ had to miss my play right I've gotta go
93 Alan: ⌊ (with mine   )

94   (2.5) ((Ms J must now have left the room))

→ 95 Asif ((Creole influenced)): ll:unch (.) you don't need no=
                ((f.))
                [ll: ʌntʃ]

→ 96   =lunch ⌈ not'n grow anyway ((laughs))
                          [nat2n gɹəʊ]
97 Alan: ⌊ ((laughs))

98 Asif: have you eat your lunch Alan

Lines 80–88 involve a verbal tussle in which Asif and Alan use questions to undermine the positions that Ms Jameson stakes out in what she says. Asif's question in line 81 treats the account she gives of her late arrival as inadequate; she rebuts his inquiry as illegitimate in line 82 but this is then undermined by Alan in lines 83 and 84; and in lines 85–87, Ms Jameson is delayed in the departure she announced in line 84 by a question that upgrades the query over her initial excuse into an explicit challenge. All this time, she has been locked into the interaction by the adjacency structures set up by the boys' questions, but at line 89 she breaks out of this pattern, ignores Asif's line 88 repair initiation, again announces her departure and leaves without saying anything more. With the co-operative exchange structure now disrupted and Ms Jameson apparently disattending to him, Asif launches into some 'muttering' 'afterburn':

> Afterburn . . . is a remonstrance conveyed collusively by virtue of the fact that its targets are in the process of leaving the field . . . (Goffman, 1971: 152–3)

and

> In muttering we convey that although we are now going along with the lines established by the speaker (and authority), our spirit has not been won over, and compliance is not to be counted on. (Goffman, 1981: 93)

In this afterburn, Asif uses some Creole/Black English. Admittedly, it can sometimes be hard trying to distinguish Creole from the local multiracial vernacular, and Asif's stopped TH in 'dat's sad man' is ambiguous. But in lines 95 and 96, he uses a characteristically Creole unrounded front open vowel in 'not' (cf. Wells, 1982: 576; Sebba, 1993: 153–4), and the stretched and heavily voiced L in his first 'lunch' maybe connects with a black speech feature first noted by Hewitt in South London (1986: 134).

Those, then, are some examples of language crossing. How does crossing fit with Bakhtin's notion of double-voicing?

Double-voicing and Some Further Clarification on Language Crossing

Bakhtin's ideas about different languages, discourses, voices and words struggling with one another for dominance in the individual's consciousness[2] are already fairly familiar in applied linguistics (e.g. Cazden, 1989; Wertsch, 1991; Fairclough, 1992; Maybin, 1994), and double-voicing is a term that Bakhtin uses to describe some of the ways that this heteroglossia acts upon the *utterance*. With double-voicing, speakers use someone else's discourse (or language) for their own purposes,

> . . . inserting a new semantic intention into a discourse which already has . . . an intention of its own. Such a discourse . . . must be seen as belonging to someone else. In one discourse, two semantic intentions appear, two voices. (Bakhtin, 1984: 189)

Bakhtin describes several kinds of double-voicing, and one of these is described as 'uni-directional'. With uni-directional double-voicing, the speaker uses someone else's discourse 'in the direction of its own particular intentions' (1984: 193). Speakers themselves go along with the momentum of the second voice, though it generally retains an element of otherness which makes the appropriation conditional and introduces some reservation into the speaker's use of it. But at the same time, the boundary between the speaker and the voice they are adopting can diminish, to the extent that there is a 'fusion of voices'. When that happens, discourse ceases to be double-voiced, and instead becomes 'direct, unmediated discourse' (1984: 199). The opposite of uni-directional double-voicing is *vari-directional* double-voicing, in which the speaker 'again speaks in someone else's discourse, but . . . introduces into that discourse a semantic intention directly opposed to the original one'. In vari-directional double-voicing, the two voices are much more clearly demarcated, and they are not only distant but also opposed (Bakhtin, 1984: 193).

Bakhtin's account of these two kinds of double-voicing meshes closely with a great deal of the data on Creole crossing and on stylised Asian English.

Creole was much more extensively integrated into multi-racial peer group recreation than either SAE or Panjabi: it had no place in the school curriculum and it was used much more by members of ethnic outgroups. Creole symbolised an excitement and an excellence in youth culture that many adolescents aspired to, and it was even referred to as 'future language'. In line with this, Creole crossing generally resembled uni-directional double-voicing. For a great deal of the time, there certainly was some reservation in the way it was used by whites and Asians, and this was most noticeable in the way that they generally avoided it in the presence of black peers. Even so, crossers tended to use Creole to lend emphasis to evaluations that synchronised with the identities they maintained in their ordinary speech, and in line with this, as Hewitt underlines, their Creole was often hard to disentangle from their local multi-racial vernacular (Hewitt, 1986: 148, 151). In Bakhtin's terms, crossing in Creole came close to the point where uni-directional double-voicing shifted over into direct unmediated discourse.

In contrast, stylised Asian English often constituted double-voicing of the vari-directional kind. From interviews and other evidence, it was clear that Asian English stood for a stage of historical transition that most adolescents felt they were leaving behind, and in one way or another it consistently symbolised distance from the main currents of adolescent life. In line with this, stylised Asian English was often used as what Goffman calls a 'say-for' (1974: 535): a voice not being claimed as part of the speaker's own identity, but one that was relevant to the identity of the person being addressed or targeted. This is certainly consistent with Extract 2: in what ways would Cyril advance his attempt to embarrass Surjit if he was claiming a stylised Asian English identity for himself?

Since Bakhtin's ideas are hardly very new, it is worth pointing to the value of trying to connect Creole crossing and stylised Asian English to double-voicing. Firstly, I am not aware of analyses in which the distinction between uni- and vari-directional double-languaging is quite as clear and consistent as it is with these two varieties.[3] Secondly, we can use Bakhtin's larger theoretical apparatus to conceptualise the emergence of mixed multi-racial youth culture in a way that ties small acts into both the 'ideological development' of individuals (Bakhtin, 1981: 345; Maybin, 1994: 132–3) and into a much wider historical sense of migration, contact and race politics. And thirdly, the interactional data actually points to significant limitations in Bakhtinian analyses (e.g. Bakhtin, 1984; Hill & Hill, 1986; Wertsch, 1991).

Michael Gardiner (1992: 177) notes:

> . . . although the early Bakhtin railed against such linguists as Saussure for ignoring the embeddedness of discourse in concrete social practices, his analyses often (though not always) remain at a curiously rarefied level, as if linguistic communication essentially consisted in the inter-action between disembodied individual 'consciousnesses'.

In line with this, when Hill and Hill use the notion of double-voicing in their masterly study of Mexicano, they suggest that hesitations and dysfluencies around code-mixing reflect the fact that the utterance has become 'a trans-linguistic battlefield upon which two ways of speaking struggle for dominance' (1986: 392–3). Here, it sounds as though the speaker is simply a vessel, and no account is taken of the role played by interlocutors. In contrast, a more fully interactional account would need to consider the extent to which, for example, hesitations and dysfluency were influenced by preference organisa-tion, and so rather than being at the mercy of conflicting voices, these patterns could actually reflect the speaker's fully controlled display of the dispreferred status of the code-selection coming next.

Returning to my own data, one of language crossing's most important characteristics might be missed if the analysis went no further than 'voices' and neglected detailed examination of situations and the interaction order.

In Extract 1, in combination with friendship and a number of other factors (cf. Rampton, 1995a: Chs 7.3, 7.4, 7.8), the formulaic use of song meant that – for a brief interlude – the exchange of abuse was ritual and jocular rather than personal/serious (cf. Labov, 1972; Goodwin & Goodwin, 1987, and also, for contrast, lines 15–16 and 29–30). In the other two extracts, crossing was closely tied up with breaches of some kind or other: Cyril's comment on the boyfriend in Extract 2 amounted to a jokey attribution of impropriety, and in Extract 3 it is an explicit sense of injustice and injury that leads into Asif's semi-resilient Creole in lines 95 and 96. As both Goffman and Garfinkel make abundantly clear, breaches, improprieties and transgressions disrupt our everyday sense of social reality, and in fact, in one form or another, routine assumptions about ordinary life seemed to be temporarily relaxed, suspended or jeapardised *whenever* adolescents code-crossed. These inter-ruptions to the routine flow of normal social order took a wide range of different forms, and varied very considerably in their scale and duration. As well as cueing or being cued by delicts, transgressions and ritual abuse, adolescents code-crossed at the boundaries of interactional enclosure, in self-talk and response cries, in games, in cross-sex banter, and in the context of performance art. In all of these moments and events, 'the world of daily life known in common with others and with others taken for granted' (Garfinkel, 1984: 35) was problematised or partially suspended.

We can summarise this aspect of language crossing by saying that it was profoundly connected with liminality and the 'liminoid' (Turner, 1982).[4] The importance of situating Bakhtinian voices in a detailed analysis of the interaction order is indicated by the central political implication of this location: crossing's position in the liminoid margins of interactional and institutional space means that in the social structures which were dominant and which adolescents finally treated as *normal*, the boundaries around ethnicity were relatively fixed. Although it varied a lot in its insistence and intensity, a sense of anomaly was always close at hand whenever crossers moved outside the identities displayed in habitual vernacular speech, and so crossing *can't* be seen as a runaway deconstruction of ethnicity. Ethnicity was certainly questioned and destabilised, but it was neither transcended nor emptied of meaning.

This is sufficient, I think, as a description. What kind of significance could crossing have for applied linguistics?

Relevance for Applied Linguistics

Though I actually think there are quite a few more, here I would like to suggest two ways in which crossing could make a more general contribution to applied linguistics.

First – and maybe more relevantly for local debates within BAAL – where does crossing stand in current discussion about ideology and play? So far, there has been a tendency to express polar views: caricaturing them a bit, one says that sport has got nothing to do with politics, while the other says there's no difference between Smith Square and White Hart Lane.[5] The first position derives from the liberal, literary anti-functionalism of Widdowson and Cook (e.g. Widdowson, 1984; Cook, 1994), the second position forms the baseline for Critical Discourse Analysis (e.g. Fairclough, 1989, 1992). Fairclough (1992: 223) points to the conflict when he refers to an alternative 'mosaic' image of discourse which:

> impl[ies a] fragmentation of conventions [and] emphasises the con-
> sequential space for creative play, for combining discourse elements in
> ever new ways to achieve momentary impact, for pastiche. . . . From

this perspective, [the hegemony models of critical discourse analysis] are overinterpretations . . . premissed on assumptions about the rationality and centredness of social processes which may no longer hold in contemporary society.

But in fact, when set against the data on code crossing, neither perspective seems adequate. On the one hand, crossing involved a lot of creative play, it drew on a range of languages, it subverted conventional speech practices and it occupied liminal spaces in which the demands of commonsense reality were relaxed. But on the other, it was also profoundly ideological: its linguistic materials were heavily indexed politically and socially; it was strategically performed in institutional and interactional power negotiations; and it was precisely because ethnic boundaries were problematic that it occurred in liminal moments and spaces (cf. Rampton, 1994, 1995a, forthcoming b).

So in the first instance, it looks as though the relationships between language, politics and play that were manifest in crossing were too complex to be fitted in any kind of simple politics versus play dichotomy. This in turn raises the question: what progress can we expect to make towards a general understanding of the relationship between politics and play in the absence of regular and systematic cross-reference to the interpretive procedures displayed in sequential interaction in a range of different groups and settings (cf. Hymes, 1979: xii, xvi; Bauman & Briggs, 1990)?

A second possible contribution to applied linguistics is more methodological. As a concept, crossing can maybe help to integrate the analysis of code-switching with the study of second language learning – two traditions that, up to a point, have been blinded by their opposition to one another.

Code-switching research certainly recognises a lack of linguistic proficiency as one explanatory factor, but, empirically, it has been overwhelmingly preoccupied with the conduct of groups in which the use of two or more languages is a routine expectation, either because they have grown up with a multilingual inheritance or because they have moved into areas or institutions where the use of additional languages is an unremarked necessity (cf. Woolard, 1988: 69–70). In fact, if one looks closely at the literature, there are a few studies which focus on code-alternation by people who aren't native speakers and who aren't accepted members of the group associated with the second language that they're using, and the interactional practices they describe are remarkably similar to the ones that Hewitt analysed in South London and I identified in Ashmead (cf. Hill & Combs, 1982; Hill & Hill, 1986; Hewitt, 1986; Heller, 1992; Woolard, 1988, 1989; Mertz, 1989; for a full discussion, cf. Rampton, 1995a: Ch. 11.3). Even so, I don't think that their significance and distinctiveness have been properly appreciated. Maybe this is because these studies inevitably pay a lot of attention to linguistic incompetence, a notion that code-switching research has generally worked hard to refute or avoid.

Linguistic incompetence is of course the central issue for SLA, but here I think, there has been only fairly limited interest in taking on the political and ethnographic perspectives that are common in the research on code-switching. Once these perspectives are introduced, a substantial number of fairly basic SLA concepts fall open to revision: the 'target language', the 'learner', the 'native speaker', 'natural acquisition', 'variability', 'achievement and avoidance communication strategies' (cf. Bourne, 1988; Rampton, 1987, 1990, 1991, 1995a: Ch. 11.5, forthcoming a). Taking the dichotomy that Street uses in his study of literacy (Street, 1984), SLA seems to be dominated by an 'autonomous' model of language learning and use, and, because of this, there is still quite a lot of scope for research that introduces more ideologically sensitive ways of looking at second language activity (cf. Rampton, 1995b). It seems to me that, as a concept, crossing could play quite a significant role in helping to bring about this kind of expansion. It would do so by putting social boundary negotiation right at the heart of the second language learning process, and as a result analysis would address the relationship between the groups on either side of a boundary, the boundary's strength and character, the wider processes maintaining or diminishing the boundaries, the bridge building resources, the interests of participants in either getting to the other side or just peering across, and finally of course, the interactional practices with which this sensitivity to boundaries was inextricably entwined.

Overall, I think that by insisting on a link-up between SLA and code-switching research, crossing foregrounds difference and incompetence in a way that neither tradition can shy clear of or neglect. In crossing, participants themselves engage actively in the complex and unpredictable politics of deficit and otherness, and their lead in doing so is one that analysis can't refuse.

Notes

1. Cross-sex interaction was a relatively privileged site for language crossing (see below), and in fact, in my data, it was one of the only contexts in which non-Panjabis addressed stylised Asian English to Panjabi bilingual friends. For further discussion, see Rampton, 1995a.
2. 'a variety of alien voices enter into the struggle for influence in an individual's consciousness . . . [they] enter into an intense interaction, a struggle with other internally persuasive discourses. Our ideological development is just such an intense struggle within us for hegemony among various available verbal and ideological points of view, approaches, directions and values' (Bakhtin, 1981: 348, 345).
3. Admittedly, with more space, several qualifications could be added to this. The reader probably also needs to see quite a bit more interactional evidence (though

Rampton, 1995a tries to provide this). And finally, it is harder to apply the concept of double-voicing to Panjabi, perhaps because the socio-ideological horizons it evoked were more indeterminate (again see Rampton, 1995a).

4. 'Liminality' is a concept developed by Victor Turner in particular, drawing on anthropological studies of initiation rites in tribal and agrarian societies. These rites have three phases: separation, in which initiands leave their childhood life behind; transition; and then incorporation, in which they are returned to new, relatively stable and well-defined positions in society, now a stage further on in life's cycle (Turner, 1982: 24). Turner concentrates on the middle phase, designated 'liminal': 'during the intervening phase of transition . . . the ritual subjects pass through a period and area of ambiguity, a sort of social limbo which has few . . . of the attributes of either the preceding or subsequent social statuses or cultural states . . . In liminality, [everyday] social relations may be discontinued, former rights and obligations are suspended, the social order may seem to have been turned upside down' (Turner, 1982: 24, 27). It is not possible to argue directly from this account of traditional ritual to the kinds of urban social relationship addressed in my own research. But Turner extends the notion of liminality into a form that fits more easily with practices common in industrial society, and he calls these 'liminoid' ('-oid' meaning 'like', 'resembling' but not identical). The distinction between liminal and liminoid is often hard to draw, but while, for example, liminal practices tend to contribute to the smooth functioning of social systems, liminoid practices are often creative, containing social critiques and exposing wrongs in mainstream structures and organisation (1982: 45). Similarly, liminality tends to involve symbols with common intellectual and emotional meaning for all members of the group, while 'liminoid phenomena tend to be more idiosyncratic, quirky, to be generated by specific named individuals and in particular groups' (1982: 54). For fuller discussion in the context of language crossing, see Rampton 1995a: Ch. 7.9.

5. The headquarters of the Conservative Party are in Smith Square. White Hart Lane is the home ground of Tottenham Hotspur Football Club.

References

Bakhtin, M. (1981) *The Dialogic Imagination*. Austin: Texas University Press.
— (1984) *Problems in Dostoevsky's Poetics*. Minneapolis: University of Minnesota Press.
Bauman, R. and Briggs, C. (1990) Poetics and performance as critical perspectives on language and social life. *Annual Review of Anthropology* 19, 59–88.
Bourne, J. (1988) 'Natural acquisition' and a 'masked pedagogy'. *Applied Linguistics* 9/1, 83–99.
Cazden, C. (1989) Contributions of the Bakhtin circle to 'communicative competence'. *Applied Linguistics* 10/2, 116–28.
Cook, G. (1994) Language play in advertisements: Some implications for applied linguistics. In D. Graddol and J. Swann (eds) *Evaluating Language* (pp. 102–16) (British Studies in Applied Linguistics 8). Clevedon: Multilingual Matters.
Fairclough, N. (1989) *Language and Power*. London: Longman.
— (1992) *Discourse and Social Change*. Oxford: Polity Press.
Gardiner, M. (1992) *The Dialogics of Critique: M. M. Bakhtin and the Theory of Ideology*. London: Routledge.
Garfinkel, H. (1984) *Studies in Ethnomethodology*. Oxford: Polity Press.

Goffman, E. (1971) *Relations in Public*. London: Allen Lane.
— (1974) *Frame Analysis*. Harmondsworth: Penguin.
— (1981) *Forms of Talk*. Oxford: Blackwell.
Goodwin, M. and Goodwin, C. (1987) Children's arguing. In S. Philips, S. Steele and C. Tanz (eds) *Language, Gender and Sex in Comparative Perspective* (pp. 200–48). Cambridge: Cambridge University Press.
Heller, M. (ed.) (1988) *Codeswitching: Anthropological and sociolinguistic perspectives*. The Hague: Mouton de Gruyter.
— (1992) The politics of code-switching and language choice. *Journal of Multilingual and Multicultural Development* 13:1, 123–42.
Hewitt, R. (1986) *White Talk Black Talk*. Cambridge: Cambridge University Press.
Hill, J. and Coombs, D. (1982) The vernacular remodelling of national and international languages. *Applied Linguistics* 3, 224–34.
Hill, J. and Hill, K. (1986) *Speaking Mexicano: The dynamics of syncretic language in Central Mexico*. Tucson: University of Arizona Press.
Hymes, D. (1979) Foreword. In K. Basso *Portraits of 'the Whiteman': Linguistic play and cultural symbols among the Western Apache*. Cambridge: Cambridge University Press.
Labov, W. (1972) *Language in the Inner City*. Oxford: Blackwell.
Maybin, J. (1994) Children's voices: Talk, knowledge and identity. In D. Graddol, J. Maybin and B. Stierer (eds) *Researching Language and Literacy in Social Context* (pp. 131–50). Clevedon: Multilingual Matters.
Mertz, E. (1989) Sociolinguistic creativity: Cape Breton Gaelic's linguistic tip. In N. Dorian (ed.) *Investigating Adsolescence* (pp. 103–16). Cambridge: Cambridge University Press.
Rampton, B. (1987) Stylistic variability and not speaking 'normal' English. In R. Ellis (ed.) *Second Language Acquisition in Context* (pp. 47–58). Oxford: Pergamon.
— (1990) Displacing the 'native speaker': Expertise, affiliation and inheritance. *ELT Journal* 44/2, 97–101.
— (1991) Second language learners in a stratified multilingual setting. *Applied Linguistics* 12/3, 229–48.
— (1994) Language crossing and the problematisation of socialisation and race. Paper given at 13th World Congress of Sociology, Bielefeld, June 1994.
— (1995a) *Crossing: Language and ethnicity among adolescents*. London: Longman.
— (1995b) Politics and change in research in applied linguistics. *Applied Linguistics* 16/2, 233–56.
— (forthcoming a) A sociolinguistic perspective on L2 communication strategies. In G. Kasper and E. Kellerman (eds) *Advances in Communication Strategy Research*. London: Longman.
— (forthcoming b) Youth, race and resistance: A sociolinguistic perspective. *Linguistics and Education*.
Sebba, M. (1993) *London Jamaican: A case study in language interaction*. London: Longman.
Street, B. (1984) *Literacy in Theory and Practice*. Cambridge: Cambridge University Press.
Turner, V. (1982) *From Ritual to Theatre: The human seriousness of play* (pp. 20–60). New York: PAJ.
Wells, J. (1982) *Accents of English* Vols 1–3. Cambridge: Cambridge University Press.
Wertsch, J. (1991) *Voices of the Mind*. London: Harvester Wheatsheaf.

Widdowson, H. (1984) The use of literature. In *Explorations in Applied Linguistics 2* (pp. 160–74). Oxford: Oxford University Press.

Woolard, K. (1988) Codeswitching and comedy in Catalonia. In M. Heller (ed.) *Codeswitching: Anthropological and sociolinguistic perspectives* (pp. 53–76). The Hague: Mouton de Gruyter.

— (1989) *Double Talk*. Stanford: Stanford University Press.

Appendix: Transcription symbols and conventions

Subjects

AC	Afro-Caribbean
An	Anglo
F	Female
In	Indian
M	Male
Pa	Pakistani

Prosody

     ⟋ low rise

     ı low stress

     ⟋ high rise

Segmental phonetics

[ ]   IPA phonetic transcription (revised to 1979)

Conversational features

[	overlapping turns
=	two utterances closely connected without a noticeable overlap, or different parts of a single speaker's turn
(.)	pause of less than one second
(1.5)	approximate length of pause in seconds
l.	lenis (quiet) enunciation
f.	fortis (loud) enunciation
CAPITALS	fortis (loud enunciation)
(( ))	'stage directions'
( )	speech inaudible
(text)	speech hard to discern, analyst guess
Bold	instance of crossing of central interest in discussion

9 Developing Grammars in Their Social Context: The L2 acquisition patterns of three Chinese learners of English

CHRISTINE RASCHKA and LESLEY MILROY
University of Newcastle upon Tyne and *University of Michigan*

Introduction

The aim of this chapter is to provide a socially sensitive and reasonably comprehensive account of the grammatical characteristics of the English of three bilingual women from the Tyneside Chinese community.[1] These women are selected from a larger sample to illustrate a range of ability from low to a higher standard, and the data reported here represent only part of a study of the grammatical patterns of English language use of 10 women from two ethnic minority groups (Punjabi and Chinese). Although we shall not be able to comment in detail here on the social correlates of this linguistic variability, we shall suggest that certain features of the social networks of individuals are likely to be highly relevant to their level of English language ability.

Over the second half of this century the developed countries have witnessed a massive population shift through politically, economically and socially motivated migration. This has led in turn to a pattern of language learning, often referred to as 'natural language acquisition', which contrasts with learning in stable and highly structured classroom situations. Most research in L2 acquisition deals with learning of the latter type.

Typically, migrant workers at the time of migration do not speak or understand the official or legitimised language of their host country, and very often there has been little or no systematic provision by the authorities for migrants to learn it. Thus, in everyday transactions with both native and non-native speakers of the host language and in the workplace and other domains, they acquire forms of the language that are situated in specific social contexts. In Europe and elsewhere many ethnic minorities continue to speak their mother tongue as well as the language of their host country. The speakers with whom we are chiefly concerned in this chapter belong to a community where Cantonese is spoken alongside English (for further details, see Li, Milroy & Pong, 1992).

Contemporary linguistic research in the field of SLA tends to concentrate on explaining selected grammatical characteristics of the learner's 'inter-language' by relating observations to theoretically motivated frameworks which aim to model an underlying linguistic knowledge. Hence, they are not concerned with socially situated language behaviour or with the effect of social context upon patterns of language use (see further Larsen-Freeman & Long, 1991; Cook, 1993).

In contrast to these theoretically motivated frameworks, there are a small number of studies which resemble the work reported here in that they have attempted to describe regularities in large bodies of naturalistic data, representing the language actually used in specific social contexts by learners in the community. The best known and most detailed studies of this type were carried out in Germany in the late 1970s, namely the 'Heidelberger Forschungsprojekt: Pidgin Deutsch' (HPD, 1975) and the ZISA project in Wuppertal (Clahsen, Meisel & Pieneman, 1983). The study most similar to our own however is that of Klein & Dittmar (1979); they used a fairly complex grammatical framework to account for the structural properties of the constantly changing grammatical systems of the migrant workers as they progressed through developmental stages of adult second language acquisition. From our point of view, an interesting feature of this research is Klein & Dittmar's sensitivity to the effects of social factors on L2 acquisition; for example they comment that social ties with German speakers is a better predictor of ability in German than variables such as duration of residence in Germany (1979: 203f.).

Data Analysis Procedures

A substantial corpus of naturally occurring (English) conversational data collected in the women's homes was analysed with the aid of a modified version of the Language Assessment, Remediation and Screening Procedure (LARSP), which yielded a descriptive account of the (English) grammatical patterns of each woman, based on a sample of 150 utterances per speaker. An example of a completed, modified chart is provided as Figure 9.1. Based on the descriptive categories set out in the Quirk grammar (Quirk, Greenbaum,

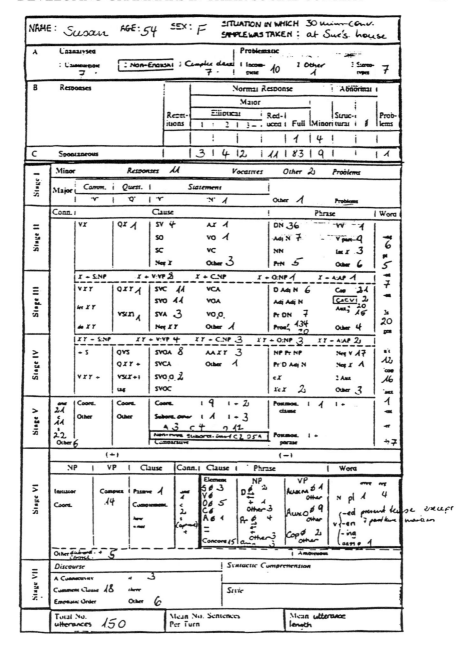

Figure 9.1 Completed modified LARSP profile summary chart

Leech & Svartvik, 1985) and organised around the normal sequence of syntactic development in children, LARSP was originally conceived as a tool for analysing the syntactic character of developmental language disorders. However, it has proved to be a useful framework for analysing *adult* pathological language data (for instance Penn & Behrmann, 1986), and can also be applied to adult second language data (Clahsen, 1985). Such an extension of LARSP's application should not be interpreted as embodying a claim that L1 and L2 developmental sequences correspond, although as we shall see the stages set out in the profile chart are able to characterise remarkably well, with the minimal adaptations shown in Figure 9.1 (see further below), the levels of English language ability which we distinguish in this chapter. LARSP provides a systematic account of the informants' strengths and weaknesses of particular structures at word, phrase and clause level with respect to the sample represented on the profile sheet. It also allows variation between individuals with respect to such structures to be considered (see further Crystal, Fletcher & Garman, 1989).

The alterations to the LARSP chart were motivated by recurrent patterns in our data. These were:

(a) inclusion as follows of two additional categories in Section A (Unanalysed Utterances):
    (i) non-English utterances
    (ii) complex clause structures which fall beyond the scope of the chart. These are characteristic of the most able English speakers.
(b) the addition of the categories Catenative Verbs at Stage III, and Non-finite Subordinate Clauses at Stage V
(c) A restructuring of the 'Error' box at Stage VI.

Note also that clause structures profiled separately under 'Other' at Stage VI are those which include co-ordinate and/or finite subordinate and/or non-finite subordinate structures.

On the basis of a preliminary analysis of their grammatical profiles as set out in the modified chart, the 10 women studied in our project were assigned to low, intermediate or higher English language ability groups. Tai Chan, Zoe, and Susan, whose developing grammars we discuss below, were selected as exemplars of each of these three ability levels. Like the developmental stages of the original LARSP profile chart, these ability levels should be interpreted as overlapping continua rather than discrete categories. Although the order in which speakers are presented below broadly matches the order of acquisition of constructions as they appear in the LARSP chart, it is important to remember that their locations on such an acquisitional continuum reflect a dynamic and ordered process of change. This is evident from their variable performance on a range of grammatical features, of which some are just beginning to be acquired, others are further advanced, and yet others are already established.

In addition to conversational data, general biographical and social information were gathered through informal interviews. A summary of the social characteristics of the three speakers described in Section 3 below is provided in Table 9.1.

Table 9.1 Summary of social characteristics of participants from Hong Kong

Characteristics	Susan	Zoe	Tai Chan
Age	54	48	50
Origin	Hong Kong	Hong Kong	Hong Kong
Urban/Rural	Urban	Urban	Rural
Mother tongue	Cantonese	Cantonese	Cantonese
Other languages	English	English	English
Education	5 years	Secondary	Primary
Occupation	Housewife and child-minder for local Chinese families	Housewife	Housewife, previously worked in Chinese take away
Length of residence	32 years	36 years	5 years
Husband's occupation	Worked in Chinese restaurant	Works in Chinese restaurant	Works in Chinese restaurant
Children	5	4	3
Engl. medium teaching	no	yes	no
Engl. language classes	no	yes	yes
Additional information	Learned Engl. from talking to neighbours, shopkeepers and children's teachers and friends	Social contacts mainly within Chinese community, Engl. for transactional purposes	Social contacts mainly within Chinese community, Engl. for transactional purposes

We shall comment only briefly on this social dimension of our analysis, as space restrictions do not permit a systematic account. The social characteristics most relevant to level of English language ability appear to be occupation, husband's occupation, and some of the details provided in the Additional Information category. These characteristics all bear directly on level of social contact with L1 English speakers, thus supporting Klein & Dittmar's (1979) conclusions that amount of contact to native German speakers was an important indicator of proficiency of non-native speakers in German.

Results

In our introduction and discussion of data analysis procedures above we outlined reasons for selecting LARSP as an analytic tool and described adaptations to the profile summary chart. We turn now to patterns emerging from the linguistic analysis of the conversational data. The completed LARSP summary charts were scanned to assess those categories on which the women seemed to differ from each other, and differences relating to response types, ratio of major to minor utterances, preference for simple rather than complex clause structures, and use of inflectional morphology were identified. We focus in the following subsections on an analysis of each of the three speakers' profiles first with respect to Response Types (i.e. as full, reduced, minor, ellipted, and unanalysed responses) and second with respect to Clause Types (i.e. in terms of grammatical functions of clausal elements such as Subject, Verb, Object, Adverbial).

Analysis of response types

Response types were analysed following the LARSP procedure presented by Crystal et al. (1989), slightly adapted as follows. Any utterance was identified as Full if obligatory constituent slots at *clause* level were filled. Thus (1) below was analysed as Full despite the lack of obligatory expansion in the verb phrase. However, (2) is analysed as Reduced utterance because a full constituent (the subject) has been omitted. Crystal et al. would classify both utterances as Reduced:

(1) He been here/
(2) Is my husband now/

The decision to distinguish between Reduced and Full utterances at clause level rather than at both Clause and Phrase level was taken as a consequence of the large proportion of reductions at clause level in the data, particularly in the lower language ability range. Since data for all speakers contains examples of phrase level reductions as in (1), this dimension of variation was less useful for discriminating between speakers of different abilities.

Tai Chan

The following salient characteristics of this speaker's language are evident from Figure 9.2:

First, 15% of her utterances are Unanalysed; these consist chiefly of stereotyped responses such as 'pardon', 'sorry' and 'I don't know'.

Second, 44% of all utterances are minor responses, the majority of these being spontaneous interjections such as 'uhuh', 'mmh' or 'yeah'.

Third, there are three times as many Reduced as Full utterances; while 18% are reduced, Full utterances constitute only 6% of Tai Chan's responses. (3) and (4) below exemplify respectively Reduced and Full utterances:

(3) because it a lot money/
(4) oh the children all go to London/

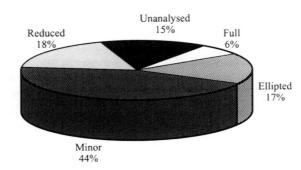

Total number of responses = 150

Figure 9.2 Quantitative analysis of response types used by Tai Chan

Zoe

Figure 9.3 differs from Figure 9.2 most clearly in displaying a shift away from minor utterances which account for only 19% of Zoe's responses, to the use of Ellipted (26%) and Full (35%) utterances. The largest increase can be seen in the use of Full utterances, from 6% by Tai Chan to 35% in Zoe's sample. We shall comment shortly on the grammatical characteristics of these utterances, of which an Ellipted and a Full example are set out as (5) and (6) below:[2]

(5) ((are those your oldest children/ [pointing to a photograph]))
     Zoe: no. my youngest/
(6) erm/. yeah/ her husband used to be a car salesman/

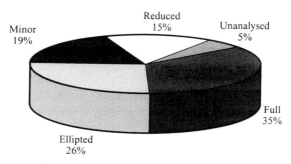

Total number of responses = 150

Figure 9.3 Quantitative analysis of response types used by Zoe

Susan

We see here a further marked increase in the use of Full utterances. More than half (or 56%) of Susan's responses fall into this category compared to a proportion of 35% for Zoe.

Another notable feature of Figure 9.4 is the relatively large proportion of Unanalysed Responses (22%). Recall that this category has been adapted to include Complex Clauses. Seven of Susan's Unanalysable responses fall within this category, and these full complex clauses are not further analysed, simply because relatively able speakers such as Susan produce utterances which fall beyond the scope of the chart.

In conclusion, the use of Response types by the three speakers analysed here show a clear shift from predominantly minor contributions of the type characteristic of Tai Chan, to the Full and often grammatically complex utterances characterising the responses produced by Susan. This shift reflects both an increasing ability to produce structurally more complex English utterances and (from the perspective of conversational roles) a tendency for more able speakers to shift from utterances which can function only as responses to prior conversational contributions. Examples respectively of Full utterances and grammatically complex utterances classified as Unanalysable are presented as (7) and (8) below:

(7) she wrap the Christmas present in the drawer/
(8) you know/ if they follow me/ like my daughter/ ((mmh)) she say I don't care ((mmh)) you understand or not I still talk/

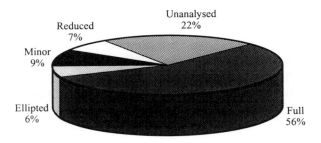

Total number of responses = 150

Figure 9.4 Quantitative analysis of response types used by Susan

In the following section we shall show that the pattern of increasing structural complexity of utterances evident in the use of response types is reflected also in the clause structure patterns characteristic of the three women. We begin again with Tai Chan, the speaker with the lowest English language ability.

Analysis of clause types

Tai Chan

We saw above that Tai Chan's language was characterised by a predominance of Stage 1 structures. Of her sample of 150 utterances, only 109 could be analysed at clause level, the remainder being clause fragments and unanalysed tokens. As shown in Figure 9.5, Stage I structures (69% of this smaller set) predominate, consisting of interjections (classified as minor utterances) and single lexical items (classified as major clause elements). In

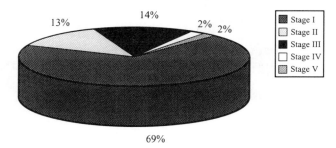

Total number of clauses profiled in Stages I–IV is 109;
excluding Stage I, N = 33

Figure 9.5 Quantitative analysis of clause types used by Tai Chan

Tai Chan's case this latter category is realised mainly as 'Other' Stage I struc-tures such as adverbials ('now'), adjectives ('dizzy'), the demonstrative Pronoun ('this') or Prepositions ('in').

There are only 33 examples of clauses realised by more than a single element in Tai Chan's sample of 109 analysed utterances. Most of these fall between Stages II and III, with a preference for clauses containing adverbial expressions (see for example (5) above).

Zoe

A considerable decrease in Stage I utterances is evident when Figure 9.6 is compared with Figure 9.5 above, even though these still constitute the largest single category of clause types in Zoe's sample of analysed utterances. Furthermore, the total number of clauses (excluding Stage I utterances) has increased from 33 in Tai Chan's sample to 90 in Zoe's sample. Most of these 90 utterances are simple clause structures with three element utterances forming the largest single category type (31%). A much smaller proportion of clause structures are realised with two elements (16%) and four elements (7%) respectively. Here are examples of Zoe's two, three and four element clauses:

(9) Jonathan called/ (SV)
(10) my.my friend live in Lemington/ (SVA)
(11) erm. my English. is OK sometimes/ (SVCA)

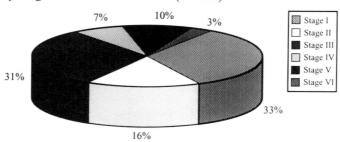

Total number of clauses profiled in Stages I–IV is 132;
excluding Stage I, N = 90

Figure 9.6 Quantitative analysis of clause types used by Zoe

A further difference between Tai Chan and Zoe is Zoe's more frequent use of complex clauses (13% compared to Tai Chan's 2%). These include (singly or in combination) Stage V coordinated constructions and both finite and non-finite subordinate clauses, as exemplified by (12), (13) and (14):

(12) so he take it home and put it on and take a photograph/ (Stage V: Coord.+1)
(13) yes. it's nice that I bring the photograph/ (Stage V: Subord. clause as C)
(14) she want to go out with me tonight/ (non-finite subordinate clause as O)

We also find attempts at Stage VI passive utterances:

(15) the girl call Alexis/((mhm)) and the boy. called. Marcus

Susan

In contrast to the previous two speakers we can see in Figure 9.7 a preference for complex clause structures falling into Stage V of the LARSP chart (42 out of 115 clause structures or 37% fall within this category).

Note also that in (16) below the subordinate clause is realised without a complementizer as direct speech:

(16) and *the man say* oh '*you don't speak like that*'
     S   V   subord. O

Subordinate clauses functioning as objects are in fact usually realised as direct speech. Although this poses some analytical problems, our analysis is supported by Quirk *et al.*, who point out that the grammatical function of direct speech can be similar to that of subordinate clauses (1985: 1022).

Of all Susan's analysed clause structures, 54% are located at Stage IV or at more advanced stages. This compares with 20% of Zoe's sample and 4% of Tai Chan's sample. When we look only at complex clauses, a clear contrast between the three speakers is also evident, the proportions of the total sample for the three women being as follows: 42% (Susan); 13% (Zoe) and 2% (Tai Chan). Thus, the proportion of clauses located at Stage IV and

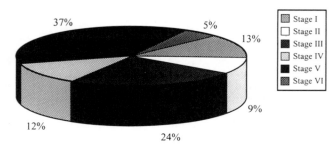

	Stage I
	Stage II
	Stage III
	Stage IV
	Stage V
	Stage VI

37%   5%   13%   9%   12%   24%

Total number of clauses profiled in Stages I–IV is 115;
excluding Stage I, N = 100

Figure 9.7 Quantitative analysis of clause types used by Susan

above and the proportion of complex clauses both emerge as accurate diagnostics of the developing grammars of English L2 learners from this community.

Conclusion

We conclude by summarising briefly the main points of this chapter, where we have presented a subset of data from a larger study. We have attempted to characterise differences in the L2 abilities of three women who are acquiring a second language in everyday contexts by adapting the grammatical profiling procedures developed by Crystal, Fletcher & Garman (1989). We have presented a two level structural analysis of the women's utterances, dealing respectively with response types (i.e. as Full, Reduced or Minor clauses) and clause types (in terms of grammatical functions of elements such as Subject, Verb, Object Adverbial). In Sections 2 and 3 we documented a shift across the acquisitional continuum with respect to the following: single lexical items and interjections are extensively deployed by Tai Chan, the speaker with the poorest English language ability; evident in the language sample of Zoe, the more advanced (intermediate) speaker are a more even spread of single lexical items, interjections, simple clause structures (with a preference for three element clause structures) and a few complex clauses. The most advanced speaker, Susan, shows clear evidence of an ability to handle complex clause structures.

We have suggested that LARSP provides a useful methodological tool for the researcher who wants to investigate L2 acquisition in its social context, providing a relatively comprehensive analytic framework which can grant insight into some important differences in the language behaviour of speakers of different abilities. Ultimately, we would wish to use data of the type presented here to construct a continuum which might in turn serve to model the L2 developmental trajectories of speakers in linguistic minority communities.

Notes

1. The data reported here contribute to a larger project 'A two level analysis of language choice in the Tyneside Chinese community' (ESRC Grant Number R0002956). The first author is supported in part by an ESRC Research Studentship. We are happy to acknowledge the support and also the contribution of Li Wei, our co-worker in this project.
2. The transcription conventions used in examples cited in this chapter are as follows:
   - a micropause is indicated by a full stop (.)
   - a tone group boundary by a slash (/)
   - interviewer's minimal responses are enclosed in double parentheses (( ))

References

Clahsen, H. (1985) Profiling second language development: A procedure for assessing L2 proficiency. In K. Hyltenstam and M. Pienemann (eds) *Modelling and Assessing Second Language Acquisition*. Clevedon: Multilingual Matters.

Clahsen, H., Meisel, J. and Pienemann, M. (1983) *Deutsch als Zweitsprache. Der Spracherwerb auslaendischer Arbeiter*. Tuebingen: Gunter Narr.

Cook, V. (1993) *Linguistics and Second Language Acquisition*. London: Macmillan.

Crystal, D., Fletcher, P. and Garman, M. (1989) *The Grammatical Analysis of Language Disability* (2nd ed.). London: Cole and Whurr.

'Heidelberger Forschungsprojekt: Pidgin Deutsch' (HPD) (1975) *Sprache und Kommunikation auslaendischer Arbeiter*. Kronberg/Ts.: Scriptor Verlag.

Klein, W. and Dittmar, N. (1979) *Developing Grammars*. Heidelberg: Springer Verlag.

Larsen-Freeman, D. and Long, M. H. (1991) *An Introduction to Second Language Acquisition Research*. London: Longman.

Li Wei, Milroy, L. and Pong Sin Ching (1992) A two-step sociolinguistic analysis of code-switching and language choice: The example of a bilingual Chinese community in Britain. *International Journal of Applied Linguistics* Vol. 2, 1: 63–86.

Penn, C. and Behrmann, M. (1986) Towards a classification scheme for aphasic syntax. *British Journal of Disorders of Communication* 21, 21–38.

Quirk, R., Greenbaum, S., Leech, G. and Svartvik, J. (1985) *A Contemporary Grammar of the English Language*. London; New York: Longman.

10 The Oral Language Development of Instructed Second Language Learners: The quest for a progress-sensitive proficiency measure

ALAN TONKYN
University of Reading

Introduction

Academic asides can be devastating. One such aside comes in Politzer & McGroarty's (1985) report on a study of 37 students on an eight-week pre-study English language course in the United States. This study included a pre- and post-test of oral communicative competence. Gains recorded were minimal, and the researchers commented that one reason for this may have been the fact that:

> . . . for intermediate students like these, great gains in communicative competence during a relatively short period such as the 8-week program under consideration here are unlikely.
>
> (Politzer & McGroarty, 1985: 110)

If this is true, then it is a truth which most people in the world of second language teaching are studiously ignoring. Teaching institutions are happy to offer intensive courses in oral communication skills of less than eight weeks and authors and publishers are not fighting shy of producing materials designed for such courses. The issue of likely performance gains by students lies at the heart of second language planning, teaching and testing, but is still bedevilled by considerable uncertainty.

Background

Cognitive theory

If we view language learning from the standpoint of cognitive (information-processing) theory, as researchers such as McLaughlin, and O'Malley & Chamot (e.g. McLaughlin, 1987; O'Malley & Chamot, 1990) have urged, then there are grounds for some pessimism as to what gains in speaking skills – or at least the linguistic competence aspect thereof – are possible on a relatively short intensive course with upper intermediate students, especially if that course is held in the country of the target language. McLaughlin sees language learning as involving, amongst other things, the transfer of language plans from controlled to automatic processing. Such 'automatised' plans in long-term memory are difficult to alter (McLaughlin, 1987: 134). Intermediate students will have a number of automatised and semi-automatised second-language plans in long-term memory. Pressure on the students to communicate, both inside and outside the classroom, is likely to lead to the use and further automatisation of these existing interlanguage skills, rather than their subjection to reanalysis and renewed controlled processing.

Longitudinal studies of progress

In spite of what has been said so far, we expect instructed students to make progress at all levels, and a key activity – probably *the* key activity – in Second Language Acquisition (SLA) research has been the attempt to chart the nature of second language development.

'Narrow focus' SLA studies have examined the acquisition of particular morphemes (e.g. Dulay & Burt, 1974; Felix & Hahn, 1985), or of grammatical constructions (e.g. Cancino *et al.*, 1978; Milon, 1974; Pienemann, 1984; Ravem, 1974). Such research, while of great interest, cannot give us a picture of overall progress in skill development. 'Broader focus' studies (e.g. Hawkey, 1982) have used proficiency tests, often allied to rating scales of various kinds, to measure progress. Such scales may, however, lack validity, as Bachman (1987) has commented, and are relatively insensitive to progress over short periods. In response to this latter problem, Alderson (1990) has called for the establishment of 'progress-sensitive' proficiency tests as a major task for the 90s.

A third approach to the measurement of second language progress has been to look at L1 development studies for an index, or indices, of L2 acquisition. The Mean Length of Utterance (MLU), much used in L1 work,[1] is not appropriate for cognitively mature L2 learners, but work in detailed performance profiling (e.g. Crystal *et al.*, 1976; Vorster, 1980) and the development of measures based on the T-unit (e.g. Hunt, 1970) have proved influential.

(The T-unit consists basically of a main clause and its associated sub-ordinate clauses; co-ordinated main clauses would not count as one unit. Thus the following speech excerpt would be counted as two T-units, divided as indicated: '*It is cheaper if the raw material is available in the country // but there is a scarcity of cows at the village level.*')

It is hypothesised that average T-unit length will provide a measure of language development. Stephen Gaies (1980: 58) has commented:

> . . . language development involves an increasing ability to incorporate and consolidate more information into a single grammatically inter-related unit – to put more chunks of information in a sentence.

Lennon (1987, 1990, 1991) has used T-unit-based measures and a detailed profiling approach in a longitudinal study of the natural acquisition of English by four advanced level learners over a six-month period. Other researchers (e.g. Larsen-Freeman & Strom, 1977; Larsen-Freeman, 1978, 1983; Dean, 1994) have focused on the Error-free T-unit and have found measures based on it (e.g. average length and relative frequency in the text) to correlate well with different levels of spoken and/or written performance.

Thus, T-unit-based measures have shown some promise as second language proficiency indicators. Some commentators have issued warnings about the use of such measures (e.g. Gaies, 1980; Crookes, 1990), but their value as progress-sensitive proficiency measures for use in research on instructed students remains relatively untested. The study reported here has made use of T-unit-based measures in an attempt to chart the progress of instructed learners in a way that is both relatively detailed but also potentially widely interpretable.

The Aims of this Study

This research was aimed at providing answers to the following questions:

- What is the nature of the changes, if any, in the spoken performance of typical adult students on a three-month intensive course?
- What is the relationship between particular types of change and global impressions of change on the part of the subjects themselves?
- Will the background of the students influence their ability to improve in spoken skills? In particular, will those who have already had to use spoken English to a considerable degree in their own countries be more resistant to improvement in spoken performance than those who have not? (For convenience the former group have been dubbed 'ESL' students, and the latter 'EFL' students.)

Subjects and Procedure

Accordingly a longitudinal study of the performance of eight adult students on a pre-study English language course at Reading University was carried out over a period of 10 weeks in the summer of 1984. Of these, four (three from Bangladesh and one from Sudan) used English in their home country as a medium of education, and have therefore been termed 'ESL' students; the other four (from Chile, Brazil, Morocco and Mexico) did not use English as a medium of education in their home countries and have been labelled the 'EFL' students.

The students were interviewed in weeks 1, 5 and 10 of the course. In addition, the students filled in questionnaires which elicited, *inter alia*, their assessment of their gains in spoken proficiency during the course. The first part of each interview was devoted to a discussion of some aspect of the interviewee's academic subject, and the second was based on a discussion of responses to one or two of the researcher's questionnaires.

Interviews 1, 2 and 3 (i.e. 'Pre-', 'Mid-' and 'Post-') have been orthographically transcribed and subjected to a preliminary analysis, and the results of this analysis are reported here. In each case, 60 T-units were selected for analysis: the first 30 coming from that part of the interview which dealt with the student's own subject and the second 30 coming from that part which dealt with matters related to language learning.

Twelve parameters ((a)–(l)) were selected for this initial analysis; they fall into three distinct groups. (The bracketed labels and the figure numbers relate to the graphs in Figures 10.1–10.2.)

The first group are all parameters which relate to the length and syntactic complexity of the T-units:

(a) Words per T-unit (after pruning of repetitions and self-corrections) (mean) **(Words/T-u) Figure 10.1**
(b) Subordinate clauses per T-unit (mean) **(Sub. cl./T-u) Figure 10.2**
(c) Non-finite clauses per T-unit (mean) **(N-F cl/T-u) Figure 10.3**
(d) CoVerbs per T-unit (i.e. Modals and Catenative verbs) (mean) **(CoVbs/ T-u) Figure 10.4**

The choice of parameter (a) was dictated by previous research, mentioned above, into T-unit length as indicator of first and second language development. The measures relating to clausal subordination within the T-unit – (b) and (c) – were chosen because of the importance, in the eyes of researchers, of this aspect of complexity as an indicator of first and second language development (e.g. Bowerman, 1979; Scarborough, 1990; Schachter, 1974;

Monroe, 1975; Lennon, 1987). The CoVerbs per T-unit measure was selected on account of its promising showing in the work of Lennon (1987) as a progress-sensitive feature.

The next group relates to fluency:

(e) Repetitions per T-unit (mean) **(Repet./T-u) Figure 10.5**
(f) Self-corrections (e.g. false starts) per T-unit (mean) **(S-corr/T-u) Figure 10.6**
(g) Filled pauses (e.g. 'er', 'um') per T-unit (mean) **(Filled p/T-u) Figure 10.7**
(h) The ratio of extraneous words (i.e. words in repetitions and sub-sequently self-corrected segments) to non-extraneous words **(Extr. W:W) Figure 10.8**

The first three features in this group – (e), (f) and (g) – are typical of normal, fluent, native-speaker speech but, it may be confidently asserted, will be present to a significantly greater extent in the utterances of intermediate non-native speakers, and can thus serve as indices of fluency. Features (e) and (f) constitute what L1 researchers have termed 'mazes' (e.g. Fletcher, 1991: 173) which can be seen, *inter alia*, as evidence of on-line monitoring by a speaker of the production process to see whether what is being uttered matches the speaker's intentions, as Levelt (1983) has proposed. Less proficient speakers, it is hypothesised, are more likely to encounter problems than more proficient ones, and therefore to produce false starts or functionless repetitions. Where syntactic control and lexical knowledge are relatively limited, there will be a greater tendency to enter linguistic cul de sacs, and hence a greater need to make repairs, or to buy time with repetitions. Feature (h), which is a measure of the extent of mazes in relation to 'non-maze' speech, was chosen as a way of showing the relative amount of non-informative speech, bearing in mind Starkweather's dictum that speech will be labelled as low in fluency where information is not conveyed at some expected rate (Starkweather, 1987). Filled pauses – feature (g) – 'are frequently taken to be associated with difficulties in formulation and/or word-finding difficulties' (Garman, 1990: 116) and thus appear to be a useful index of second language fluency.

The final group relates to grammatical and lexical accuracy (based on researcher's judgement), and its interaction with T-unit length:

(i) Errors per T-unit (mean) **(Errors/T-u) Figure 10.9**
(j) The ratio of errors to (non-extraneous) words **(Errors:Words) Figure 10.10**
(k) Words per error-free T-unit (mean) **(W/Err.-free T-u) Figure 10.11**
(l) The ratio of error-free T-units to total T-units **(Err.-free T-u:T-u) Figure 10.12**

Graphs: Selected aspects of spoken proficiency development over a 10-week course

* = Gain (Improvement) of $\geq 20\% < 30\%$; ** = Gain of $\geq 30\%$
(B, C, H and U: 'ESL' subjects; D, F, K, T: 'EFL' subjects)

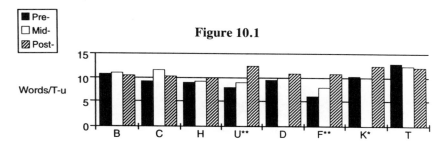

Figure 10.1

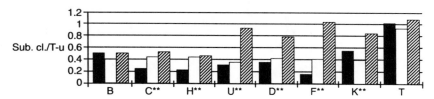

Figure 10.2

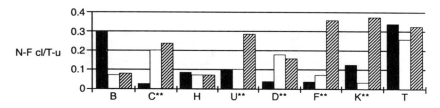

Figure 10.3

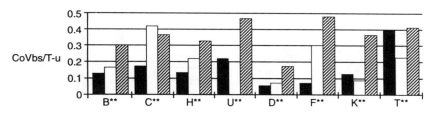

Figure 10.4

Figure 10.5

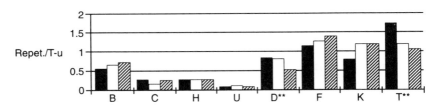

Figure 10.6

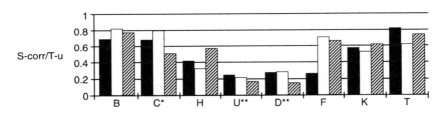

Figure 10.7

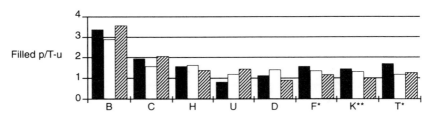

Figure 10.8

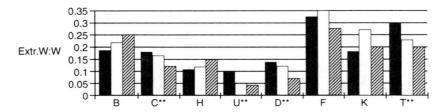

Figure 10.9

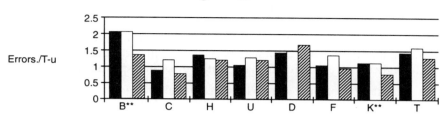

Figure 10.10

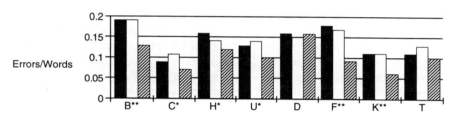

Figure 10.11

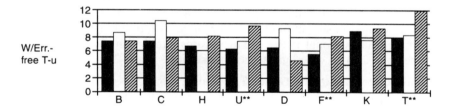

Figure 10.12

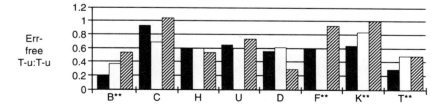

As mentioned above, researchers such as Larsen-Freeman (1983) and Dean (1994) have found that the addition of the error factor to Kellogg Hunt's T-unit-based measures of proficiency renders the latter more powerful indices of second language development, and therefore features (i)–(k) were selected for attention. It was hoped that features (j) and (l) in particular would provide useful indications of the relative amount of error in a spoken performance.

An example of an analysed T-unit is the following:

{but} *er* they don't have *er* a [(a) really (a really) idea or] <u>actual</u> idea about what <u>happen</u> in the field. (13 words, pruned of mazes)

({ } = not counted; [ ] = self-correction; ( ) = repetition; *er* – filled pause _ = error.)

It must be admitted that there is much which has not been captured in this preliminary analysis. No account has been taken of pronunciation, which can be an overriding factor in determining communicative effectiveness. Lexical range has not so far been assessed, and errors[2] have been left uncategorised. Strategic competence has not been measured in any way, though the interviews were designed not to place a premium on this.

Results

Complexity/Productivity (see Figures 1–4)

Words per T-unit. Though Larsen-Freeman and others have expressed doubts about the validity of T-unit length by itself as an index of ESL development, one notes that in six out of eight of the subjects T-unit length does increase over the course, though in three of these cases gains are small. A certain ceiling effect may also be noted in the cases of subjects B and T.

Subordinate clauses per T-unit. This appears to be a potentially interesting index of progress, in that seven out of the eight subjects make gains, with six making significant gains (against an arbitrary 30% benchmark). For five of the subjects, gains in **non-finite clause** use are particularly marked. (These results replicate those of Lennon, 1987.)

The one specific syntactic structure selected for study, **CoVerbs**, (= modal and catenative verbs) showed a marked gain pattern for all the subjects. Since many CoVerbs were followed by non-finite clause structures, there was obviously a link between gains in these two areas.

Fluency (see Figures 5–8)

It is interesting to look at **repetitions and filled pauses** together, since both probably signal a need for planning and word-search time. Non-proficient speakers would be distinguished from proficient speakers by the number (and placement) of these features.

The results are somewhat difficult to interpret. In both cases, there is a distinction between the ESL and EFL groups, but the distinction is not of the same kind in each case. The ESL group tend to make much less use of repetition than the EFL group, and there is little room for gain by the former. Subjects F and K possibly pay for their marked increases in syntactic complexity with increased use of repetition. The filled pause results, however, do not show the same trend. Filled pause use is a notable feature of both groups, but while the EFL group all improve, three significantly, only one of the ESL group shows any improvement, and that is a slight one. Taken together, the results for these features could be said to show an expected advantage for the EFL group with regard to fluency *improvement*, but closer examination of pause placement and length might be necessary to disentangle these results.

The results for instances of **self-correction** show no clear gain trend for either group of students, and fluctuations of performance are noticeable. It is possible that this feature is particularly sensitive to conversation topic: to avoid false starts, for example, a speaker needs to know where he or she is going.

The **ratio of extraneous to non-extraneous words** may provide the best measure of a certain kind of dysfluency, in that it reflects the proportion of a speaker's utterances which actually 'pay off' in an interaction. These results show a slightly stronger improvement tendency, but two subjects show fluctuations, and three a performance which worsens overall.

Error (see Figures 10.9–10.12)

In examining **errors per T-unit**, we notice a general, but not overwhelming, tendency for improvement. Six of the subjects show an improvement from the pre- to the post-interview, but three of these are slight improvements with a mid-course fluctuation. The **error:words ratio** is perhaps a better indicator of overall accuracy, and shows a clearer improvement trend, with no subjects worsening, and seven showing improvements, six of which are substantial or fairly substantial.

The **length of error-free T-units** and the proportion of such T-units in the whole speech sample are measures which, as has been mentioned above, Larsen-Freeman & Dean have found significant indices of proficiency. According to each of these measures, six of the eight subjects show an improving trend. The **proportion of error-free T-units** shows somewhat fewer fluctuations, and suggests a stronger gain tendency in the EFL group.

Looking at the error results overall (see Figures 10.9–10.12 and Table 10.2), and comparing them with the impression ratings in Table 10.1, it is interesting to note that those two subjects who gave themselves the highest overall improvement ratings, namely F and K, were notable for *both* increasing the length and complexity of their units of speech *and* showing improvements in accuracy. It is also interesting that the two subjects rated highest and lowest (of this group) by ELTS examiners[3] prior to the course, namely C and B respectively, also come top and bottom of the group according to most of the error measures in this study. This suggests that prevalence of error in a speaker's speech is a significant factor in impression ratings by the student him/herself and by others.

Looking at the results overall (see Table 10.2), there is certainly evidence of improvement. Of the 96 pre-/post-comparisons reported here, 68 show a gain, with 42 of those gains being at the 30% level or better, and 49 at 20% or better. It must also be noted, however, that in 47 cases the mid-course interview shows an unexpected rise or fall in performance.

The EFL group, as predicted, performs somewhat better than the ESL group in terms of improvement, with 37 gains and 11 losses or no-gains against the latter group's 31 gains and 17 losses or no-gains. EFL group gains tend also to be more significant in crude percentage terms.

If we examine the performance of individuals, we find evidence of the kind of trade-offs in development which Lennon (1987) noted in his subjects. Looking at the three areas of complexity, fluency and accuracy (see Table 10.2) we find that only two subjects, C and U, show a predominant gain pattern in all areas, with U showing a greater measure of improvement. Subjects H, F and K show gains in the areas of complexity and accuracy,

Table 10.1 Impression ratings

| | —— 'ESL' group —— | | | | —— 'EFL' group —— | | | |
	B	C	H	U	D	F	K	T
Pre-course ELTS oral band	4	6	5	5	5	—	5	5
Self-assessed gain in oral social English†	1	1	0	2	1	2	2	2
Self-assessed gain in oral seminar English	1	1	1	1	2	2	2	1

† 0 = none; 1 = some; 2 = high

which seem to be paid for in the fluency area. Subject D makes strong complexity and fluency gains, but has a pattern of losses in accuracy. Subject T, capable initially of fairly complex speech units, makes few gains in this area, but improves strongly in fluency and accuracy. Subject B, perhaps the most disappointing performer, makes definite gains in accuracy, but shows no real improvement in complexity or fluency.

Table 10.2 Summary of performance changes (pre- to post-course)

| | *'ESL' group* | | | | *'EFL' group* | | | |
Complexity	*B*	*C*	*H*	*U*	*D*	*F*	*K*	*T*
W/				**		**	*	
T-u	−	+	+	+	+	+	+	−
SubC/		**	**	**	**	**	**	
T-u	/	+	+	+	+	+	+	+
N-f C/		**		**	**	**	**	
T-u	−	+	−	+	+	+	+	−
CoV/	**	**	**	**	**	**	**	**
T-u	+	+	+	+	+	+	+	+
Fluency								
Rep/					**			**
T-u	−	+	/	/	+	−	−	+
S-C/		*		**	**			
T-u	−	+	−	+	+	−	−	+
FP/						*	*	**
T-u	−	−	+	−	+	+	+	+
Extr W/		**		**	**			**
T-u	−	+	−	+	+	+	−	+
Error (accuracy)								
Err/	**						**	
T-u	+	+	+	−	−	+	+	+
Err:	**	*	*	*		**	**	
W	+	+	+	+	/	+	+	+
W/ Err-f				**		**		**
T-u	−	+	+	+	−	+	+	+
Err-f T-u:	**					**	**	**
T-u	+	+	−	+	−	+	+	+

(+ = gain (improvement); / = no change; − = loss; * = gain of ≥ 20% < 30%; ** = gain of ≥ 30%)

Conclusions

Thus, overall, the pessimism of Politzer & McGroarty regarding possibilities of gain in oral skills on a relatively short intensive course at intermediate level is not supported by these data. However, the data also emphasise the complexity of the patterns of improvement, with gains in some areas being 'paid for' by a standstill, or even a decrement, in others. These complex 'trade-offs' appear to give support to the idea of multi-parameter rating scales for oral skills, rather than global impression scales, even though Richards & Chambers (1992) have cast some doubts on the reliability of the former.

The data give only limited support to the notion that what has been termed here an 'ESL' background may make improvement on a subsequent English language course more difficult because of automatisation of skills. Obviously the labelling of my subjects was somewhat crude in this respect, and other factors such as aptitude were ignored.

It is hoped that further data analysis will render the study more revealing. In particular, a planned comparison of these transcription-based measures with raters' impression-based assessments could serve to highlight particular features of speech which 'trigger' impressions of gain. Such findings could contribute to the empirical validation of rating scales called for by Bachman (1987).

The research method itself is not without its problems, some of which stem from the nature of the T-unit. In particular, with subjects of this kind, spoken T-units tend to fluctuate greatly in size, with standard deviations of half the mean being common. This can mean that a few very large T-units, especially in a relatively small sample, can affect the mean disproportionately. Occasionally spoken T-units may be difficult to segment, and there are times when something like the utterance – as described by Crookes (1990: 186–8) – might seem a better unit of planning. It is possible that the length of fluent 'runs' between filled, or lengthy unfilled, pauses could be a useful additional index of development.

This type of analysis is obviously never going to be part of the normal language tester's armoury. It might, however, lead to the development of slimmed-down versions which, like Vorster's TOLP in the L1 field, are practical research tools for anyone wanting to state a learner's stage of development, or to measure progress, with more precision and in a fashion which will be widely understood.

Notes

1. The MLU is not uncontroversial in studies of L1 development, however, as Snow (this volume) demonstrates.

2. It must also be admitted that, as Lennon (1991) has shown, the identification of errors and assessment of their scope can be problematical.
3. All but one of the group (F) had taken the University of Cambridge/British Council English Language Testing Service (ELTS) test prior to arrival in the UK. A 9-band scale is used in each of the skill areas, with Band 7 being held to indicate completely adequate English for tertiary-level study in the medium of English.

References

Alderson, J. C. (1990) Language testing in the 1990s: How far have we come? How much further must we go? Paper presented at the Regional Seminar on Language Testing and Programme Evaluation, RELC, Singapore.

Bachman, L. F. (1987) Problems in assessing the validity of the ACTFL oral interview. Paper presented at the Symposium in the Evaluation of Foreign Language Proficiency, Indiana University, March 1987.

Bowerman, M. (1979) The acquisition of complex sentences. In P. Fletcher and M. Garman (eds) *Language Acquisition: Studies in first language development*. Cambridge: Cambridge University Press.

Cancino, H., Rosansky, E. J. and Schumann, J. H. (1978) The acquisition of English negatives and interrogatives by native Spanish speakers. In E. M. Hatch (ed.) *Second Language Acquisition: A book of readings*. Rowley, MA: Newbury House.

Crookes, G. (1990) The utterance, and other basic units for second language discourse analysis. *Applied Linguistics* 11, 183–99.

Crystal, D., Fletcher, P. and Garman, M. (1976) *The Grammatical Analysis of Language Disability: A procedure for assessment and remediation*. London: Edward Arnold.

Dean, K. (1994) A study of the written interlanguage of intermediate EFL learners. University of Reading: Unpublished MA dissertation.

Dulay, H. and Burt, M. (1974) Natural sequences in child second language acquisition. *Language Learning* 24, 37–53.

Felix, S. and Hahn, A. (1985) Natural processes in classroom second-language learning. *Applied Linguistics* 6, 223–38.

Fletcher, P. (1991) Evidence from syntax for language impairment. In J. Miller (ed.) *Research on Child Language Disorders*. Austin, TX: Pro-Ed.

Gaies, S. J. (1980) T-Unit analysis in second language research: Applications, problems and limitations. *TESOL Quarterly* 14, 53–60.

Garman, M. (1990) *Psycholinguistics*. Cambridge: Cambridge University Press.

Hawkey, R. (1982) An investigation of inter-relationships between personality, cognitive style, and language learning strategies: with special reference to a group of adult overseas students using English in their specialist studies in the UK. University of London: Unpublished PhD thesis.

Hunt, K. (1970) Syntactic maturity in schoolchildren and adults. *Monographs of the Society for Research in Child Development* Serial no. 134, Vol. 35, No. 1.

Larsen-Freeman, D. (1978) An ESL index of development. *TESOL Quarterly* 12, 439–48.

— (1983) Assessing global second language proficiency. In H. Seliger and M. Long (eds) *Classroom-oriented Research in Second Language Acquisition*. Rowley, MA: Newbury House.

Larsen-Freeman, D. and Strom, V. (1977) The construction of a second language acquisition index of development. *Language Learning* 27, 123–34.

Lennon, P. (1987) Second language acquisition of advanced German learners. University of Reading: Unpublished PhD thesis.
— (1990) Investigating fluency in EFL: A quantitative approach. *Language Learning* 40, 387–417.
— (1991) Error: Some problems of definition, identification and distinction. *Applied Linguistics* 12, 180–96.
Levelt, W. (1983) Monitoring and self-repair in speech. *Cognition* 14, 41–104.
McLaughlin, B. (1987) *Theories of Second-Language Learning*. London: Edward Arnold.
Milon, J. P. (1974) The development of negation in English by a second language learner. *TESOL Quarterly* 8, 137–43.
Monroe, J. H. (1975) Measuring and enhancing syntactic fluency in French. *The French Review* 48, 1023–31.
O'Malley, J. M. and Chamot, A. U. (1990) *Learning Strategies in Second Language Acquisition*. New York: Cambridge University Press.
Pienemann, M. (1984) Psychological constraints on the teachability of languages. *Studies in Second Language Acquisition* 6, 186–214.
Politzer, R. and McGroarty, M. (1985) An exploratory study of learning behaviours and their relationship to gains in linguistic and communicative competence. *TESOL Quarterly* 19, 103–23.
Ravem, R. (1974) The development of *Wh*-questions in first and second language learners. In J. C. Richards (ed.) *Error Analysis: Perspectives on second language acquisition*. London: Longman.
Richards, B. and Chambers, F. (1992) Assessing open-ended tasks in foreign languages: An empirical study of reliability in the GCSE examination. University of Reading, Dept of Arts and Humanities in Education: Unpublished paper.
Scarborough, H. S. (1990) Index of productive syntax. *Applied Psycholinguistics* 11, 1–22.
Schachter, J. (1974) An error in error analysis. *Language Learning* 27, 205–14.
Starkweather, C. W. (1987) *Fluency and Stuttering*. Englewood Cliffs, NJ: Prentice Hall.
Vorster, J. (1980) *Manual for the Test for Oral Language Production*. Pretoria: South African Human Sciences Research Council.

11 Elaborating Elaboration in Academic Tutorials: Changing cultural assumptions[1]

JOAN M. TURNER and MASAKO K. HIRAGA
Goldsmiths College, University of London and *The University of the Air, Japan*

Introduction

This paper looks at how cultural assumptions change the rhetorical effects of particular utterances, and, as a result, how a change of awareness is necessary for interlanguage pragmatic development. The rhetorical function looked at is that of elaboration in spoken interaction in academic contexts. The motivation for rhetorical effects is analysed in terms of sociopragmatic (Thomas, 1983; Leech, 1983; Kasper, 1992) assumptions, that is culturally evolved ways of using and interpreting linguistic utterances. Such assumptions are deep-rooted and for the most part unconscious, so that their motivation needs to be probed.

We found that the motivation for elaboration in the British context was essentially critical appraisal, both in terms of what was expected by tutors (elaboration prompts) and in terms of how students elaborated (elaboration strategies); that elaboration on the part of the student in this way was not expected in the Japanese context, but that elaboration did take place, motivated by differing sociopragmatic assumptions.

Elaboration Prompts and Sociopragmatic Assumptions

In the attempt to probe the deeper level assumptions regarding elaboration, we looked at the kinds of utterances intended to elicit it in authentic data from tutorials in Britain. This included 12 video-recorded tutorials, 20 audio-recorded tutorials, and observation notes from over 60 tutorials in both cross-cultural (British tutor/Japanese student) and native speaker (British tutor and British student) contexts in fine art, music, drama, dance, and communications.

We found frequent occurrences of wh-questions, yes/no questions, comments, tag questions, either/or questions, and hypothetical questions, which we characterised as elaboration prompts. The following example shows how they function:

(1)

BT (British Tutor):	What kind of music do you like best?
JS (Japanese Student):	Minimalism.
BT:	I wonder what it is about minimalism that you like so much?

(audio-taped tutorial)

The initial prompt was breadth-affording, leaving the student scope to tailor an elaboration. When elaboration did not occur, a second prompt of a similar nature, but linguistically more opaque, followed. This suggests that the initial prompt was intended as a request for a more wide-ranging analysis. When it was not forthcoming, the use of an ultra-polite formula possibly covered up a sense of exasperation at the lack of an appropriate response to what seemed an obvious request. This combination of negative politeness (Brown & Levinson, 1987) and linguistic opacity seems to be the result of taken-for-granted assumptions. Ultimately, it is not conducive to effective cross-cultural communication.

The next examples show a contrasting take-up of the comment as an elaboration-cuing prompt:

(2)

BT: Em .. This has all the feeling .. of em, er, techniques of Nihonga.

JS: Ah. [After a pause, the tutor went on to elaborate.]

(video-taped tutorial)

(3)

BT: You seem not to be using the circular device any more.

BS: Yeah, that kinda stems from when I was trying to work with the image of the pebble dropping in the water, and the kind of rhythm that ensued . . . , but that wasn't getting me anywhere, I'm not really sure where I'm going . . .

(video-taped tutorial)

While the Japanese student does not take the tutor's observation further, the British student is obviously aware of the demands of the genre (the fine art tutorial) that he is participating in. In, no doubt unconsciously, picking up the need to explain what is happening in his work, he shows his awareness of the sociopragmatic assumptions shaping the communicative rationale of the tutorial.

The tag question works similarly, being a more implicit comment on the part of the tutor. This example from a tutorial on dance, 'stillness is not the same as doing nothing, is it?' demands that the student agree as well as show that she understands the difference between stillness and doing nothing in dance-analytical terms, by elaborating that explanation. In other words, the more explicit request, 'can you tell me the difference between stillness and doing nothing?' is sociopragmatically assumed, but not uttered.

All of these elaboration prompts show a conflict between the pragma-linguistic function of the speech acts deployed, which appear to be straight-forward requests or comments, and the deeper underlying sociopragmatic purpose of getting students to evaluate, and to develop ideas. It seems that the linguistic action of elaboration in academic contexts in Britain relates to the deeply embedded cultural demand for critical appraisal. The valorisa-tion of critical thinking has been documented in research (Entwistle, 1984) into lecturers' perceptions of what study of their various disciplines promoted. A closer study of the linguistic strategies of elaboration may therefore enhance the understanding of what critical thinking entails. This is supported by the case of a PhD candidate (Street, 1994) who did not seem to have the same understanding as her examiners of what was meant by the encouragement to 'elaborate' or 'tease out' the argument. She felt she was being asked to reiterate things she had already said.

While it seems that the extent to which the request for elaboration is hidden linguistically reveals the extent to which it is taken for granted, two prompt strategies in particular constrain the making of judgments and choices crucial to critical appraisal. One is the either/or question, which obviously limits the field of choices to two, and the other is the hypothetical question, which takes the student out of the present situation and enforces a judgment. The either/or question, 'are you more interested in working two-dimension-ally or three-dimensionally?' asked of a fine art student entails an analytical choice which will determine the future development of the student's work. The following extract shows the progression of a tutor's strategies, from an apparently simple information-eliciting wh-question, to a rather dramatic hypothetical scenario, as he successively fails to get the student to make the required appraisal.

(4)

BT: Which is the best one?

JS: Mm, I can't say that because, –

BT: Which is the worst one? . . . Are there any that are not here because they were no good?

JS: Just . . . these . . . [meaning I have only done these]

BT: They're not all of the same value.

JS: Yeah?

BT: Understand? . . . Mm, if we were to say, I'm going to ask you to choose four . . .

JS: Mm-m.

BT: Let's say. And I've got a big bonfire over here,

JS: Mm, right.

BT: And I'm going to put eight of them on the fire. And save four. . . . Which four would we keep?

JS: I cannot choose.

BT: Yes, you can. You must.

JS: Why do you know, why do you want to know that? Because, . . .

BT: Because it will tell me something.

JS: Mm. It's a universe, they're part of the universe. I like to show . . . eh, construction –

BT: . . . But, but if you say, 'because I made it, it therefore is OK –'

JS: Mm-m.

BT: You will never develop any . . . critique.

(video-taped tutorial)

The misunderstanding appeared to arise because the initial question was taken at face value and resisted by the student at that level. However, it was ultimately only a ploy, opening up the route to appraisal rather than being of any moment in itself. As that route was continually blocked in terms of what the tutor wanted, the hypothetical question became a last desperate strategy. The function of the hypothetical question then, is to sharpen the kind of judgment that has to be made.

Differing Sociopragmatic Assumptions

The problems that the Japanese students appeared to have with elaboration in the British context were partly explained when the different prompts were translated into Japanese and used in interviews conducted by Japanese tutors with their undergraduate linguistics students. Wh-questions such as 'what do you think of your essay?' or 'how are you going to prove your claim in the latter part of your paper?' were most frequent, followed by imperatives ('please explain what you want to discuss in this paper') and yes/no questions ('could you elaborate section 1 a little bit more?'). They are all used directly as information elicitors rather than as implicit prompts for critical appraisal. The comment strategy ('I think you should do it this way rather than that way, but . . .'), negative yes/no questions ('don't you think it is a good idea to . . . ?'), and tag questions ('comparison with the German data will make your essay more convincing, won't it?') function as strong recommendations, propelling the student in a particular direction, rather than eliciting from him/her how they have oriented themselves in the field.

Either/or and hypothetical questions also do not appear to demand analysis on the part of the student. In the former, the tutor has usually formulated a contrasting analysis and the student need only make a choice. The following example is illustrative of how a tutor is likely to formulate an either/or question, and shows how the burden of analysis is differently placed in the two cultures. 'This part of your work is more 3-dimensional and this is more 2-dimensional, which area are you more interested in?'

Hypothetical questions tend to be interpreted as advice, as in 'what do you think would happen if you used a role play as data elicitation?' answered by 'I think I should do that.' These differences appear to result from differing sociopragmatic assumptions, which were further revealed in the kinds of elaboration strategies used in a discourse completion test.

Elaboration Strategies

The aim of the discourse completion test (DCT) was to find out by larger-scale elicitation, how students actually elaborated in five tutorial situations cued by different prompt types.[2] As the aim was to detail the kinds of elaboration strategies used rather than analyse at a micro-level the varying aspects of spoken language use, we felt that the instruction to fill in as if speaking would give us adequate data, and at the same time would ease the administrative procedure. The test was administered to both British (36) and Japanese (169) informants. 88 of the Japanese informants answered in English while 81 responded to a translated version in Japanese. The Japanese informants who answered in English were further broken down into those who had at least one year's experience of study in an English speaking country (24) and those who hadn't (64). The DCT was answered by students and tutors of literature, linguistics, geology, and a number of other science and social science areas. The level of English of the students varied from intermediate to advanced.[3]

The elaboration strategies that we arrived at (Table 11.1) were the result of a three-stage process. The present authors initially coded the English language data individually. Upon agreement of the strategies at the fourth reformulation, the Japanese language data was looked at in the light of the coding system by two Japanese researchers and two research assistants independently. The final scoring of this data was agreed by discussion. We divided the resulting elaboration strategies into two broad groups, analytical, and non-analytical elaboration. The following example of elaboration elicited from a British fine art lecturer after the coding procedure on the DCTs seemed both to validate and to epitomise the analytical strategies we had defined – developmental, comparative, evaluative and delimiting:

(5)

Tutor: Have you visited any art galleries recently?

Student: Yes, I went to see the X exhibition at the Y gallery. I'd seen a previous exhibition of her work about three years ago [COMPARATIVE] and I wanted to see how it had changed [DEVELOPMENTAL]. It seems to have become more architectural [EVALUATIVE and COMPARATIVE]. The objects are much larger in scale, less like furniture and more to do with architectural space [COMPARATIVE], relating to the whole body being able to walk round, under, or through them [DELIMITING]. It's quite an unexpected turn for her work to take [EVALUATIVE], much less predictable than it used to be, much richer than the previous formula [COMPARATIVE].

Such a fully elaborated example rarely occurred in the DCTs (Hiraga & Turner, 1994), but it encapsulates the analytical strategies used, which occurred despite differences in the disciplinary content. The contrasting constructed example below illustrates the non-analytical elaboration strategies used, which we labelled technical, personal, informative and conciliatory:

(6)

Student: Yes, I went to see the X exhibition at the Y gallery. It was very impressive [PERSONAL]. The gallery also featured the Z as a special display of the month [INFORMATIVE]. As I didn't have enough time [PERSONAL] to go to both, I just saw the X, because it was what Prof. A recommended in class [CONCILIATORY]. I would certainly like to go back there [PERSONAL] in one of the mornings next week when the gallery is relatively empty [TECHNICAL].

Table 11.1 Strategies of elaboration

Types	Strategies	Definitions	Examples
Analytical	Developmental	to develop ideas	'I'm interested in gender difference in language use. They say women's speech and use of language are different from those of men. I want to study why such difference exists.' (2/J)
	Comparative	to compare two ideas, authors, etc.	'I don't see how it fits with the overall argument in the book.' (1/B)
	Evaluative	to evaluate ideas	'I felt that [his] theories were relevant to what we've been looking at recently in the course.' (2/B)
	Delimiting	to show an awareness of scope, to narrow the focus	'. . . at least I've read one or two of her recent papers on . . .' (2/B)
Non-Analytical	Technical	to refer to technical (non-substantial) points	'It was really hard how to incorporate it with the presentation, because I was allowed to have just a few minutes to to present.' (3/J)
	Personal	to display personal opinion or feelings	'I like the work of him very much. I wanted to incorporate it into my essay for a long time, and the chance has come finally. I'm really glad to do it, and happy that you like it' (3/J)
	Informative	to give information	'I am interested in his study. And I have thought why the difference between each class ours. He has the conclusion that it is because especially people in the upper class have prestige and they do not want to pronounce in the same way as people in the lower class.' (2/J)
	Conciliatory	to relate or reconcile the interests of two different parties	'But even then you suggest so, I will try to make it shorter.' (5/J)

Summary of Discourse Completion Test Results

Four major findings emerged. Firstly, in terms of analytical elaboration, the different types of prompts made very little difference to the kinds of strategies deployed by the British informants. All the situations in the DCT elicited analytical strategies. By contrast, non-analytical strategies were used regardless of the type of prompt by the Japanese groups, while they occurred less frequently in the British data. It is assumed therefore that the elaboration strategies used do not depend on the grammatical form of the prompt, but more on the sociopragmatic assumptions underlying the prompts in each culture.

Secondly, when we compared the variation of strategies according to the informant groups, the British informants employed analytical strategies of a comparative and evaluative nature more often than the other groups. The Japanese informants did not entirely avoid analytical strategies, but it is notable that the comparative strategy was extremely rare in the Japanese-language and the English-language Japanese respondents with no study abroad, whereas it occurred in four out of five situations in the British data. This preference for the comparative strategy along with the analytical use of the either/or prompt in the British context seems indicative of a predilection for dialectical thinking.

What is interesting in terms of interlanguage pragmatics is that the English-language Japanese respondents with more than one year's study abroad, showed an overall similar disposition of analytical and non-analytical strategies to the British data. This would seem to suggest that direct exposure to the western academic system had influenced their elaboration strategies. Conversely, there appears to be a transfer from Japanese sociopragmatic assumptions in the other English-language respondents, as their variation profile in analytical and non-analytical strategies indicated considerable resemblance with the Japanese-language data.

Thirdly, the most salient non-analytical strategies in all the data groups were technical and personal strategies. The personal strategy occurred in almost all the situations in the Japanese data and the English-language but no experience abroad data, but in only two situations in the British and the English-language experience abroad data. It seems that in Japan, elaborating on personal grounds is more widely acceptable, while in Britain it is more restricted to contexts such as compliments, which demand it.

Fourthly, the use of the informative and the conciliatory strategies seemed to be particularly Japanese. The informative strategy was used by the Japanese groups in four out of five situations. This appears to be operating against the background sociopragmatic assumption that what is required is the display of knowledge. The conciliatory strategy has two rhetorical effects, namely keeping the peace and complying with what the tutor seems to want. In a situation where the prompt demanded a choice out of two interpretations of the student's essay, the Japanese informants tended to avoid choosing, saying for example, 'when I wrote this sentence, I didn't mean that I completely agreed with the author, but it doesn't mean I was criticising him', or 'I cannot agree nor criticise. I wrote just what I felt', declining to see things in an antithetical way. This seems to show a preference for a holistic way of thinking which interrelates with the lack of comparison as an analytical strategy.

In response to the question 'what would you say if I suggested you made the concluding section a bit shorter?' some students answered as if they were following the suggestion because it came from the tutor rather than giving it their consideration. For example, 'thank you for giving me your invaluable opinions. Because my conclusion is quite simple, I will express it in a shorter manner as you suggest'. The use of the conciliatory strategy here shows sensitivity to the authoritative role of the tutor.

Elaboration Strategies and Sociopragmatic Structuring

The difference in occurrence of analytical and non-analytical strategies operating in the DCT data seems to indicate that each culture emphasises different aspects of the academic process. While British academic culture is predominantly thinking-centred, valuing the process of critical appraisal by means of such analytical strategies as comparison, evaluation, and probing further, Japanese academic culture is predominantly knowledge-centred, valuing the demonstration of knowledge gained by following the correct procedures in adequate detail and technique. This is seen in the desire to be informative, and the greater use, over all the situations, of the technical strategy. Furthermore, the valorisation of dialectical thinking on the one hand and holistic reasoning on the other seem to be diametrically opposed.

To sum up, changing from one academic context to another makes for an interchange of differing, sometimes conflicting assumptions. In such an encounter, it is necessary for the participants to develop an awareness of their own cultural assumptions as well as those of the other culture. We hope that in elaborating the differing sociopragmatic assumptions underlying elaboration in academic contexts in Britain and Japan, we have contributed to such a development.

Notes

1. We would like to express our thanks to the following people: Peter Cresswell, Jane Harris and Brian Falconbridge at Goldsmiths, Yoko Fujii and Yoshie Sogo at the University of the Air, and Hiroko Takanashi at Japan Women's University.
2. With contextualisation, the prompts in the DCT are: (1) Oh, what exactly are you having problems with in the chapter? (2) Are you familiar with the work of (relevant name)? (3) I like the fact that you incorporated the work of (relevant name). (4) When you wrote this [pointing to a particular sentence], were you implying that you agreed with the author or were you criticizing him? (5) I think you're doing good work. What would you say if I suggested you made the concluding section a bit shorter?
3. Our assessment of the language level of the informants was based on a representative sample (20%) of the students for whom we had either TOEFL or IELTS scores. We estimated that a minimum score of 480 (TOEFL) and 5 (IELTS) was intermediate.

References

Brown, P. and Levinson, S. (1987) *Politeness: Some universals in language usage.* Cambridge: Cambridge University Press.
Entwistle, N. (1984) Contrasting perspectives on learning. In F. Marton, D. Hounsell and N. Entwhistle (eds) *The Experience of Learning* (pp. 1–18). Edinburgh: Scottish Academic Press.
Hiraga, M. K. and Turner, J. M. (1994) The problem of elaboration for Japanese students of English: A study in interlanguage pragmatics. Paper presented at the 33rd Annual Meeting of JACET.
Kasper, G. (1992) Pragmatic transfer. *Second Language Research* 8(3), 203–31.
Leech, G. (1983) *The Principles of Pragmatics.* London: Longman.
Street, B. (1994) Academic literacy: A case study. Unpublished ms.
Thomas, J. (1983) Cross-cultural pragmatic failure. *Applied Linguistics* 4, 91–112.

Section 3:
Change, Language Education and the Developing World

Introduction

This sub-theme of the Conference explored the complex relationships between language education and social change in developing countries. Issues raised included the choice of national languages, the role of English as the medium of contact in development activities, and the role of agencies such as the British Council in language education in the developing world. The focus of attention in this sub-theme, therefore, was on the way in which language education and language policy influence, support or hinder the planned or deliberate social change which constitutes the essence of development activity.

The starting point for this discussion is D. P. Pattanayak's rousing discussion of 'Change, Language and the Developing World'. Pattanayak argues that in order to understand the language situation in many developing countries it is necessary to appreciate that multilingualism and multiculturalism are an absolutely fundamental phenomenon. If we can adopt this perspective – and Pattanayak suggests that many Western commentators may have difficulty in doing so – then it becomes apparent that monolingualism is an exceptional state of affairs. A multilingual society, for Pattanayak, is a rich and diverse society. One implication of this argument is that, in planning change, we must strive to ensure that variety is maintained; any diminution in the multilingual and multicultural character of society leads to an impoverishment of that society as a whole and the cultural dispossession of individual members of it. This argument leads Pattanayak to fear the growing international hegemony of English.

The contribution by Martin Cortazzi and Lixian Jin, 'Changes in Learning English Vocabulary in China', provides an interesting contrast with Pattanayak's chapter. Cortazzi and Jin demonstrate that over recent years there has been a massive increase in the numbers of people in China who are learning and teaching English. They do not share Pattanayak's concern regarding the increasing importance of English, but they do argue convincingly that Chinese learners have their own distinct and effective learning style – a style which is coherent with Chinese culture. Their conclusion thus offers a parallel to Pattanayak's, in that they are arguing in favour of variety in fundamental pedagogic approaches. The international homogenisation of teaching approaches may be counter-productive.

The final contribution in this section is Clinton D. W. Robinson's 'Winds of Change in Africa: Fresh air for African languages?' Robinson uses the language situation in Cameroon as a case study in which to explore a range of issues surrounding the relative functions of indigenous and former colonial languages. In so doing, he picks up on several of the points raised by Pattanayak. He also proposes an important agenda for further research into community structures in African societies and the roles of African and other languages in those same societies. Robinson concludes his chapter with the upbeat suggestion that the increasing use of African languages constitutes an essential element in 'the continent's search for its own path of development'.

12 Change, Language and the Developing World

D. P. PATTANAYAK
Indian Institute of Applied Language Sciences

Introduction

I must begin with an anecdote. I was presenting a paper on mother tongue in an international seminar at Uppsala. Suddenly a member of the audience interrupted me and, pointing his finger at me, said, 'You, people from the third world countries, make unsubstantiated statements. Can you give me one example of difference between dominant monolingual and multilingual countries?' It took me a minute to absorb the shock, as I did not expect such behaviour from the audience. I composed myself and told him that since he had asked for one example, I would give him two. I said, 'For you the mono- lingual, one language is the norm, two languages is a quantum jump being a hundred per cent achievement over your one language, three languages are tolerable, more than three languages are absurd. For us, many languages are facts of existence, three languages are a compromise, two languages are a tolerable restriction, one language is absurd.' He was about to sit down. I asked him to remain standing until I gave the second example. I said, 'An American political scientist asked, "How much diversity can this culture tolerate?" If any social scientist asked such a question in my country, he would not be worth his salt. A social scientist in my country must ask, "How much uniformity can this culture tolerate?"' This episode prompted me to be cautious about the biases inherent in Western formulations.

The first questions to which I shall draw attention are the so-called con- cepts of 'development' and 'Third World countries'. After the developed countries appropriated the first and the second Worlds for themselves, they lumped together the countries of Asia, Africa and Latin America and called them the Third World. Since the developed countries are the point of refer- ence for gauging development and since development is measured in terms of *per capita* GNP/GDP, PIQL or rate of growth, the Third World countries are also called the Developing World.

143

Acceptance of Third World status results in the construction of a social reality which is permanently inferior to the developed countries. It sets up an education system which seeks to create skills, knowledge and competences congruent to the dominant world and not to solve its own problems and set its own standards. Change is considered as replacement of everything indigenous by everything dominant and developed. Modernisation is equated with Westernisation. A low self image and lower assessment of tradition as well as performance are what characterise them.

The developing world is multilingual, multiethnic as well as multicultural. The first and second Worlds are equally diverse, but they are not perceived as such. The European Nation State built around unitary symbols, the American experiment of the Melting Pot, Salad Bowl or Distant Stranger are nothing but euphemisms for homogenisation and assimilation. Even though the pot has melted leaving the identities intact, still the American effort at declaring English as the sole official language through the Hayakawa Amendment – failing which pushing it through the state legislatures – is evidence of pursuance of a dominant monomodel.

The developed countries are models for the developing countries to emulate. As a result of this emulation many languages are perceived to be a threat to national cohesion, administrative integration and barriers to economic growth. The theoretical formulations by Fergusson, Fishman, Neustupny, Kelman and Kloss (see Pattanayak, 1984) are samples of formulations of monomodels. The theories propounded by these writers neither fit with the social realities in the developing world nor do they explain the socio-political development of the developing world. The more they seek to universalise their own experience, the greater becomes the gap between the limited elite resulting from the appropriation of rank, status and wealth by one language among many and the masses speaking diverse languages in the developing world. The developed world is the producer of theories and the developing world is consumer. The consumption of such theories gives rise to a sense of inequality, powerlessness and helplessness.

The use of the term 'development', amazingly, demonstrates its extreme vagueness and often its contrary use. A cursory glance at current journals in a small social service institution yielded the following: development, physical development, mental development, spiritual development, political development, economic development, social development, cultural development, rural development, urban development, tribal development, agricultural development, industrial development, regional development, child development and development for the people. Added to these are educational development, language development, curriculum development. The scope of 'development' presents confusion and contradiction.

It is interesting to see how 'development' affects multilingual pluricultural countries. The many languages result in small zones of communication. When one or two languages are chosen for mega-communication, the small communication zones wither away, resulting in loss of culture. The land-holding pattern in the developing countries presents a similar picture. The average land size is five hectares in the tropical belt and three hectares in Asia. When super-farm technology is imposed on them the smallholdings become uneconomic. The tribal communities present a tragic case of death of language and loss of culture. The tribals live in small clusters in the midst of large forests. In the name of development, the erection of bunds (dams) for electricity generation, opening of the land for tourist promotion, exploitation of minerals located in hills and jungles all result in the tribals being dispossessed and dislocated. This in turn, results in the death of their language and cultures.

Another important marker of modernisation is urbanisation. It is projected that in 2000 AD the world's urban population will be 2,917 million out of which the share of the developing countries will be 1,967 million. With the growth of urban population (India's urban population has doubled during the last two decades, from 109 million in 1971 to 217 million in 1991), the appalling growth of urban poverty is mind boggling. In India the growth of urban poverty between 1982 and 1988, estimated by government sources, is 20.1%, while according to independent scholars it is 37%. According to independent scholars during this period the number of persons in absolute poverty has grown from 69.2 million to 77 million. The urban population in general and the urban poor in particular are pulverised, homogenised and confronted with the loss of their languages and cultures. The gap between the urban rich and the urban poor goes on increasing. Whether one looks at development from the vantage point of language use, land use or urbanisation, the conclusion is inescapable that the gap between developed and developing countries as well as the developed and undeveloped sectors within a country is on the increase. The language of the rich grows richer and the language of the poor becomes poorer. Having access to the media, the rich become information rich. The poverty of information of the poor becomes phenomenal.

Talking about development journalism Prof. Cairncross (quoted by Jhingan, 1975: 4) says, 'Development is not just a matter of having plenty of money, nor is it a purely economic phenomenon. It embraces all aspects of social behaviour, the establishment of law and order, the relationship between family, literacy and scrupulousness in business dealings, familiarity with mechanical gadgets and so on.'

Rogers (1976: 133), quoting Wilbur Schram and Daniel Lerner, says 'Development is simply a purposeful change towards a kind of social and economic system that a country decides it wants.' Gunnar Myrdal defines development as 'upward movement of the entire social system'. As Ramaswamy (1992: 17) observes:

> Development cannot be imposed from above. It has to be generated from within. The particular process implies partnership in development by two parties, namely the people themselves and the Government organisations or non-government organisations. The participatory process refers to a host of development functions, like collection of data, processing and analysing, determination of needs and their prioritisation, planning programmes and budgeting, raising of resources, implementation and monitoring and impact evaluation; all done in a participation manner.

Meanwhile Quabral (1975: 2) argues:

> Development requires effective vertical and horizontal flow of information within a country and full communication to and from, as well as within and away from the village.

In spite of the different parameters of Development Communication recognised by scholars from the East and the West, the Indian scenario is symptomatic of the developing countries. As Dua (1993: 7) says:

> While there was no mention of Journalism Education and training in Indian languages in the recommendations of the 1954 Rajadhyaksha Press Commission, the 1984 Press panel headed by Justice K. K. Mathew made only a passing reference to journalism in Indian Languages in chapter 12 of its Report.

Thus, the transformation of English from a colonial language to a National language results in the dwindling of the Indian languages.

A study of the state of the art of educational planning shows that the context of the socio-economic basis of education has changed considerably during the last three decades. The resource crunch all over the world and the developing countries in particular has raised questions about the role of the State in determining the quality of education, in preparing people for work and employment, in funding strategies and in management. It is sad but true that education has been bureaucratised all over the world, more so in the developing countries. Politicians, ignorant of the changing contexts, unsure of a second term and changing their portfolios more often than necessary, rely more and more on the civil servants. In India, for example, the *National Policy on Education* (Government of India, 1986) as well as the *Programmes of Action* (Government of India, 1986, 1992) are bureaucratic documents.

Ever since then whenever a Report has been prepared by experts on education, a bureaucratic committee sits over it and emasculates it in the name of feasibility. This has happened to all the Reports since the 1986 *National Policy on Education*, the latest being the Report of the Empowered committee to comment on the Report submitted by Yaspal, former chairman of the University Grants Commission.

A report of the Indian Institute of Educational Planning (IIEP, n.d.) states that, 'Improving the quality of education is one of the necessary conditions of development.' In the developing countries this means improving the quality of teaching conditions whereas in the developed countries it is mainly a matter of the achievement and maintenance of higher levels of knowledge. The developed countries are moving from a manpower based system to one based on knowledge and intelligence. The developing world finds itself in a spot as it is threatened by losing its twin advantages of abundance of low cost labour and abundance of natural resources.

Both the developed and the developing worlds suffer from over-education and underemployment. As higher education graduates take the jobs of secondary school graduates the plight of the developing world is accentuated. The under-education of the labour force and the over-education at the tertiary level result in the repatriation of labour to developed countries for doing lower level work and doing higher level technical work at a much lower cost of training per unit.

In the West multilingualism is taboo. Shapson & D'Oyley's 1984 study of the situation in Canada is entitled *Bilingual and Multicultural Education*. A notice in the University of Leeds, announcing a lecture, says that the speaker will speak on 'monolingualism', 'bilingualism', and 'multiculturalism'. In Europe 'intercultural education' is a preferred term. However, 'intercultural' cannot be a substitute for 'multicultural', since only the recognition of multiculturalism validates intercultural education. Multiculturalism is given reluctant recognition.

In the West, nations were formed around unitary symbols. Therefore it is difficult to reconcile the concept of the nation with multilingualism, multiculturalism or variations of different sorts. The treatment of intercultural education as a problem specific to capitalist systems by the Eastern Europeans absolved them of the responsibility of recognising multilingualism and multiculturalism.

Economic liberalisation in the developing countries has resulted in the expansion of the most effective schools and the withering away of the least effective schools. The most effective schools in the process lose their small size and reasonable teacher:student ratio, whereas the less effective schools impart poor education.

Another factor flowing from the free market economy is that neither the provider nor the customer have adequate financial capacity to negotiate acceptable contracts. Under these circumstances, there is no wonder that literacy and primary education are reduced to targets rather than being a commitment and a duty. In the primary stage, after years of emphasis on enrolment, we have turned our mind towards retention. And yet the drop out rate is 70%–80% at the VIIth standard stage. There is no recognition of language being a major factor in the high drop out rate. In the secondary stage in India, the pass rate ranges between 35% and 55%. With around 2% of the student population in the colleges and universities coming from socially backward sectors, it is evident that education means education for some. 'Education for all' is a mere adjunct of 'education for some'.

Language and society are mutually constitutive categories. There are significant correlations between a developed economy, monoculturalism, unitary symbolism and language dominance on the one hand and between a developing economy, multilingualism, multiculturalism and multimodel society on the other. The formations of Language and State are intimately connected. The creation of different states after the collapse of the Soviet Union and the break-up of Pakistan into Pakistan and Bangladesh bear eloquent testimony to this.

Grierson, in his *Linguistic Survey of India* (undertaken from 1886 onwards and published between 1903 and 1927), identified 179 languages and 544 dialects. The Indian Census of 1961, the last to give mother tongue information, identified 193 languages corresponding to 1,652 mother tongues. If one adds together all the different mother tongues identified from the earliest surveys till the present time, one comes across nearly 3,000 mother tongues. To match with this linguistic diversity one finds nearly four thousand castes and communities and an equal number of faiths and beliefs. The management of this diversity has been possible through 18 constitutionally recognised languages, one National Official language and one Associate National Official language, 34 literary languages and a host of non-literary languages, 87 languages used for publication, 71 languages used for broadcasting, 58 languages used in school curricula and 41 languages used as media of instruction at different levels. All these languages, belonging to four language families, written in 10 major writing systems and a number of minor ones, present a picture of diversity unparalleled in the world.

Language use defines zones of communication. The small zones of communication survived because of autonomy of groups and flexibility of communicative function. When mono models were imposed on such diverse structures, diverse minority and minor languages were required to be assimilated to the majority languages, while diverse languages were kept in a permanent antagonistic posture, so facilitating the control of the colonial language, be it the language of external or internal colonisation.

It is necessary to distinguish between the tremendous changes that have been occurring in the social process and the deliberate change which the state seeks to bring about through intervention. The changes that take place in the socialisation process, in transmitting beliefs, skills and techniques to newer generations, are so subtle that from the broad perspective of society it looks as though society has remained static. That is why, although many changes occur in a language across generations, still people claim that they are speaking the same language. Societal changes brought about by state intervention are often rapid as well as drastic.

The theories of social change propounded by the Western scholars – Comte's logical positivism, Spencer and Hobhouse's evolutionism, and Marx's historical materialism – are linear theories which assumed that there is social evolution and social progress which in turn assumed that 'each succeeding age in a society, and each succeeding society in human history are "better" or "superior" to the preceding ages and societies' (Kuppuswamy, 1972: 6). All three theories provided justification for the Europeans coming to Asia, Africa, and Latin America to 'civilise', 'modernise' and 'protect' the indigenous populations. For the New World and the Colonised World this meant the advent of various processes of domination, exploitation, war, slavery and extermination. In the developing world the substitution of everything indigenous by everything Western was perceived as 'change' and as 'modern'. The developing world suffered from perpetual self-denial and self-deprecation and accepted low status in a hierarchical system.

Today the developing world stands at the cross-roads. In spite of lip service to development, the nuclear weaponry of the developed world is poised against the developing world. The developing third world has 72% of the world's population and 14% of the world's wealth; 90% of world energy and 90% of audio frequency are enjoyed by 10% of the world's population. This has resulted in the saturation of development for a few and deprivation for many. There is no wonder that in the developing world peoples' voices are gagged, their languages are derided, their autonomy is pulverised, their cultures are homogenised and assimilated, and the changes brought about by state intervention are aimed at killing diversity.

One interesting example of indigenous languages and cultures being threatened by the intrusion of a language, partly through State support and partly by popular acclaim, is provided by the case of English. The British Council's missionary approach has now given way to exportability through the British trade authority. What could be better sales talk than statements like '403 million people use it as a first language'; '1.5 billion people use it as a second language' and '60 countries have given it the status of official language'? It is the language of development. It is the language of upward socio-economic mobility. It is the international link language, a language of wider communication and a bi-directional window on the world. In a country as diverse as India, it enjoys the status of Associate Official Language.

It is often forgotten that English in the world is now being spoken of as 'Englishes of the World'. This has given recognition to different types of learners. Learners with no English, those who have had their entire education through a Regional Language, learners with six to eight years of frozen, passive English resulting in the acquisition of bookish English, learners with fractured English, learners with pidginised and creolised varieties of English: these are some of the examples of variation obtaining within English. Added to this are the dialectal varieties which are seldom recognised by the standard language supporters. There is no effort at bridging the gap between diverse home languages and the standard language of the school. No one assumes responsibility for the creation of such a link.

English is backed by international groups which treat English as an instrument of colonisation and as a commodity for trade. Intra-nationally it is the support system for the managerial mini-sector for the preservation of privileges. It promotes the generation, sustenance, and socialisation of a conspicuously consumeristic life style. It interprets skill migration as brightening life chances, and it accentuates the divide between (1) rural and urban, (2) the developing and the developed, and (3) elites and masses. It permits better education for a miniscule minority. At the same time, it inhibits interaction between science and society and it inhibits the creation of appropriate technology. As an adversary to many languages sharing communication, it promotes alienation, anomie, and blind spots in cultural perception. It is the carrier of values antithetical to indigenous cultures and results in the atrophy of cultures. It makes non-English cultures permanent parasites on English and English-speaking countries. In the process, indigenous languages become anaemic and move towards certain death. While speaking about the efficacy and efficiency of English education, language acquisition as proficiency is measured in terms of the English language. Language results are compared with those achieved by the English-only schools. Accreditation is denied if results are below the English-only standard.

It may thus be seen that there is a parallel between, on the one hand, English as a colonial imposition supported by a segment of the elite and receiving stiff nationalist opposition, and, on the other, the current elitist imposition acclaimed by a segment of the population aspiring to achieve access to elitist privileges and opposed by a larger segment of the population. Change has completed the circle.

There are misconceptions about the development of a language in a multilingual setting. Unlike economic development, where historically the development of a region or a sector is achieved at the cost of another, linguistic and cultural development operate differently. It is true that in monolingual countries even bilingualism has been considered subtractive and the recognition or empowerment of another language are considered to be threats to the dominant language. But a multilingual pluricultural country thrives on respect for the different. All languages complement and supplement one another. The question to be asked is whether we make change our friend or our enemy. When under the pressure of the dominant we make it impossible for minor and minority languages to survive and so make their cultures wither, we are not making change our friend. When we adopt a colonial language to displace the mother tongue and even a dominant indigenous language, we are not making change our friend. When through policy and planning we put two or more languages in adversary posture, we are not making change our friend. It is only when we recognise that one language is not for all functions, all languages are not for all functions, but functions and power are distributed among all languages, then we make change our friend. It is only when we recognise that languages are different yet equal that we make change our friend. As empowerment of women does not take away power from men, similarly empowering all languages does not take away power from some. Empowering all languages is both a sine qua non for the maintenance of multilingualism and pluriculturalism and at the same time is synonymous with this maintenance. The developing world must correct its sight and cope with change without diluting its multilingual and pluricultural character.

References

Dua, M. R. (1993) Current trends in journalism and communication education in Indian languages. In Department of Communication and Journalism, *Commemorative Volume of a National Seminar on Current Trends in Journalism and Communication Education in Indian Languages*. Hyderabad: Department of Communication and Journalism, Osmania University.

Government of India (1986) *National Policy on Education*. New Delhi: Department of Education, Ministry of Human Resource Development.

— (1986) *Programme of Action*. New Delhi: Department of Education, Ministry of Human Resource Development.

— (1992) *Programme of Action*. New Delhi: Department of Education, Ministry of Human Resource Development.

Grierson, Sir George A. (1903–1927) *Linguistic Survey of India*. 11 volumes. Calcutta.

IIEP (Indian Institute of Educational Planning) (n.d.) *The Prospects for Educational Planning: Report of the workshop organised by IIEP on the occasion of its XXVth anniversary*. New Delhi: IIEP.

Jhingan, M. L. (1975) *Economics of Development and Planning*. New Delhi: Vikas Publishing House.

Kuppuswamy, B. (1972) *Social Change in India*. New Delhi: Vikas Publishing House.

Pattanayak. D. P. (1984) Language policies in multilingual states. In Andrew Gonzalez (ed.) *Language Planning, Implementation and Evaluation: Essays in honour of Bonifacio P. Sibayan on his sixty-seventh birthday*. Kuala Lumpur.

Quabral, Nora C. (1975) Development communication. In Juan F. Jamais (ed.) *Readings in Development Communication*. Los Banos: University of the Philippines Press.

Ramaswamy, A. S. (1992) Community organisation for development. *The Hindu* Tuesday 18 February 1992, p. 17.

Rogers, Everett M. (1976) *Communication and Development: Critical perspectives*. London: Sage.

Shapson, S. and D'Oyley, V. (1984) *Bilingual and Multicultural Education*. Clevedon: Multilingual Matters.

13 Changes in Learning English Vocabulary in China

MARTIN CORTAZZI and LIXIAN JIN
University of Leicester and *De Montfort University*

Introduction

'*When Chinese students learn a language they think that vocabulary is the most important thing.*' This typical comment from a student in China does not reveal *how* Chinese students learn foreign language vocabulary and whether their approaches have changed in the rapid recent expansion of ELT and the use of communicative approaches to language teaching.

There has been little research about vocabulary learning in developing countries and, in general, comparatively little seems to be known about the cultural aspects of language learning strategies, despite calls for more research in this area (O'Malley & Chamot, 1990: 165). This paper focuses on Chinese learners' perceptions of methods of learning vocabulary, with some emphasis on cultural aspects.

We first give a brief background of recent changes in English teaching in China. Then we outline a framework of some current Western notions about vocabulary learning which are contrasted with Chinese approaches. Finally we report a recent questionnaire study of Chinese university students' learning of English vocabulary, contrasting their present approaches with how they recall learning vocabulary in middle school. This will give a perspective on changes in learning vocabulary in China.

Changes in ELT in China

The most significant recent change in ELT in China is the rise in the number of learners. In 1957 there were only 843 full time secondary school teachers of English in the whole country (Ross, 1992: 252) compared to current estimates that there are over 310,400 such English teachers (ibid: 251) with over

57 million full time school and university students (Zhu & Chen, 1991) and 150 million part time students learning English (Dzau, 1990: 32). Three reasons for this rise are: the general perception of the need for English as part of China's modernization, and hence the present key role of English in education; new job opportunities requiring English in the rapid development of a 'socialist market economy'; and, of course, China has a large population, still increasing, which is now 1,202 million.

There are other important changes within the *culture of learning and teaching* in the foreign language classroom (Cortazzi & Jin, 1996). A culture of learning might be defined as the system of expectations and interpretations which are used by learners and teachers regarding their classroom roles, the nature of learning and how to learn. Such a culture of learning has its roots in educational tradition and cultural practices (Jin, 1992). It is often taken for granted, so that classroom participants are unaware of its influence on learning.

A Chinese culture of learning English is fundamentally concerned with mastery of knowledge focused on four centres (see Figure 13.1). Learners see themselves as apprentices: their study is strongly based on imitation of the teacher as 'master' or model. They internalize knowledge through close attention and memory, believing that understanding meanings and the ability

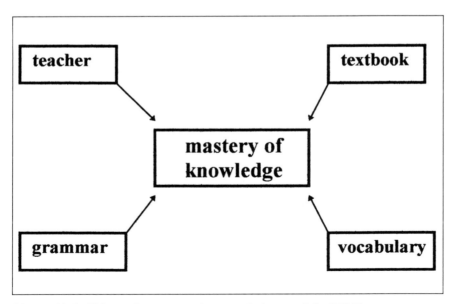

Figure 13.1 Chinese four-centred transmission model of ELT

to use English creatively will come later. The verb 'teach' in Chinese is '*jiao shu*', literally 'teach the book', although for many teachers this is balanced by a more humanistic term '*yu ren*', meaning 'cultivate a person'.

This Chinese four-centred approach focuses on the transmission of knowledge through: *teacher-centredness* – the teacher is an authority, a source of knowledge, an intellectual and moral example; *textbook-centredness* – texts are taught and learned (often memorized) in exhaustive detail; *grammar-centredness* – where grammar-translation approaches are commonplace and the teacher and textbook transmit this subject knowledge to students; and *vocabulary-centredness* in which students engage heavily in memorizing hundreds, even thousands, of words each year. The culture of learning associated with this long-standing transmission model is, however, changing or at least it is now in tension with a Western more communication-focused model (see Figure 13.2).

This Western culture of learning is fundamentally concerned with the development of language skills. It is sensitive to learners' needs, creative expression and contextual appropriateness. This model is much more *learner-centred*; *task* or *problem-centred*; it pays more attention to language *functions* and *uses*: and many activities involve learners in classroom *interaction*. Many Chinese teachers of English are well aware of this model. It has been

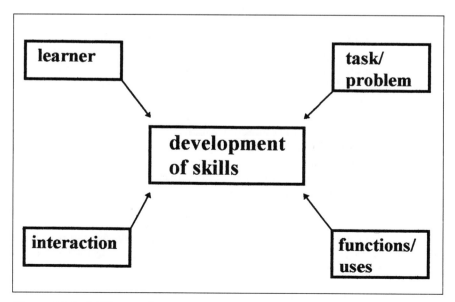

Figure 13.2 A Western four-centred communication model of ELT

disseminated through such courses as the British Council's Advanced Teacher Training courses, teachers' seminars and conferences (Wang, 1990; Dzau, 1990) and through Chinese-produced materials, e.g. *Communicative English for Chinese Learners* (Li *et al.*, 1987).

It is difficult to assess how far Chinese ELT has moved in the direction of this second model. Some teacher trainers have been disappointed at the lack of impact of communicatively oriented courses. However, among Chinese teachers there is now a fairly widespread belief in 'eclecticism': a Chinese approach to ELT which attempts to combine knowledge of English with the ability to use it in genuinely communicative contexts. Such eclecticism minimizes tension between the two models of learning. The development of practical innovations is, however, heavily constrained by several factors: the present examination system (which emphasizes grammar and vocabulary); institutional resistance to change on the part of decision-makers; perceived limitations in resources and teacher training; and the difficulty in teaching large classes. Some teachers may well perceive change towards Western methods as part of a process of Westernization, which is not necessarily in China's interests, culturally, and which might be perceived as post-imperialist imposition.

Approaches to Learning Vocabulary

A sampling of books widely used in teacher training (Gairns & Redman, 1986; Nation, 1990; McCarthy, 1990; Harmer, 1991) shows that current Western approaches to teaching vocabulary include a variety of techniques to demonstrate meaning and emphasize the organization of vocabulary through lexical relations, collocation and word formation. The importance of interacting with words is stressed; however, memorization and how to learn words seem to be de-emphasized. From research, the complexity of lexical organization is becoming more widely known: in cognition, as prototypes or schemas (Taylor, 1989; Aitchison, 1994); at discourse levels as text organizers (Hoey, 1983; Carter, 1987); and as pre-fabricated chunks (Pawley & Syder, 1983), or lexical phrases (Nattinger & DeCarrico, 1992) in the idiom principle (Sinclair, 1991). A current Western framework for vocabulary learning would therefore include these aspects in a continuous, dynamic process. Knowing a word is much more than simply knowing its isolated meaning: students need to see the ecology of words, their function in networks and contexts of meaning.

In contrast Chinese approaches to learning English vocabulary seem fixed on memorization of lists of individual words. This is reinforced by the syllabus and exam system at middle school and university level: middle school students are required to learn 5,000 words (Hua, 1992: 43). Thorne & Thorne (1992: 38) confirm that 'most Chinese learners would probably identify this acquisition of "new words" as their single greatest source of problems in learning English'. Not surprisingly, many students give up learning English 'because they are bored by vocabulary lists and are tired of memorizing words every morning' (Yue, 1991: 60). Rote memorization is emphasized by students: 'mechanical memorization is the most efficient way of learning words, and that is what they do most of the time. They said that the more time you spend on memorizing, the more you will learn' (Li & Li, 1991: 69). In contrast, there were no such statements among a group of American students learning Chinese, rather they 'always try to find new interesting ways of memorizing new words' (ibid). Publishers in China have identified a healthy market for books concerned with learning English vocabulary: recent bestselling titles include *How to Increase Word Power* (Huang, 1991), *How to Memorize English Vocabulary using Etymology* (Zhao, 1991), *Vocabulary Fundamental* (Liu, 1993), *Vocabulary 22,000* (Liu, 1993).

Further evidence of the Chinese approach can be found in Chang's (1990) study of 40 prominent Chinese professionals, who were reckoned to have mastered English. Two strategies dominate their accounts of how they had learnt vocabulary: *extensive constant reading* and *memorizing words*, either by noting new words in a vocabulary book or by learning words from review cards. Some had learned words directly from the dictionary.

The Present Study

In conducting the present study we had several points in mind. O'Malley & Chamot (1990: 165) note that cultural background can be expected to play a part in identifying the set of learners' strategies. This remark implies: first, that researchers need to be cautious about imposing a framework on subjects; second, that the kinds of strategies which learners themselves identify may be influenced by their own background.

On the first point, we are properly cautious (in part since one of the authors of this chapter is Chinese and the other British). We therefore initially asked Chinese university students about their strategies using an open-ended question: How do you learn English words? Replies were then listed to make a questionnaire, using the students' terms. This involves the subjectivity of self-report data, which is offset by a reasonable sample of questionnaire responses (N = 212).

On the second point, it is assumed that common patterns of response are influenced by cultural background, and this is exactly one focus of interest – to explore students' culture of learning.

A further point is the need to move from description to explanation. Therefore we attempted to elicit students' perceptions of the efficiency of each method, as a step towards investigating their evaluations or explanations about which strategies work. Further, having analysed the initial data, 30 interviews were conducted with students in a different university in order to obtain their explanations of the results. We quote from these interviews later.

Since our focus is on change in vocabulary learning we asked the students in the study to fill in two versions of the questionnaire: the *first* asked them to recall how they learned English vocabulary when they were in the middle school, i.e. at least three or four years earlier; the *second* asked them how they learn English vocabulary now. Students did not know they were to fill in a second questionnaire when they received the first one. (Ideally, of course, we would have conducted a full longitudinal study of the same group of students over several years, spanning their transfer from school to university but the present study, with this retrospective element, may indicate directions of change as a preliminary to a fuller study later.)

The 212 questionnaires were collected from three universities in China: Nankai University in Tianjin, the People's University in Beijing, and Hangzhou Institute of Commerce in Hangzhou. The first two are key universities and can be considered to be at the forefront of educational change: many students at these three universities have access to Western teachers for at least part of their English course and the presence of foreign teachers using more communicative methods may be a significant factor in any changes in vocabulary learning.

Table 13.1 displays the results in five main columns: the first enumerates the students' initial listing of their vocabulary learning methods. The second column shows in percentages ratings of how *frequently* they had used each of these methods in the *past*, i.e. in middle school. The second column shows the frequency in two categories, 'hardly' and 'often', reduced from a more extended Likert scale. The third column shows the *frequency* of each method *now*, i.e. at university. The fourth column shows in percentages the students' ratings of the *efficiency* of each method in the *past*, rated as 'positive' or 'negative', or 'unsure'. The fifth column gives students' ratings of the *efficiency* of each method *now*, i.e. whether they would recommend the methods to fellow university students.

Table 13.1 Changes in learning English vocabulary in China

I studied English vocabulary by using the following methods:	Past — Frequency of use (%) Hardly	Often	SS	Now — Frequency of use (%) Hardly	Often	Past — Efficiency of use (%) Neg.	Posi.	Unsure	SS	Now — Efficiency of use (%) Posi.	Neg.	Unsure
read English 1. newspapers/mags	88.5	11.5	**	19.8	80.2	11.0	40.0	49.0	**	83.0	3.8	13.2
2. textbooks	3.8	96.2	**	17.9	82.1	1.0	93.3	5.8	**	68.9	6.6	24.5
3. literature	90.4	9.6	**	37.1	62.9	16.8	27.7	55.4	**	73.3	4.8	21.9
4. non-fiction	92.3	7.7	**	57.1	42.9	14.0	23.0	63.0	**	46.2	10.6	43.3
listen to 5. audio cassettes	56.4	43.6	**	22.1	77.9	8.2	62.9	28.9	**	78.6	6.8	14.6
6. radio programme	71.2	28.8	**	12.4	87.6	9.1	46.5	44.4	**	86.7	3.8	9.5
7. native speakers	86.5	13.5	**	29.1	70.9	6.1	49.5	44.4	**	83.5	4.9	11.7
8. other learners	61.8	38.2	**	35.9	64.1	22.0	30.0	48.0		50.5	13.5	35.9
9. teachers of English	6.6	93.4		11.7	88.3	1.0	87.5	11.5		78.6	4.9	16.5
speak to 10. native Eng. speakers	92.2	3.8	**	42.9	57.1	6.3	56.3	37.5		77.1	1.9	21.0
11. teachers of English	47.6	52.4	**	19.8	80.2	7.8	66.7	25.5		74.5	5.7	19.8
12. other learners	70.5	29.5	**	37.1	62.9	23.3	29.1	47.6		51.4	11.4	37.1
write 13. essays, compositions	55.8	44.2	**	18.3	81.7	6.9	60.8	32.4	**	83.3	7.8	8.8
14. taking notes	21.2	78.8	**	17.1	82.9	5.8	75.7	18.4		79.0	5.7	15.2
watch/read English 15. films/video cassettes	84.2	15.4	**	26.7	73.3	19.0	37.0	44.0		70.5	8.6	21.0
16. TV programmes	77.9	22.1	**	59.0	41.0	17.0	43.0	40.0		50.5	4.8	44.7
17. cartoons/comics	91.3	8.7	*	81.9	18.1	16.6	32.0	52.0		39.4	8.7	51.9
18. vocabulary cards	34.9	65.1	**	62.9	37.1	10.5	59.0	30.5		40.0	19.0	41.0
memorize 19. words in dictionaries	64.1	35.9		57.1	42.9	34.0	31.1	35.0		40.0	23.8	36.2
20. words in voca. books	33.7	66.3		33.3	66.7	10.8	54.9	34.3		53.3	15.2	31.4
21. words in categories	49.5	50.5		31.8	61.9	11.8	48.0	40.2		58.1	13.3	28.6
22. translation/interpreting	48.1	51.9	**	43.3	56.7	7.6	55.2	37.1		67.3	3.8	28.8
23. word formation	61.5	38.5	**	35.0	65.0	7.8	52.0	40.2		65.0	7.8	27.2
24. games	90.6	9.4		49.0	51.0	13.6	38.8	47.6		55.8	9.6	34.6

N = 212. neg. = negative; posi. = positive; SS = statistical significance
*: P ≤ 0.05–0.01 – The differences are statistically significant. **: P ≤ 0.01–0.000 – The differences are statistically highly significant.

This arrangement of the data permits a ready analysis of the students' perceptions of changes in learning vocabulary in terms of frequency and efficiency. If there are changes, several interpretations are possible: this is change reflecting learners' development across phase; or this is a diachronic change in vocabulary teaching and learning reflecting changes in ELT in China; or (less likely, given the number of subjects) this reflects differences in students' memory of what they do now compared with several years previously.

Table 13.1 additionally shows statistically significant differences between the second and third columns, and between the fourth and fifth columns: two stars represents significance at the $p \leq 0.01$ level, one star represents significance at the $p \leq 0.05$ level.

It is clearly apparent that the *majority* of the learning methods are significantly different between columns two and three, i.e. there are *major changes* in the frequency of use of vocabulary learning methods between middle school and university. The most frequently used methods in the middle school are reading textbooks, listening to the teacher and taking notes; there is clearly a much wider range of methods frequently used at university. Methods which have *not* significantly changed, for frequency, are *listening to the teacher, taking notes* and methods focusing on *memorization*, although the use of *vocabulary cards* has significantly declined. In other words, some traditional features of the Chinese culture of learning have carried over from middle school to university, in spite of the fact that the use of *radio, films and audio cassettes* are used with dramatically more frequency, as are peer learning and the use of *essays, newspapers and literature*.

The students' ratings of efficiency for different methods show fewer significant changes. Only methods 1 to 7, and 13, have dramatic shifts, with a notable devaluing of textbooks accompanied by positive evaluations of *essays*; *using radio, audio cassettes* and *newspapers*; and *listening to native speakers*.

It is interesting to note that large percentages of students were unsure of many vocabulary learning methods when they were in middle school, and that still in university many remain unsure about using *cartoons* or *TV programmes*. This can be explained by the fact that few Chinese students have access to a TV, since most live in university dormitories. Surprisingly high percentages of students are unsure about whether *non-fiction* is useful, and there appear to be divided opinions about *vocabulary cards*.

To show the patterns of change more clearly we have taken the figures for *frequent* use and those for *positive* replies about *efficiency* and plotted

☐ = past

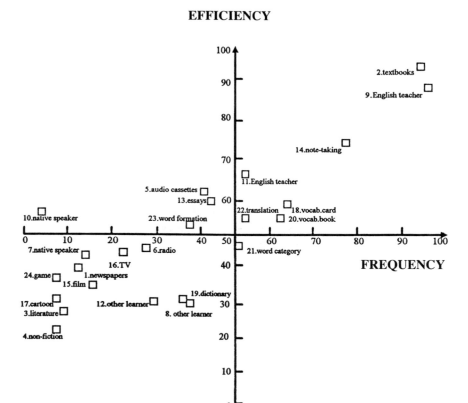

Figure 13.3 The frequency and efficiency of methods of learning English vocabulary in China in the past

them on two axes (see Figures 13.3 and 13.4) which intersect at the 50 per cent level. This gives a clear impression of the changes in vocabulary learning, since many methods are in the lower left quadrant (less frequent, less efficient) for the *past* (in middle school) but have shifted to the upper right quadrant (more frequent, more efficient) *now* (in university). The methods of using *vocabulary books*, doing *translations, listening to the teacher* and *memorizing words from dictionaries*, however, have changed little.

■ = now

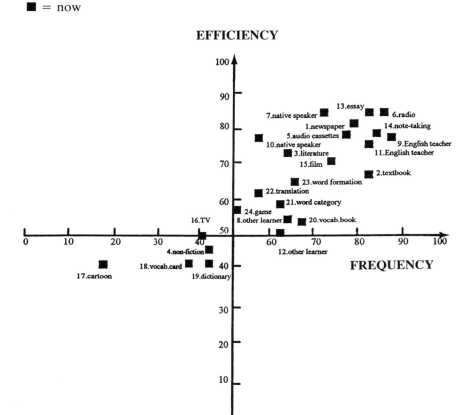

Figure 13.4 The frequency and efficiency of methods of learning English vocabulary in China surveyed in 1994

Interviews

In interviews, students emphasized memorization: '*Listen and remember. That is most Chinese students' conception of study.*' This was sometimes likened to stuffing a Beijing duck; '*We Chinese get used to a pouring and filling teaching way.*' Many students emphasized that they had been taught to *remember* vocabulary but not given the opportunity to *use* it. '*The result of Chinese ways of teaching . . . students remember more words but they don't know how to make use of them.'* 'Reciting the vocabulary word by word is easy; learning the correct usage of words is more difficult.' When they compared their Chinese teachers of English with Western teachers, some students thought that the Chinese teachers were better at teaching vocabulary since they were *'in the habit of explaining more about the meanings of words'*, whereas Western teachers were inclined to underestimate the students' knowledge of English vocabulary and therefore tended *'to use simple and easy words'*. Other students welcomed the new and varied approaches which Western teachers brought, *'We should absorb some fresh elements from Western ways of teaching to adjust to Chinese ways of learning.'*

Students maintained that reliance on listening to the teacher and memorizing from books would *'only work for tests and exams'*. Such methods were *'efficient to enlarge vocabulary in a short period to pass tests'*, *'since time is limited'*. Those who used vocabulary books did so *'because vocabulary books can cover words that might not appear in other English materials, but would appear in exams'*.

Apart from helping to pass exams, students doubted the efficiency of their ways of memorizing, since they did not relate to realistic practice. *'We don't use the words in real life after memorizing so it's easy to forget.'* *'We don't know how to use the words in real life. If we use them in the wrong way it is hard to correct them.'* *'Memorizing is dull, boring, mechanical. We get no explanations for the usage, or context, of words. It is not very impressive.'*

Students lacked confidence and, in the absence of an English-speaking environment, practice was difficult. If they tried to practise with each other it was difficult to find a partner who was at a suitable level and they needed *'a friendly stranger – we feel embarrassed to talk to people we are familiar with in English'*. Practising English could lead to loss of face, they would feel *'strange'*, *'foolish'*.

Conclusions

Several brief conclusions can be drawn: there are wide-ranging and highly significant differences between Chinese students' reports of how they learn English vocabulary in the middle school and in the university; reasons for this seem to be a combination of developmental change, diachronic change, and differences in provision of facilities and language level reached. The students' perceptions of vocabulary learning are seen in terms of activities rather than cognitive strategies; the textbook and teacher are dominant as sources of words in the middle school, but the range of sources and methods used by over half the university students is much more diverse. Some ways of learning seem remarkably constant (listening to the teacher, note-taking, memorization from vocabulary books), indicating that some aspects of a Chinese culture of learning have not changed in recent years. Reliance on textbooks and vocabulary cards has diminished, however, where it might have been expected that students would continue to use these heavily. It would be tempting to show the students that vocabulary development is not simply a matter of learning new words (as the Chinese students almost universally assume), but is also a matter of learning new uses for known words and of learning to link words in lexical sets, collocations and lexical phrases, since learning a word is a continuous process. It is tempting, too, to encourage them to be more active and interactive in their vocabulary learning. However, such proposals, although enlightened in terms of Western models of language learning, need to be related to the Chinese culture of learning, which stresses mastery of knowledge and the authority of teacher and textbook. It is worth pondering why it is that many students prefer Chinese teachers for vocabulary learning: Chinese teachers not only systematically teach new words and require students to memorize them, but also teach students methods of memorizing them. It is worth asking if methodological innovations would help students pass their exams. Those concerned with future developments in Chinese approaches to vocabulary learning might also consider that a strength of students' current approaches is the use of highly retentive memories – many students *do* acquire very high levels of active vocabulary and these are not only those who have learnt to recite a dictionary. How can Western frameworks for learning words build on Chinese students' memorization? For productive change, the culture of learning needs to be borne in mind, otherwise it is doubtful if the students will be convinced of the efficacy of innovation.

References

Aitchison, J. (1994) *Words in the Mind*. Oxford: Blackwell.
Carter, R. (1987) *Vocabulary, Applied Linguistic Perspectives*. London: Unwin Hyman.
Chang, C. K. (1990) *How I Learned English*. Taipei: Bookman Books.
Cortazzi, M. and Jin, L. (1996) Cultures of Learning: Language classrooms in China. In H. Coleman (ed.) *Society and the Language Classroom*. Cambridge: Cambridge University Press.
Dzau, Y. F. (ed.) (1990) *English in China*. Hong Kong: API Press.
Gairns, R. and Redman, S. (1986) *Working with Words, a Guide to Teaching and Learning Vocabulary*. Cambridge: Cambridge University Press.
Harmer, J. (1991) *The Practice of English Language Teaching*. London: Longman.
Hoey, M. (1983) *On the Surface of Discourse*. London: George Allen & Unwin.
Hua, Y. (1992) Teaching vocabulary, a discussion. *Teaching English in China, ELT Newsletter* 24, pp. 43–5.

Huang, X. F. (1991) *How to Increase Word Power*. Beijing: Zhong-wen Books Ltd.

Jin, L. (1992) *Academic Cultural Expectations and Second Language Use: Chinese postgraduate students in the UK – A cultural synergy model*. PhD thesis, Leicester University.

Li, J. and Li. J. (1991) Memory strategies. *Teaching English in China, ELT Newsletter* 23, pp. 64–71.

Li, X. *et al.* (1987) *Communicative English for Chinese Learners*. Shanghai: Shanghai Foreign Language Education Press.

Liu, Y. (1993) *Vocabulary Fundamental*. Beijing: San Huan Publishing House.

— (1993) *Vocabulary 22,000*. Beijing: San Huan Publishing House.

McCarthy, M. (1990) *Vocabulary*. Oxford: Oxford University Press.

Nation, I. S. P. (1990) *Teaching and Learning Vocabulary*. Boston, MA: Heinle & Heinle.

Nattinger, J. R. and DeCarrico, J. S. (1992) *Lexical Phrases and Language Teaching*. Oxford: Oxford University Press.

O'Malley, J. M. and Chamot, A. U. (1990) *Learning Strategies in Second Language Acquisition*. Cambridge: Cambridge University Press.

Pawley, A. and Syder, F. H. (1983) Two Puzzles for Linguistic Theory: Nativelike selection and nativelike fluency. In J. C. Richards and R. W. Schmidt (eds) *Language and Communication*. London: Longman.

Ross, H. (1992) Foreign Language Education as a Barometer of Modernization. In R. Hayhoe (ed.) *Education and Modernization: The Chinese Experience* (pp. 239–54). Oxford: Pergamon Press.

Sinclair, J. M. (1991) *Corpus, Concordance, Collocation*. Oxford: Oxford University Press.

Taylor, J. R. (1989) *Linguistic Categorization: Prototypes in linguistic theory*. Oxford: Clarendon Press.

Thorne, C. and A. (1992) Vocabulary Learning and Memorization; helping learners to help themselves – a role for the teacher. *Teaching English in China, ELT Newsletter* 24, pp. 38–42.

Wang, Z. L. (ed.) (1990) *ELT in China*. Beijing: Foreign Language Teaching and Research Press.

Yue, C. (1991) An alternative to rote learning in teaching vocabulary. *Teaching English in China, ELT Newsletter* 23, pp. 60–3.

Zhao, G. Q. (1991) *How to Memorize English Vocabulary Using Etymology*. Chang-Chung: North-East Normal University Press.

Zhu, W. and Chen, J. (1991) Some Economic Aspects of the Language Situation in China. *Journal of Asian Pacific Communication* 2, 1: 91–102.

14 Winds of Change in Africa: Fresh air for African languages? Some preliminary reflections

CLINTON D. W. ROBINSON
Summer Institute of Linguistics

Introduction[1]

The enormous changes and challenges facing Africa today raise major questions: what is the future for African development? What is education for in Africa? What is the future of African culture and identity in a world where strong globalising tendencies are evident? The purpose of this paper is to ask some preliminary questions about the impact of the current changes and challenges on the use and development of African languages. The basis for this debate is the complementary role of languages, African and non-African. The question is how each of the languages available to a group of speakers can best be integrated into their multilingual communication needs. Up to now, African languages have not always been viable choices in written communication, in education and the media. With the current changes in Africa, are such choices becoming more viable? Is there a greater or lesser possibility that African languages will become genuinely available as options for use in a wider variety of social institutions?

The paper will first examine the nature of the changes currently taking place in Africa, seeking to show some of the implications for the use and development of African languages. The situation in Cameroon will serve as a case study, and the paper will conclude by drawing out some questions for research, as a means of setting parameters in the search for a way forward.

Change in Africa

Over the past five years immense changes have taken place in Africa. The most significant of these has been the rapid transition towards reshaping the political landscape as democratisation movements have gathered pace. Decalo (1992: 9) remarks that 'the political *atmosphere* in Africa today is radically different: exhilarating, ebullient, optimistic'. Decalo's emphasis on the *atmosphere* signifies his and others' ambiguity about the outcome of this transition – indeed although the movement is unstoppable, the political 'big bang' has not yet cooled into its final shape. Predating the political changes and still continuing has been the economic decline of Africa: persistently low commodity prices, economic growth rates outstripped by population growth, static inflows of aid, rising external debt, currency devaluation (Wall, 1994) – all these contribute to increasing economic hardship for vast numbers of Africans. Thus a certain amount of political optimism is immediately tempered by a pessimistic economic assessment. Less well known, but equally disturbing is the educational crisis: huge numbers of school-age children at a time of falling resources. UNESCO (1993) notes:

> Of the 38 countries worldwide with gross enrolment ratios in first level education of less than 90% in 1990, 24 are located in that region, and in nearly half of these the ratio was lower in 1990 that it had been a decade earlier. (UNESCO, 1993: 33)

Each of these three areas – political transition, economic decline and educational crisis – will be examined in turn with regard to factors which might impact language issues.

Political transition

The fall of the Berlin Wall in Europe in 1989 heralded massive political change in Africa. Mounting internal and external pressures challenged the many one-party and military regimes across the continent. Some countries, such as Benin, made the transition in a peaceful way, while in many others incumbent governments showed reluctance to move in the direction of multi-party democracy (e.g. Cameroon, Niger, Togo). Two critical questions in this transition are of special importance as far as language issues are concerned: pluralism and accountability.

Pluralism

Wiseman (1993) argues that it would be wrong to see the current democratisation process in Africa as the emergence of pluralism, since at independence 'relatively democratic and pluralistic political structures had been hastily constructed' (p. 439). These quickly gave way in most countries to the more authoritarian regimes which are now being challenged. However, there is an older pluralism – that of the many ethnic groups which make up most of the African countries. In seeking to forge nation-states the colonisers faced the question of the integration of the many ethnic groups within them. That same question remains in the current democratisation process: how can ethnic pluralism be integrated with democratic pluralism in a multi-party system?

The ethnic question is of the utmost importance in the language debate, since language is readily available as a symbol of ethnicity, and any promotion of African languages can be interpreted as a desire to enhance the political power of their speakers. On the other hand, genuine pluralistic policies must make space for communities to choose to use their own language. In many countries there is a fear – and in some cases a trend – that political parties will form along ethnic lines, leading to a fragmentation of national political life (Rijnierse, 1993). In other places there is a growing recognition of the strength of ethnic loyalties and an acceptance of diversity. Village-level development committees have been promoted in Cameroon on the basis of people's commitment to their home village; these committees have replaced former bodies based on administrative divisions (Robinson, forthcoming). In terms of language, the new regime in Ethiopia has begun planning bilingual education which recognises all Ethiopian languages (UNESCO, 1993). In Burkina Faso efforts are put into mobilising local communities in rural development, with local-language literacy projects as an educational component.

Such positive respect for ethnic diversity and the harnessing of loyalties for local development does not minimise the ambivalent or even negative outworkings of ethnic distinctions. Long-standing patterns of domination and subordination are being challenged as each ethnic group seeks to assert its rights. In northern Ghana groups which have long paid tribute to other, more dominant groups are refusing to go on doing so, and localised conflicts have occurred. At worst, ethnically based power-seeking has led to outright conflict, as in, for example, Somalia, Rwanda, Liberia and Angola. These situations stand as frightening examples to other African nations, as democratisation gives more freedom for the expression of ethnic differences. However, such examples hardly demonstrate the failure of democracy in pluralist African societies; in some cases they emphasise the need for dialogue and democratic processes. With reference to Liberia and Somalia, Clapham (1993: 435) remarks that 'the self-defeating efforts of autocratic regimes to retain power in the face of popular opposition eventually led to their overthrow . . .' It is noteworthy that language is not a central issue in any of these conflicts which span monolingual and multilingual contexts. Both Somalia (Somali) and Rwanda (Kinyarwanda) are amongst the few countries on the continent with a single African language.

Accountability

Decalo (1992: 13) points out that the authoritarian regimes in Africa are 'fundamentally unaccountable'. The political models bequeathed by the colonial powers demonstrated an upward, hierarchical accountability. Ultimately, local administrators were accountable to the metropole of the colonial power. The democratisation movement implies, more than anything else, a change in the direction of accountability. Administrators, government officials and even members of elected bodies such as national assemblies depended for their appointment and survival on the patronage of those holding the strings of power, not on those they were called to serve or to represent. Further, even democratic change itself is called into question by the mass of the people when it is initiated and controlled by those who have most interest in maintaining their own power as Munslow (1993) argues.

Accountability to the people implies increased communication, as politicians and others listen to people's concerns and seek to put across their own proposals. This will mean using the people's language. In Cameroon the multi-party elections since 1990 have seen political candidates for the first time choosing to use the local language, rather than the official language which they know only a small proportion of village people readily understand.

Implications

Moves towards social and political pluralism, associated with increased downward accountability, are likely to create more space for local identity and for local initiative, and so provide both an opportunity and an incentive for local communities to work towards developing their language for new purposes, such as adult education, primary education and development communication. However, a question hangs over this scenario: how far will central governments, even democratically elected, allow such local political space to develop? In terms of language this has implications for policy and for perspective. Will a pluralist stance result in policies which genuinely promote the full development of African languages if communities manifest the desire and the will to do so? Or will policies, on the other hand, continue to be bound by the fear that the use of local languages will increase ethnic divisions, and by the maintenance, deliberate or unwitting, by the élite of their privileges based in part on their wider linguistic repertoire? The question of perspective is crucial. Up to now, language policies in Africa have been based largely on the perspective of the state and its need to manage the multilingual 'problem'. For African languages the new climate of pluralism and accountability, however tentatively espoused, could offer an opportunity for the perspective to be reversed. Instead of basing policies on the management needs of the state, the focus may shift to the needs of communication, of education and of the sociocultural identity of the speakers of the languages themselves.

Such speculation immediately raises questions about the resources which would be needed to support African language development at the local level. The economic situation, to which we now turn, is unpromising.

Economic decline

Current trends

Even a cursory glance at certain indicators shows how Africa is declining economically relative to the recent past as well as in relation to the rest of the world. The inexorable rise of debt in sub-Saharan Africa is a sign of economic decline and of how shackled the economy is; other economic indicators paint a dark picture. (See Table 14.1.)

Table 14.1 Economic decline in Africa

External debt	1982	1992
	$70bn	$183bn
Real GDP per capita:	1960	1990
relative to Northern levels	14%	8%
GNP per capita growth	1965–80	1980–92
	1.5%	−1.1%
Annual average rate of inflation	1980–91	1992
	14.7%	24.5%
Resource flows – aid	1989	1992
	$458m	$727m
Food import dependency ratio	1970	1990
	6.5%	10.2%

Sources: UNDP 1994; OECD 1994

Development strategies

Into this assessment of the economic state of Africa in general must be introduced the growing appreciation in development circles that development is certainly not only about economics, and may not even be primarily about economics. In development which is essentially people-centred (Sadik, 1994; UNRISD, 1994), social and political development are seen as the underpinnings of economic development at least as much as the other way round (and probably more). This is not to sidestep the huge economic disparities and overwhelming needs in Africa, but to redefine human security as essentially multidimensional – as much about culture as commodities, identity as internal rates of return and self-esteem as self-financing. As these realisations gain currency, human resource development is foregrounded as the goal of development activity. Thus, the promotion of education, participation and communication becomes a central pivot of development intervention (Bhola, 1993; OECD, 1994). In multilingual settings this immediately puts language issues centre stage. As I have argued elsewhere (Robinson, 1992), a participatory approach to development requires that language issues be addressed at the design and planning stages.

Implications

Such bleak economic prospects in Africa augur badly for the maintenance of current programmes by African governments, let alone envisaging new initiatives requiring injections of fresh resources. Is this lack of central resources entirely a negative phenomenon? In the blackness left by the extinction of the arc lights of government funding, two small candle flames may end up burning brighter: use of people's own resources, and the contribution of non-governmental organisations (NGOs).

The need for ownership by local people of development initiatives affecting their lives is a mainstay of current development thinking (Batchelor, 1993; Oakley, 1991; Rahman, 1993). In addition, the unavailability of government resources is now plainly evident, and local communities are taking seriously the need to evaluate what resources might be generated locally. These remain small; the same crisis which has depleted government coffers affects local people just as much. Nevertheless, this candle flame has begun to shed a little light; perhaps the biggest benefit is the recognition by local people that even the small resources they command can make a difference.

The second candle flame is the role of NGOs. As the ability of government to meet grassroots needs is curtailed, space is created for NGOs to develop creative and contextually appropriate strategies which support local initiative and build capacity. A higher proportion of international aid is being channelled through NGOs, and they have a significant role to play in strengthening respect for local cultures. NGO projects are more likely to use the local language in their communication, since their actions are premised on the participation of the people.

The one positive effect of the economic crisis is the incipient reversal of perspective – towards greater local initiative and responsibility. Thus we can look for a greater impetus for the use of local resources, however small, and greater space for the flexible approaches of NGOs.

Educational crisis

As African countries became independent, education was seen as a way of consolidating independence by providing the skills and training necessary to run the state and to move forward in development. Educated élites were created, but hopes for the ongoing role of education have been disappointed as the systems have not kept pace with the demands made on them:

> . . . the education systems that were to initiate and sustain that [social] transformation by developing new skills and technologies, innovative ideas, and new values in most countries still do not reach all of the school-age population and are unable to provide sufficient teachers and text-books for those who are in school. (Samoff, 1993: 188)

Educational statistics show that huge progress has been made, particularly in literacy rates. Under the pressure of increasing population and declining resources not only has progress slowed, but there is the danger of slipping backwards. (See Table 14.2.)

Table 14.2 Educational crisis in Africa

Literacy rate	1970	1992
	28%	51%
Total first level enrolment	1980	1989
	47.8m	55.9m
Proportion of first level age group enrolled	1980	1989
	79%	67%
Ratio of school enrolment relative to Northern levels	1980	1990
	56%	46%
Proportion of government budgets on education	1985	1990
	17%	15.7%

Sources: UNDP 1994; UNESCO 1993

It is well known in international research that use of the first language is a factor in educational achievement (Baker, 1993; Corson, 1993; Skutnabb-Kangas, 1981; UNESCO, 1953) and African educators have made the same point (Bamgbose, 1991; Elugbe, 1994; Tadadjeu, 1990). The need for the cultural contextualisation of education has long been argued (Diambomba, 1989; Gfeller & Robinson, 1992; UNESCO, 1990a). The question then must be asked whether the language issue is peripheral to the current educational crisis in Africa or part of it. While the huge issues of population growth and dwindling resources dominate the horizon, and the long-term problems of pedagogical quality (teacher training, material development) cast long shadows, the crisis should provide added stimulus to factor research and experimentation on the language question into the search for the way forward.

The language of instruction has been a major factor in making education a culturally alienating process (Gfeller & Robinson, 1992; Skutnabb-Kangas, 1990). The lack of integration of educational goals with the cultural context and African values has contributed to the present crisis – education which is geared mainly to the (re)production of ruling élites has increasingly shown itself to be irrelevant to Africa's development. Language is a critical issue in bringing education close to the learner and therefore in motivating learners to invest energy and time in 'the intrinsic excitement and self-regenerating dynamo of learning' (Samoff, 1993: 213). Language and community are inseparable, and in Africa evoke ties of identity and origin – in today's crisis situation the way forward will need to include and harness the linguistic, material, cultural and human resources of the community in promoting an educational model rooted in the local context (Tadadjeu, 1989).

Policy and Practice: The case of Cameroon

Cameroon presents the situation of a highly multilingual country, complicated by the use of two official languages, French and English, the legacy of a divided colonial tutelage. The number of Cameroonian languages is put at 270+ (Grimes, 1992) with a population of 12.5m (UNESCO, 1993). There is no nation-wide lingua franca; seven regional lingua francas are used in different parts of the country, the most widespread being Pidgin English (Wes Cos) in the west, along the coast and in some southern towns. The country has enjoyed considerable stability and relative economic prosperity since independence – it has nevertheless been hit hard by the recent economic decline. Its ethno-cultural diversity, and especially its lack of any dominant ethnic groups,[2] makes it particularly interesting from the point of view of the relationship between Cameroonian languages. The relative political stability permits an observation of the evolution of language policy and practice over time, without the influence of major upheavals. The current effects of political transition, economic decline and educational crisis emerge all the more clearly.

Some of the chief indicators of the state of development of Cameroon are given in Table 14.3, with Chad, a neighbouring country, and the United Kingdom added for comparative purposes (data from UNDP Human Development Report 1994).

Table 14.3 Comparative development indicators

(1992 data)	*Cameroon*	*Chad*	*United Kingdom*
Life expectancy at birth (years)	55.3	46.9	75.8
GNP *per capita* – US$	860	210	16,600
Adult literacy rate (% of population)	56.5	32.5	99
Human development ranking	124	168	10
Newspapers per 100 people	0.7	<0.1	40
TVs per 100 people	2.3	0.1	43
Daily calorie supply (% of requirements)	93	69	100+

Source: UNDP 1994

Figure 14.1 indicates the disparity between population growth and economic growth in the decade 1980–1990. While the rate of population growth in Cameroon has increased slightly (2.6% to 2.8%), the rate of growth of GNP/capita has plummeted from +2.4% to −1.1%.

Figure 14.1 Percentage change in population and GNP/*capita* in Cameroon

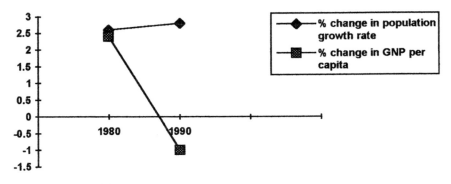

Source: UNDP, 1994

Compounding these basic realities is a downward movement in the proportion of the (smaller) government budget spent on education in the same period (1980–1990): 20.3% to 19.6% (UNESCO, 1993). Taken together, 'la crise', as it is popularly known, forms a gloomy framework for the policy debate.

The language policy debate

The language policy debate in Cameroon has its roots in the practices and communication strategies of the early missions and the first colonial powers. Based on Stumpf (1979) and Robinson (forthcoming), suffice it here to sketch an outline of the earlier debate, against which to set recent developments.

In the 1880s missions used African languages, but quickly saw it as too demanding a task to use and develop each language in their mission area. As their work spread, missions, both Catholic and Protestant, began to promote certain languages as church languages. In the 1970s local people began to advocate the use of their own language and since that time churches and missions of all persuasions have given attention to all Cameroonian languages.

Mission strategy came into conflict early on with the desire of the colonial administrators to educate Cameroonians in the metropolitan language. Although each colonial authority gave serious consideration to the use of local languages, in fact all the incentives of the educational system pointed people in the direction of acquiring the language of the colonial power.

At independence, French and English were *de facto* the languages of education, enshrined in the constitution as the official languages. Cameroonian languages had no mention in this constitution, which has remained unchallenged until recently. Through the 1960s and 1970s the 'national language debate', as it is termed, was muted. Concern for national unity made official circles reluctant to raise the language question for fear of provoking ethnic division.

In the 1980s the debate began to move into a different phase. Increasing linguistic research and development work undertaken by governmental and non-governmental agencies began to raise the possibility of using local languages for communication and education. Along with this came a growing acceptance that language in and of itself, while it may enhance consciousness of ethnic identity, was unlikely to exacerbate ethnic divisions. Thus a number of ministerial and presidential statements expressed support for the use of local languages (Biya, 1986; MESRES, 1985; MINFOC, 1985), though this did not result either in the formulation of an explicit policy towards Cameroonian languages or in officially sponsored initiatives for their increased use.

What effect, then, have recent political and economic changes had on the language policy debate? Firstly, in the more pluralist climate of democratisation many new political parties have formed, and they have sought to adopt policies which will bring them grassroots support. Even so, from various sources (personal communications) it has emerged that they have not included in their manifestos any proposals concerning Cameroonian languages, except for one smaller regional party. In the debate over the new constitution the language question has been more prominent. At the insistence of the newer parties, a recent draft included reference to Cameroonian languages, rather than only to French and English. However, movement on adopting the constitution is slow, and it is not publicly known at this point whether a more clear statement regarding the status of Cameroonian languages will be included.

These developments are subject to the broader political debate over what will constitute proper democratic processes and suitable structures in Cameroon. At the national level, the question of language policy, always reflecting wider social realities, will continue to depend on the jockeying for position of divergent political interests. Having said that, consensus seems to be growing informally that Cameroon's languages deserve greater attention as a sign that pluralist policies reflect a genuine respect for the identity of all ethnic groups.

Secondly, the deteriorating economic climate makes new initiatives look less possible. The openness of more pluralist approaches may be vitiated by the lack of resources to support new directions. The lack of funds limits the training of linguists and investment in research; the training and development costs of introducing Cameroonian languages into education begin to look beyond the country's means. However, initiatives at grassroots level continue.

Practice at the grassroots

The national policy debate has been informed by practical initiatives on the ground. Since the debate opened up in the 1980s, there has been increasing space for initiatives which have required no more than the approval of central government. PROPELCA[3] is an initiative of the University of Yaoundé aiming to introduce Cameroonian languages in the first three years of primary school (Tadadjeu, 1990); this has found positive echoes both with school authorities and with pupils and parents in the selected experimental schools. While the government is interested in the programme, no decision about adopting it in government schools has yet been taken. In the private school system where it was first introduced, the authorities are now moving ahead with plans to generalise the programme on a national level. The arguments presented in favour of this programme emphasise the role of language in cultural identity, the awakening of the child's spirit of enquiry with regard to its immediate environment, and the importance of these factors in African development (SENECA, 1994).

With the enlarging of 'local space' the work of the Société Internationale de Linguistique (SIL) has grown, majoring on supporting local initiatives with technical support, as well as running workshops at various levels to develop skills in local language development, literacy, material design and translation. Co-operation, once limited to one national ministry, has broadened to include local and national NGOs, as well as a number of ministries involved in education and social development (SIL, 1993).

This is further illustrated in the formation of the National Association of Cameroon Language Committees (NACALCO) which brings together local bodies concerned with the development and promotion of their language (Fosong, 1992; Trihus, 1992). Its aim is to support the work of language committees through training and the search for funds and to promote the use of local languages in social institutions.

The space for such non-governmental initiatives is a result both of growing political pluralism and economic decline. The lack of resources means that government knows it could not fund such initiatives, though it continues to have a responsibility to do so. The danger is that initiatives proliferate with little or no co-ordination or with no guiding policy framework. Growing pluralism, on the other hand, creates space for the more flexible and context-sensitive approaches of non-governmental organisations.

Ambiguities and Outlook

This example from Cameroon illustrates the ambiguity inherent in the current changes in Africa as far as their impact on African languages is concerned. Political transition and economic decline, with the associated educational crisis, present both opportunities and obstacles to the integration of African languages in a multilingual strategy of communication. These are summarised in Table 14.4.

The tensions caused by these ambiguities would appear to be long-term. There is little indication that the political change is complete, nor that economic prospects might brighten quickly. The educational crisis may not even have reached its full extent. These are not reasons for inaction, but for careful research and committed action. In the present climate of massive change it is important not only that we should understand the role that African languages can play in the future social development of the continent, but also

Table 14.4 African languages: opportunities and obstacles

	Political transition	*Economic decline*	*Educational crisis*
Oppor-tunities	New pluralism, openness to expression of local cultures	Space for local initiative, for small beginnings	Openness to radical educational alternatives
Obstacles	Energies absorbed by political process, language issues low priority	No funds available for new programmes	Breakdown of educational systems

enable African languages to be viable choices for use in social institutions. In the context of current changes, it will be important to understand what difference of approach might be feasible in education and in other areas of social development through the use of African languages. This poses a fresh challenge to research.

The challenge for research

In the current climate efforts in linguistic research must be conducted together with the speakers of the languages and combined with action; it will aim to meet the communication needs of the language community. It will be experimental in nature, analysing needs and possibilities as they are addressed practically. In the end the fruits of such research will be in the hands of the language community which will make decisions about their use. This approach borrows from participatory action research (PAR) used in development:

> At the micro level, PAR is a philosophy and style of work with the people to promote people's empowerment for changing their immediate environment – social and physical – in their favor. (Fals-Borda & Rahman, 1991: 16)

What, then are the questions which such research must address?

Some research questions

In relation to community structures and institutions:

- what organisations are emerging at local levels in the new political space which might need or sponsor communication in African languages? What are their communication strategies, in oral and written form?

- how far is political space being created for decentralising responsibility and initiative in the educational system? What is the right multilingual strategy for education in specific local contexts?
- what role does the local language have as a means of instruction in the search for educational goals and strategies which are culturally relevant?
- how far is space being created to give access to media for local communities speaking different languages?
- what kind of external help (training, capacity building, . . .) might be most appropriate to foster responsibility and capacity in emerging local organisations?
- in a situation of diminishing internal financial resources how can external resources (research, aid funds, . . .) best be managed to ensure growth of local responsibility and control?

In relation to languages:

- what languages are used or available in the local environment and what functions does each one fulfil? What are the local attitudes to languages?
- what is the state of development (written materials, didactic resources, literacy classes, . . .) of the various languages? What needs to be done to make specific languages viable as instruments of written communication?
- what needs to be done to promote a policy environment in which African languages become viable choices for purposes determined by the community?
- which national-level institutions are potential partners in the promotion of African languages?
- at the international level, which institutions can offer support to action-research of this kind?

This action-research should not be seen as addressing by itself the huge questions of African development, but rather as an attempt to understand better the opportunities and roles for African languages which the current changes open up. This will enable those concerned for communication, language and culture in Africa to maximise their contribution in Africa's overall search for ways ahead. In his helpful article on the Nigerian situation, Brann (1993) concludes:

> Never have the responsibilities and opportunities of linguists – descriptive, prescriptive, or social – been greater in Nigeria, as well as elsewhere in Africa, than in the present decade. (Brann, 1993: 656)

Conclusion

Some commentators have debated the term 'rebirth' as a description of the current changes in Africa (Decalo, 1992; Munslow, 1993), and many see the situation as more significant than the changes of the independence years. Radical change is occurring, and language policies and use are part of that. The symbolic functions of language mean that it will necessarily be a part of the redefinition of African identity as political systems and social institutions become more accountable and more responsive to the people. The crisis is deep and the problems massive, yet this should not discourage us from seeking out new opportunities, harnessing new energies and setting off in bold new directions. The use of African languages in complementary and equitable fashion, alongside other languages, will be part of the full development of Africa's own genius and of the continent's search for its own path of development.

Notes

1. Thanks are due to the late Sylvia Hedinger who sent material on Cameroon prior to her untimely death, and to Amanda Lake for much of the preparatory research.
2. The largest ethnic group (Beti) represents only 17% of the population, and some would argue (Robinson, 1992) that it must be seen as at least two language groups (Ewondo & Bulu).
3. Projet de Recherche Opérationnelle pour l'Enseignement des Langues au Cameroun.

References

Baker, C. (1993) *Foundations of Bilingual Education and Bilingualism*. Clevedon: Multilingual Matters.

Bamgbose, A. (1991) *Language and the Nation: The language question in Sub-Saharan Africa*. Edinburgh: Edinburgh University Press for the International African Institute.

Batchelor, P. (1993) *People in Rural Development*. Carlisle: The Paternoster Press.

Bhola, H. S. (1993) Policy challenges of literacy for development in Africa: Building pillars of prosperity, pyramids of peace. Paper presented at the Second African–African American Summit, Libreville, Gabon, 24–28 May 1993.

Biya, P. (1986) *Pour le libéralisme communautaire.*Lausanne/Paris: Pierre-Marcel Favre/Editions ABC.

Brann, C. M. B. (1993) Democratisation of language use in public domains in Nigeria. In *The Journal of Modern African Studies* 31(4), 639–56.

Clapham, C. (1993) Democratisation in Africa: Obstacles and prospects. In *Third World Quarterly* 14(3), 423–37.

Corson, D. (1993) *Language, Minority Education and Gender: Linking social justice and power*. Clevedon: Multilingual Matters.

Decalo, S. (1992) The process, prospects and constraints of democratization in Africa. In *African Affairs* 91, 7–35.

Diambomba, M. (1989) Universities and development in Africa: Problems and challenges for planning. In F. Caillods (ed.) *The Prospects for Educational Planning* (pp. 174–208). Paris: UNESCO/IIEP.

Elugbe, B. O. (1994) Minority language development in Nigeria: A situation report on Rivers and Bendel States. In R. Fardon and G. Furniss (eds) *African Languages, Development and the State*. London: Routledge.

Fals-Borda, O. and Rahman, A. (1991) *Action and Knowledge: Breaking the monopoly with participatory action-research*. New York: The Apex Press.

Fosong, D. (1992) Association of National Languages Created. In Cameroon Tribune (1507) 17.9.92, 11.

Gfeller, E. and Robinson, C. D. W. (1992) Which language for teaching? The cultural messages transmitted by the languages used in education. Reference paper for the International Conference on Education, 43rd session, Geneva, 14–19 September 1992.

Grimes, B. F. (ed.) (1992) *Ethnologue: Languages of the world* (12th. edition). Dallas: Summer Institute of Linguistics.

Laishley, R. (1994) Africa's debt burden continues to grow. In *Africa Recovery* 7(3/4), 112–14.

MESRES (Ministère de l'Enseignement Supérieur et de la Recherche Scientifique) (1985) Allocution d'ouverture du 4ème Congrès Régional de la SIL en Afrique. Yaoundé, 27.5.85.

MINFOC (Ministère de l'Information et de la Culture) (1985) *L'identité Culturelle Camerounaise*. Yaoundé: MINFOC.

Munslow, B. (1993) Africa: Prospects of a rebirth? In *Third World Quarterly* 14(2), 337–42.

Oakley, P. (ed.) (1991) *Projects with People: The practice of participation in rural development*. Geneva: ILO.

OECD (1994) *Development Cooperation 1993 Report*. Paris: OECD.

Rahman, A. (1993) *People's Self-Development*. London: Zed Books.

Rijnierse, E. (1993) Democratisation in sub-Saharan Africa? Literature review. In *Third World Quarterly* 14(3), 647–63.

Robinson, C. D. W (1992) *Language Choice in Rural Development*. Dallas: Summer Institute of Linguistics/International Museum of Cultures.

— (forthcoming) *Language and Rural Development: An African perspective*. Berlin: Mouton de Gruyter.

Sadik, N. (1994) Statement to the 21st World Conference of the Society for International Development. Mexico City, 6 May 1994.

Samoff, J. (1993) The reconstruction of schooling in Africa. In *Comparative Education Review* 37(2), 181–222.

SENECA (Secrétariat National à l'Education Catholique) (1994) Demande de reconnaissance officielle des programmes d'enseignement des langues nationales. Unpublished note.

SIL (Société Internationale de Linguistique) (1993) *Rapport Annuel 1992–1993*. Yaoundé: SIL.

Skutnabb-Kangas, T. (1981) *Bilingualism or Not: The Education of Minorities*. (Multilingual Matters 7) Clevedon: Multilingual Matters.

— (1990) *Language, Literacy and Minorities*. London: Minority Rights Group.

Stumpf, R. (1979) *La Politique Linguistique au Cameroun de 1884 à 1960. Comparaison entre les administrations coloniales allemande, française et britannique et du rôle joué par les sociétés missionnaires*. Bern: Peter Lang.

Tadadjeu, M. (1989) *Voie Africaine: Esquisse du communautarisme africain*. Yaoundé: Club OUA Cameroun.

— (ed.) (1990) *Le défi de Babel au Cameroun*. (Collection PROPELCA 53). Yaoundé: Université de Yaoundé.

Trihus, M. S. (1992) The role of language committees in developing the indigenous languages of Cameroon. MA thesis. University of Texas at Arlington.

UN (1993) *African Debt Crisis*. Pamphlet produced by the Africa Recovery Unit.

UNDP (1994) *Human Development Report 1994*. Oxford: Oxford University Press.

UNESCO (1953) The use of vernacular languages in education. (Cited in R. Fasold (1984) *The Sociolinguistics of Society*. Oxford: Blackwell.)

— (1990a) *World Declaration on Education for All*. Paris: UNESCO.

— (1990b) *Basic Education and Literacy: World statistical indicators*. Paris: UNESCO.

— (1992) Statistical document on education and culture. Reference document for the International Conference on Education, 43rd session, Geneva, 14–19 September 1992.

— (1993) *World Education Report 1993*. Paris: UNESCO.

UNRISD (UN Research Institute for Social Development) (1994) *The Crisis of Social Development in the 1990s: Preparing for the World Social Summit*. Geneva: UNRISD.

Wall, T. (1994) Africa agenda needs stronger support: UN. In *Africa Recovery* 7(3/4), 1 & 36–38.

Wiseman, J. A. (1993) Democracy and the new political pluralism in Africa: Causes, consequences and significance. In *Third World Quarterly* 14(3), 439–49.